Contents

D1099612

Pronunciation

This section is designed to familiarize you with the sounds of Arabic using our simplified phonetic transcription. The pronunciation of the Arabic letters and sounds is explained below, together with their "imitated" equivalents. This system is used throughout the phrase book. When you see a word spelled phonetically, simply read the pronunciation as if it were English, noting any special rules.

The Arabic language

There are over 20 countries where Arabic is the official language. These are the main areas where you can expect to hear Arabic spoken (but see notes about differences in dialects):

North Africa

Egypt (**muSr**) has the largest population of any Arab country (63 million), and Arabic is spoken by almost the entire population. The dialect is also widely understood everywhere else through Egyptian films and TV programs.

Other North African countries include Libya (**libyaa**), Tunisia (**toonis**), Algeria (**al-jazaa'ir**), Morocco (**al-maghrib**), and Sudan (**as-soodaan**). The total population of these countries is around 100 million, with Algeria, Morocco, and Sudan accounting for approximately 28 million each. Most of the population speak Arabic but often in a regional dialect. English and French are also widely spoken in the area, as well as other indiginous languages, such as Berber.

The Levant

Includes Lebanon (**lubnaan**), Syria (**sooriya**), Iraq (**al-AHiraaq**), Jordan (**al-urdunn**), and Palestine (**filasteen**). Of these countries, Iraq and Syria have the largest populations with around 20 million and 15 million respectively. Jordan has around 6 million and Lebanon only just over 3 million. The Palestinian population is scattered throughout the West Bank, Israel, the Gaza strip, and the wider diaspora. The Levant Arabic dialect is reasonably pure, but French is a strong influence in Lebanon.

The Gulf

Saudi Arabia (**as-sAHoodeeyya**) has the biggest population in the Gulf region (19 million). However, many of these are immigrant workers who may not speak Arabic. Yemen (**al-yaman**) has a population of over 15 million. The other Gulf countries have relatively small populations: Bahrain (**al-baHrayn**) – 570, 000; Kuwait (**al-koowayt**) – 1.7 million; Oman (**AHumaan**) – 2.3 million; Qatar (**qaTar**) – 560, 000; United Arab Emirates (**al-imaaraat al-AHrabeeya al-muttaHida**) – 2.3 million. Dialects vary between countries.

Uniting all these different countries and dialects is what is known as "Modern Standard Arabic" (MSA) – the more formal version of the language used for almost all written material and sometimes for oral communication, particularly if it involves different nationalities. Almost all Arabic speakers will speak their own dialect but also be able to communicate in Modern Standard.

So that you can use this *Berlitz Arabic Phrase Book* in as many countries as possible, we have chosen to use a modified Modern Standard Arabic, which includes elements of colloquial pronunciation and vocabulary.

Below you will find the sounds of the Arabic language explained. (▶ 9 for more details on how the Arabic letters are joined.)

Consonants

Letter	Approximate pronunciation	Symbol	Example	Pronunciation
ب	b as in bat	b	بنت	bint
ت	t as in tin	t	تلفون	tilifoon
ث	t as in tin (colloq.) [or th as in thin (MSA)]	t	ثلاثة	talaata
ج	soft j as in French je (g as in gate in Northern Egypt)	j	جميل	jameel
ح	strong, breathy h	H	حلو	Hilw
خ	h from back of throat as in Scottish loch	kh	خالد	khaalid
د	d as in dad	d	دار	daar
ذ	d as in dad or z as in zebra (colloq.) [hard th as in that (MSA)]	d/z	ذهب هذا	dahab haaza
ر	r as in rain	r	رجل	rajul
ز	z as in zebra	z	زبيب	zibeeb
س	s as in sun	s	سلام	salaam
ش	sh as in shut	sh	شمس	shams
ص	strong, emphatic s	S	صباح	SabaaH
ض	strong, emphatic d	D	ضاني	Daanee
ط	strong, emphatic t	T	طالب	Taalib

7

Consonants (cont.)

Letter	Approximate pronunciation	Symbol	Example	Pronunciation
ظ	strong, emphatic z	Z	ظلام	Zalaam
ع	a guttural sound made by tightening the throat	AH	عرب	AHrab
غ	like French "r," as in rue	gh	غير	ghayr
ف	like f in fan	f	فارس	faaris
ق	q pronounced from back of throat (sometimes dropped in spoken Arabic)	q	قبل	qabl
ك	k as in kart	k	كرفس	karafs
ل	l as in lip	l	لماذا	limaazaa
م	m as in man	m	مارس	maaris
ن	n as in never	n	نور	noor
ه	h as in hat	h	هنا	huna
و	win win	w	وسط	wasT
ي	y as in yet	y	يمين	yameen
ء	short pause, like the sound when you drop the ts in butter ("bu'er")	'	أسد	'asad

Short vowels

There are three short vowels which are written above or below the letter they follow. However, they are not normally shown in most Arabic text as the reader is expected to know them:

—	a as in English bat, but sometimes nearer to an e	a	وَلَد	walad
—	u as in English but	u	كُل	kul
—	i as in English bit	i	بِنت	bint

Long vowels/Dipthongs

Long vowels and dipthongs are formed by a combination
of the short vowels and the letters alif (ا), waaw (و),
and yaa (ي):

ـَـا	ar as in English far	aa	دَار	daar
ـُـو	oo as in English boot	oo	نُور	noor
ـِـي	ee as in English meet	ee	فِيل	feel
ـَـو	o as in English home	au	يَوم	yaum
ـَـي	ay as in English say	ay	سَير	sayr

Stress

In Arabic the stress in a word tends to fall on syllables with long vowels
or be relatively even. So a word like **yameen** would have the stress on the
long vowel: **yam<u>ee</u>n**; but **laban** would be pronounced with equal stress
on both syllables.

Arabic alphabet and script

Arabic is written right to left (except numbers ➤ 216). The letters also
change their shape depending on whether they are at the beginning, in
the middle, or at the end of a word. Here is the alphabet and script:

	beg:	mid:	end:		beg:	mid:	end:		beg:	mid:	end:
'alif	ا	ـا	ـا	raa'	ر	ـر	ـر	ghayn	غـ	ـغـ	ـغ
baa'	بـ	ـبـ	ـب	zaa'	ز	ـز	ـز	faa'	فـ	ـفـ	ـف
taa'	تـ	ـتـ	ـت	seen	سـ	ـسـ	ـس	qaaf	قـ	ـقـ	ـق
thaa'	ثـ	ـثـ	ـث	sheen	شـ	ـشـ	ـش	kaaf	كـ	ـكـ	ـك
jeem	جـ	ـجـ	ـج	Saad	صـ	ـصـ	ـص	laam	لـ	ـلـ	ـل
Haa'	حـ	ـحـ	ـح	Daad	ضـ	ـضـ	ـض	meem	مـ	ـمـ	ـم
khaa'	خـ	ـخـ	ـخ	Taa'	طـ	ـطـ	ـط	noon	نـ	ـنـ	ـن
daal	د	ـد	ـد	Zaa'	ظـ	ـظـ	ـظ	waaw	و	ـو	ـو
dhaal	ذ	ـذ	ـذ	AHyn	عـ	ـعـ	ـع	yaa'	يـ	ـيـ	ـي

Basic Expressions

ESSENTIAL

Yes./No.	naAHm/laa. نعم./لا.
Okay.	Hasanan. حسنا.
Please.	min faDlak/lau samaHt. من فضلك/لو سمحت.
Thank you.	shukran شكرا
Thank you very much.	shukran jazeelan. شكراً جزيلاً.

Greetings/Apologies الترحيب/الاعتذار

Hello./Hi!	as-salaam AHlaykum/ahlan السلام عليكم./أهلا!
Good morning.	sabaaH al-khayr. صباح الخير.
Good afternoon/evening.	masaa al-khayr. مساء الخير.
Good night.	tiSbaH[ee] AHla khayr تصبح [تصبحي] على خير.
Good-bye.	maAH as-salaama. مع السلامة.
Excuse me! (getting attention)	lau samaHt[ee]! لو سمحت!
Excuse me. (May I get past?)	laa mu'aakhaza. لا مؤاخذة.
Excuse me!/Sorry!	aasif[a]! آسف [آسفة]!
Don't mention it.	AHfwan عفوا.
Never mind.	walaa yuhimmak [yuhimmik]. ولا يهمك.

Communication difficulties

الصعوبة في التفاهم

Do you speak English?	tatkallam[ee] injileezee
	تتكلم [تتكلمين] إنجليزي؟
I don't speak much Arabic.	laa atkallam AHrabee kateer
	لا أتكلم عربي كثير.
Could you speak more slowly?	mumkin tatkallam[ee] bibuT'
	ممكن تتكلم [تتكلمي] ببطء؟
Excuse me?/What was that?	AHfwan/maaza qult[ee] عفوا؟/ماذا قلت؟
Please write it down.	uktubuh [uktubeeh] lau samaHt[ee]
	أكتبه [أكتبيه] لو سمحت.
Can you translate this for me?	mumkin tutarjim[ee] lee haaza
	ممكن تترجم [تترجمين] لي هذا؟
What does this/that mean?	maa maAHnaa haaza ما معنى هذا؟
Please point to the phrase in the book.	ashir [asheeree] ilaal AHibaara feel kitaab, lau samaHt[ee]
	أشر [أشيري] إلى العبارة في الكتاب، لو سمحت.
I understand.	afham. أفهم.
I don't understand.	laa afham لا أفهم.
Do you understand?	hal tafham[ee] هل تفهم [تفهمين]؟

GRAMMAR

Arabic has a masculine and a feminine form of "you," which means the sentence will change slightly depending on whether you are talking to a male or a female. In the *Basic Expressions* section you will find these changes in brackets [ ] in the Arabic column. In the rest of the book only the masculine is shown (➤ 169 for more details).

– mee'a khamsa wa arbAHeen juhayh.
– laa afham.
– mee'a khamsa wa arbAHeen juhayh.
– uktubeeh lee lau samaHtee … aah,
  "145 pounds" … tafaDDalee.

11

Questions أسئلة

Arabic questions are simple to form. There are two types:

1. Questions to which the answer is "yes" (**naAHm**) or "no" (**laa**). These are formed either by simply raising the intonation at the end of a statement or by adding the question word **hal**:

ismak sameer.   Your name is Samir.

ismak sameer?/hal ismak sameer?   Is your name Samir?

2. Other questions are formed by using the relevant question word (➤ 12–17):

maa ismak?   What's your name?

matta yiftaH al-matHaf?   When does the museum open?

Where? أين؟

Where is it?	ayn huwa/hiya أين هو/هي؟
Where are you going?	ilaa ayn tazhab[ee] الى أين تذهب [تذهبين]؟
at the meeting place [point]	AHnda nuqTit al-liqaa' عند نقطة اللقاء
downstairs	taHt تحت
from the U.S.	min amreeka من أمريكا
far away from me	bAHeed AHnee بعيد عني
here (to here)	hunaa (ilaa hunaa) هنا (إلى هنا)
in the car	fees sayyaara في السيارة
in Egypt	fee muSr في مصر
inside	daakhil داخل
near the bank	qareeb min al-bank قريب من البنك
next to the apples	bijaanib at-tufaaH بجانب التفاح
opposite the market	muqaabil as-sooq مقابل السوق
on the left/right	AHlaal yasaar/yameen على اليسار/اليمين
there (to there)	hunaak (ilaa hunaak) هناك (إلى هناك)
to the hotel	ilaal funduq إلى الفندق
outside the café	khaarij al-maqhaa خارج المقهى
up to the traffic lights	Hatta ishaarit al-muroor حتى إشارة المرور
upstairs	fauq فوق

When? متى؟

When does the museum open?	matta yaftaH al-matHaf متى يفتح المتحف؟
When does the train arrive?	matta yaSil al-qiTaar متى يصل القطار؟
10 minutes ago	munzu AHshar daqaa'iq منذ ١٠ دقائق
after lunch	bAHd al-ghadaa' بعد الغداء
always	daa'iman دائما
around midnight	Hawaala muntaSif al-layl حوالى منتصف الليل
at 7 o'clock	as-sAHa sabAHa الساعة ٧
before Friday	qabl yaum al-jumAHa قبل يوم الجمعة
by tomorrow	khilaal al-ghad خلال الغد
early	baakir باكر
every week	kull usbooAH كل أسبوع
for 2 hours	limuddit sAHatayn لمدة ساعتين
from 9 a.m. to 6 p.m.	min tisAHa SabaaHan Hatta sitta masaa'an من ٩ صباحا حتى ٦ مساء
immediately	fauran فورا
in 20 minutes	fee AHishreen daqeeqa في ٢٠ دقيقة
never	abadan أبدا
not yet	laysa bAHd ليس بعد
now	al-aan الآن
often	kateer كثيرا
on March 8	fee tamanya maaris في ٨ مارس
at the weekend	fee nihaayat al-usbooAH في نهاية الأسبوع
sometimes	aHyaanan أحيانا
soon	qareeban قريبا
then	fee haazal waqt في هذا الوقت
within 2 days	khilaal yaumayn خلال يومين

What sort of ...? ؟... ما نوع

I'd like something ...	ureed shay' ... أريد شيئاً
It's ...	haaza ... هذا
beautiful / ugly	jameel/qabeeH جميل/قبيح
better / worse	afDal/aswa' أفضل/أسوأ
big / small	kabeer/Sagheer كبير/صغير
cheap / expensive	rakheeS/ghaalee رخيص/غال
clean / dirty	naZeef/wisikh نظيف/وسخ
dark / light	ghaamiq/faatiH غامق/فاتح
delicious / revolting	lazeez/muqrif لذيذ/مقرف
easy / difficult	sahl/SAHb سهل/صعب
empty / full	faarigh/malyaan فارغ/مليان
good / bad	jayyid/sayyi' جيد/سيء
heavy / light	taqeel/khafeef ثقيل/خفيف
hot, warm / cold	saakhin, daafi'/baarid ساخن، دافئ/بارد
modern / old-fashioned	Hadees/qadeem حديث/قديم
narrow / wide	Dayyiq/waasiAH ضيق/واسع
old / new	qadeem/jadeed قديم/جديد
open / shut	maftooH/mughlaq مفتوح/مغلق
pleasant / unpleasant	murDee/ghayr murDee مرض/غير مرض
quick / slow	sareeAH/baTee' سريع/بطيء
quiet / noisy	haadi'/muzAHij هادئ/مزعج
right / wrong	SaHeeH/khaaTi' صحيح/خاطئ
tall / short	Taweel/qaSeer طويل/قصير
vacant / occupied	faarigh/mashghool فارغ/مشغول
young / old	Sagheer as-sinn/AHjooz صغير السن/عجوز

Why? لماذا؟

Why?	limaaza? لماذا؟
Why not?	lima laa لم لا؟
because of the weather	bi-sabab al-jau بسبب الجو
because I'm in a hurry	li'annee mustAHjil لأني مستعجل
I don't know why.	laa adree limazaa. لا أدري لماذا.

Arabic grammar has two genders: masculine and feminine. Most feminine nouns end with the sound **a** or obviously refer to feminine people (**umm** – mother; **bint** – girl/daughter, etc.). **al** (also pronounced **il**) means *the* and is used for both genders. There is no equivalent of the English *a/an* or of the verb *to be* in the present (*is/am/are*). This means you can have many sentences and questions with no verb at all:

ana mudarris	I (am a) teacher.
ayn al-bank?	Where (is) the bank?
bikam haaza?	How much (is) this?

Adjectives come <u>after</u> the noun. Those referring to feminine nouns also have to be feminine, again usually by adding **a**:

bayt jameel	(a) beautiful house
buhayra jameela	(a) beautiful lake

Arabic plurals are complicated and need to be learned individually (> 215 for more details).

How much/many? كم ثمن/عدد؟

How much is that?	*bikam haaza?* بكم هذا؟
How many are there?	*kam AHdadhum?* كم عددهم؟
1/2/3	*waHid/itnayn/talaata* ٣/٢/١
4/5	*arbAHa/khamsa* ٥/٤
none	*laa shay* لا شيء
about 100 pounds	*meet junayh taqreeban* ١٠٠جنيه تقريبا
a little	*qaleel* قليل
a lot of milk	*Haleeb kateer* حليب كثير
enough	*kifaaya* كفاية
few/a few of them	*bAHD/bAHDuhum* بعض/بعضهم
more than that	*aktar min zaalik* أكثر من ذلك
less than that	*aqall min zaalik* أقل من ذلك
much more	*aktar bi-kateer* أكثر بكثير
nothing else	*laa shay aakhar* لا شيء آخر
too much	*kateer jiddan* كثير جدا

Who? / Which one? مَن؟/أي واحد؟

Who's there?	man hunaak?	من هناك؟
Me!	ana!	أنا!
someone	aHad maa	أحد ما
no one	laa aHad	لا أحد
Which one do you want?	ayy waaHid tureed?	أي واحد تريد؟
this one/that one	haaza/zaalik	هذا/ذلك
one like that	waaHid misl zaalik	واحد مثل ذلك
something	shay maa	شيء ما
nothing/none	laa shay/walaa waaHid	لا شيء/ولا واحد

Whose? لمن؟

Whose is that?	liman haaza	لمن هذا؟
It's ...	innahu ...	إنه
mine/ours/yours	lee/linaa/lak [lik]	لي/لنا/لك [لك]
his/hers/theirs	lahu/lahaa/lahum	له/لها/لهم
It's ...	innahu ...	إنه
my/our/your turn	dooree/doornaa/doorak [doorik]	دوري/دورنا/دورك
his/her/their turn	dooruh/doorhaa/doorhum	دوره/دورها/دورهم

GRAMMAR

To express possession (my/your/our, etc.) in Arabic, you need to add a
particular ending to the noun, e.g.:

kitaab book   **kitaabee** my book

Here is a table of the most important endings:

	ending	example
my	ee	kitaabee
your (masculine sing.)	ak	kitaabak
your (feminine sing.)	ik	kitaabik
your (plural)	kum	kitaabkum
his/its	uh	kitaabuh
her/its	haa	kitaabhaa
our	naa	kitaabnaa
their	hum	kitaabhum

How? كيف؟

How would you like to pay?	*kayf tureed an tadfAH* كيف تريد أن تدفع؟
by credit card	*bi-baTaaqat al-i'timaan* ببطاقة الائتمان
in cash	*naqdan* نقدا
How are you getting here?	*kayf sa-taSil ilaa hunaa* كيف ستصل إلى هنا؟
by car/by bus/by train	*bis-sayyaara/bil-baaS/bil-qiTaar* بالسيارة/بالباص/بالقطار
on foot	*maashiyan* ماشيا
quickly	*bi-surAHa* بسرعة
slowly	*bi-buT'* ببطء
too fast	*sareeAH jiddan* سريع جدا
very	*jiddan* جدا
with a friend	*maAH Sadeeq* مع صديق
without a passport	*bidoon jawaaz safar* بدون جواز سفر

Is it …?/Are there …? هل هو/هل هناك ...؟

Is it …?	*hal huwa* ...؟ هل هو
Is it far?	*hal huwa bAHeed* هل هو بعيد؟
It isn't ready.	*laysa jaahiz* ليس جاهزا.
Is there …?	*hal hunaak* ...؟ هل هناك
Are there …?	*hal hunaak* ...؟ هل هناك
Is there a shower in the room?	*hal hunaak dush feel ghurfa* هل هناك دش في الغرفة؟
Are there buses into town?	*hal hunaak baaSaat ilaal madeena* هل هناك باصات الى المدينة؟
There's a good restaurant near here.	*hunaak maTAHam jayyid qareeb* هناك مطعم جيد قريب.
There aren't any towels in my room.	*laysa hunaak ayy manaashif fee ghurfatee* ليس هناك أي مناشف في غرفتي.
Here it is/they are.	*haa huwa/haa hum hina* ها هو/ها هم هنا.
There it is/they are.	*haa huwa/haa hum hunaak* ها هو/ها هم هناك.

17

ممكن؟ Can/May?

Can I have ...?	*mumkin aakhud*	ممكن آخذ ...؟
Can we have ...?	*mumkin nakhud*	ممكن نأخذ ...؟
May I speak to ...?	*mumkin atkallam mAHa*	ممكن أتكلم مع ...؟
Can you tell me ...?	*mumkin taqool lee*	ممكن تقول لي ...؟
Can you help me?	*mumkin tusaAHidnee*	ممكن تساعدني؟
Can you direct me to ...?	*mumkin tadullnee AHlaa*	ممكن تدلني على ...؟
I can't.	*laa astaTeeAH.*	لا أستطيع.

ماذا تريد؟ What do you want?

I'd like ...	*ureed*	أريد ...
Could I have ...?	*mumkin aakhud*	ممكن آخذ ...؟
We'd like...	*nureed*	نريد ...
Give me ...	*AHTeenee*	أعطني ...
I'm looking for ...	*abHas AHn*	أبحث عن ...
I need to ...	*aHtaaj an*	احتاج أن ...
go to ...	*az-hab ilaa*	أذهب إلى ...
find ...	*ajid*	أجد ...
see ...	*ara*	أرى ...
speak to ...	*atkallam mAHa*	اتكلم مع ...

– lau samaHt.
– *naAHm?*
– mumkin tusaAHidnee?
– *naAHm, TabAHan.*
– mumkin atkallam mAHa al-ustaaz sameer,
min faDlak?
– *laHZa waHda, lau samaHt*

Other useful words كلمات أخرى مفيدة

fortunately	li-Husn al-HaZZ لحسن الحظ
hopefully	atmanna أتمنى
of course	TabAHan طبعا
perhaps/possibly	rubbamaa/jaa'iz ربما/جائز
probably	min al-muHtamal من المحتمل
unfortunately	lil-asaf للأسف

Exclamations علامات تعجب

At last!	akheeran! أخيرا
Go on.	akmil. أكمل
Damn!	lAHeen! لعين
Good God!	yaa ilaahee! يا إلهي
I don't mind.	laa umaaniAH. لا أمانع
No way!	laa majaal! لا مجال
Really?	bijadd? بجد
That's enough.	haaza kifaaya. هذا كفاية
That's true.	haazihil Haqeeqa. هذه الحقيقة
Well I never!	mish mAHqool! مش معقول
How are things?	kayf al-amoor? كيف الأمور
Fine, thank you.	bi-khayr, shukran. بخير، شكرا
great/terrific	raa'iAH رائع
very good	AHZeem عظيم
fine	bi-khayr بخير
okay	mashee al-Haal ماشي الحال
not good	laysa jayyid ليس جيدا
terrible	sayyi' jiddan سيء جدا

Accommodations

There is a wide range of accommodation to choose from in the Middle East, from luxury Western-style hotels to youth hostels, rented apartments, and camping sites. You should try to reserve in advance, particularly during local holidays. In many parts of the Middle East an unmarried man and woman will not be allowed to share a room. Women traveling alone should be especially careful to reserve appropriate accommodation. Types of accommodation available vary from country to country, but the main ones are listed below:

فندق *fundooq*

Hotel. These vary from Western-style hotels, comparable to hotels in Europe and the United States and offering Western-style facilities and cuisine (as well as Arabic food), to small local hotels. Tourist information bureaus often have lists with details of price ranges. Reservations can be made through a travel agent or by directly contacting the hotel.

بنسيون *bensyoon*

Boarding house. Usually family run and often occupying part of an apartment block or the owner's house. Prices are usually reasonable, but facilities are often shared. Rates are often negotiable for longer stays.

شقة مفروشة *shaqqa mafroosha*

Furnished rented appartment. These can be found in many of the major cities in the Middle East – and can be an economic option for a longer stay. For details, contact the tourist information office for the country concerned before you leave.

بيت شباب *bayt shabaab*

Youth hostel. These can be found in many Arab countries, including Egypt, Bahrain, Qatar, and Saudi Arabia. You may need a Hostelling International card to get a discount.

Reservations الحجز

In advance مسبقاً

Can you recommend
a hotel in …?
mumkin tanSaHnaa
bi-funduq fee
ممكن تنصحنا بفندق في …؟

Is it near the center of town?
hal huwa qareeb min wasT il-madeena
هل هو قريب من وسط المدينة؟

How much is it per night?
kam ujrat il-layla? كم أجرة الليلة؟

Is there anything cheaper?
hal hunaak arkhaS? هل هناك أرخص؟

Could you reserve a
room for me there, please?
mumkin taHjiz lee ghurfa hunaak,
lau samaHt
ممكن تحجز لي غرفة هناك، لو سمحت؟

How do I get there?
kayf aSil hunaak
كيف أصل هناك؟

At the hotel في الفندق

Do you have any vacancies?
hal AHndakum ghurfa faarigha
هل عندكم غرفة؟

Is there another hotel nearby?
hal hunaak funduq aakhar qareeb
هل هناك فندق آخر قريب؟

I'd like a single/double room.
ureed ghurfa li-shakhS/li-shakhSayn
أريد غرفة لشخص/لشخصين.

Can I see the room, please?
mumkin araa al-ghurfa,
lau samaHt
ممكن أرى الغرفة، لو سمحت؟

I'd like a room with …
ureed ghurfa bi أريد غرفة بـ…

twin beds
sareerayn سريرين

a double bed
sareer muzdawij سرير مزدوج

a bath/shower
banyo/dush بانيو/دش

– *hal AHnaakum ghurfa faarigha?*
ureed ghurfa li-shakhSayn.
– *aasif, al-funduq mumtali'.*
– *wah. hal hunaak funduq aakhar qareeb?*
– *naAHm, sayyid/sayyida. al meeridiyaan qareeb jiddan.*

21

Reception الاستقبال

I have a reservation.	AHndee Hajz. عندي حجز
My name is …	ismee … اسمي
We've reserved a double and a single room.	Hajaznaa ghurfa li-shakhSayn wa ghurfa li-shakhS حجزنا غرفة لشخصين وغرفة لشخص.
I confirmed my reservation by mail.	akkadt Hajzee bil-bareed أكدت حجزي بالبريد.
Could we have adjoining rooms?	mumkin ghurfatayn maftooHayn AHla bAHDhuma ممكن غرفتين مفتوحين على بعضهما؟

Amenities and facilities التسهيلات ووسائل الراحة

Is there (a/an) … in the room?	hal hunaak … feel ghurfa هل هناك … في الغرفة؟
air conditioning	takyeef hawaa تكييف هواء
TV/telephone	tilifizyoon/tilifoon تلفزيون/تلفون
Does the hotel have (a) …?	hal feel funduq هل في الفندق …؟
cable TV	tilifizyoon kawaabil تلفزيون كوابل
laundry service	maghsala مغسلة
solarium	shurfat Hammaam shamsee شرفة حمام شمسي
swimming pool	masbaH مسبح
Could you put … in the room?	mumkin taDaAH … fee ghurfatee ممكن تضع … في غرفتي؟
an extra bed	sareer iDaafee سرير إضافي
a crib [child's cot]	sareer lil-Tifl سرير للطفل
Do you have facilities for children/the disabled?	hal ladaykum tas-heelaat lil-aTfaal/lil-muAHaaqeen هل لديكم تسهيلات للأطفال/للمعاقين؟

How long ...? كم مدة ...؟

We'll be staying for ...	*sa-nuqeem li-muddat ...* سنقيم لمدة ...
one night only	*layla waahda faqaT* ليلة واحدة فقط
a few days	*biDAHat ayyam* بضعة أيام
a week (at least)	*usbooAH (AHlaal aqall)* أسبوع (على الأقل)
I don't know yet.	*laa aAHrif bAHd.* لا أعرف بعد.
I'd like to stay an extra night.	*awadd al-iqaama layla iDaafeeya* أود الإقامة ليلة إضافية.
What does this mean?	*maa maAHna haaza?* ما معنى هذا؟

– *as-salaam AHlaykum. ismee joon nyootun.*
– *wa-AHlaykum as-salaam sayyid nyootun.*
– *awadd al-iqaama laylatayn.*
– *Hasanan. hal tasmaH bi-tAHbi'at waseeqat at-tasjeel?*

ممكن أرى جواز سفرك، لو سمحت؟	May I see your passport, please?
املأ الاستمارة، لو سمحت.	Please fill in this form.
ما هو رقم لوحة سيارتك؟	What is your car registration number?

غرفة فقط	room only
بالفطور	breakfast included
وجبات متوفرة	meals available
اسم العائلة/الاسم الاول	last name/first name
عنوان البيت/الشارع/رقم	home address/street/number
الجنسية/المهنة	nationality/profession
تاريخ/مكان الولادة	date/place of birth
رقم جواز السفر	passport number
رقم لوحة السيارة	car registration number
المكان/التاريخ	place/date
التوقيع	signature

Price السعر

How much is it …?	*kam tamanuh*	كم ثمنه …؟
per night/week	*feel layla/usbooAH*	في الليلة/الأسبوع
for bed and breakfast	*lis-sareer wal-ifTaar*	للسرير والإفطار
excluding meals	*bidoon al-wajbaat*	بدون الوجبات
for full board [American Plan (A. P.)]	*li-iqaama kaamla*	لإقامة كاملة
for half board [Modified American Plan (M. A. P.)]	*li-nuSf iqaama*	لنصف إقامة
Does the price include …?	*hal yashmil as-sAHr*	هل يشمل السعر …؟
breakfast	*al-fuToor*	الفطور
sales tax [VAT]	*aD-Dareeba*	الضريبة
Do I have to pay a deposit?	*hal aHtaaj li-dafAH AHraboon*	هل أحتاج لدفع عربون؟
Is there a discount for children?	*hal hunaak takhfeeD lil-aTfaal*	هل هناك تخفيض للأطفال؟

Decision القرار

May I see the room?	*mumkin ara al-ghurfa*	ممكن أرى الغرفة؟
That's fine. I'll take it.	*Hasanan. sa-aakhud-haa*	حسنا. سآخذها.
It's too …	*innahaa … jiddan*	أنها … جدا.
dark/small	*muZlima/Sahgeera*	مظلمة/صغيرة
noisy	*Daajja*	ضاجة
Do you have anything …?	*hal AHndak shay*	هل عندك شيئ …؟
bigger/cheaper	*akbar/arkhaS*	أكبر/أرخص
quieter/lighter	*ahda'/aktar inaara*	أهدأ/أكثر إنارة
No, I won't take it.	*laa, lan aakhud-haa*	لا، لن آخذها.

Problems مشاكل

English	Transliteration / Arabic
The ... doesn't work.	... laa yAHmal. ... لا يعمل
air conditioning	takyeef al-hawaa تكييف الهواء
fan	al-marwaHa المروحة
heating	at-tadfi'a التدفئة
light	aD-Dau النور
I can't turn the heat [heating] on/off.	laa astaTeeAH tashgheel/iTfaa' at-tadfi'a لا أستطيع تشغيل/إطفاء التدفئة.
There is no hot water.	laa yoojad maa' saakhin لا يوجد ماء ساخن.
There is no toilet paper.	laa yoojad waraq al-Hammam لا يوجد ورق الحمام.
The faucet [tap] is dripping.	al-Hanafeeya tunnaqiT الحنفية تنقط.
The sink is blocked.	al-maghsal masdood المغسل مسدود.
The window/door is jammed.	ash-shibbaak/al-baab maznooq الشباك/الباب مزنوق.
My room has not been made up.	ghurfatee lam turattab غرفتي لم ترتب.
The ... is broken.	... maksoor. مكسور ...
blind/lamp	ash-sheesh/al-miSbaaH الشيش/المصباح
lock/switch	al-qifl/miftaaH an-noor القفل/مفتاح النور
There are insects in our room.	hunaak Hasharaat fee ghurfatnaa هناك حشرات في غرفتنا.

Action تصرف

English	Transliteration / Arabic
Could you have that seen to?	mumkin tuAHaalij haazihil mushkila ممكن تعالج هذه المشكلة؟
I'd like to move to another room.	awadd al-intiqaal ilaa ghurfa ukhra أود الانتقال إلى غرفة أخرى.
I'd like to speak to the manager.	awadd at-taHaddas mAHal mudeer أود التحدث مع المدير.

General requirements

طلبات عامة

In most Middle Eastern countries the current is 220 volts, but there are variations. There are many different types of sockets and plugs in use, so it is best to take a universal adaptor.

In some countries, you could experience power cuts and may want to take a flashlight [torch] and/or candles for emergencies.

About the hotel عن الفندق

Where's …?	*ayn …*	أين ...؟
the bar	*al-baar*	البار
the bathroom	*al-Hammaam*	الحمام
the dining room	*Hujrat aT-TAHaam*	حجرة الطعام
the elevator [lift]	*al-miSAHad*	المصعد
the parking lot [car park]	*garaaj as-sayyaaraat*	كراج السيارات
the sauna	*ghurfat as-sauna*	غرفة السونا
the shower	*ad-dush*	الدش
the swimming pool	*al-masbaH*	المسبح
the tour operator's bulletin board	*lauhat maktab as-siyaaHa*	لوحة مكتب السياحة
Where are the bathrooms [toilets]?	*ayn al-Hammaamaat*	أين الحمامات؟
What time is the front door locked?	*matta yuqfal al-baab ar-ra'eesee*	متى يقفل الباب الرئيسي؟
What time is breakfast served?	*matta yuqaddam al-ifTaar*	متى يقدم الفطور؟
Is there room service?	*AHndakum khidmaat lil-ghuraf*	عندكم خدمات للغرف؟

لمكنات الحلاقة فقط	razors [shavers] only
مخرج للطوارئ	emergency exit
باب حريق	fire door
الرجاء عدم الإزعاج	do not disturb
لخط خارجي اطلب رقم ...	for an outside line dial …

26

Personal needs طلبات شخصية

The key to room ..., please.	*al-miftaaH lil-ghurfa raqm ..., lau samaHt* المفتاح للغرفة رقم.. ، لو سمحت
I've lost my key.	*aDAHt miftaaHee* أضعت مفتاحي.
I've locked myself out of my room.	*aghlaqt al-baab wal-miftaaH daakhil al-ghurfa* أغلقت الباب والمفتاح داخل الغرفة.
Could you wake me at ... ?	*mumkin tuSaHHeenee as-SaaAH* ممكن تصحيني الساعة ...؟
I'd like breakfast in my room.	*ureed al-ifTaar fee ghurfatee* أريد الفطور في غرفتي.
Can I leave this in the safe?	*mumkin atruk haaza feel khazeena* ممكن أترك هذا في الخزينة؟
Could I have my things from the safe?	*mumkin aakhud ashyaa'ee min al-khazeena* ممكن آخذ أشيائي من الخزينة؟
Where is our tour guide?	*ayn mandoobna as-siyaaHee* أين مندوبنا السياحي؟
May I have an extra ...?	*mumkin aakhud ... iDaafee* ممكن آخذ ... إضافي؟
bath towel	*minshafa* منشفة
blanket	*baTaaniya* بطانية
hanger	*AHlaaqa* علاقة
pillow	*wisaada* وسادة
soap	*Saaboon* صابون
Is there any mail for me?	*hal hunaak bareed lee* هل هناك بريد لي؟
Are there any messages for me?	*hal hunaak rasaa'il lee* هل هناك رسائل لي؟

BREAKFAST ➤ 43; CHANGING MONEY ➤ 138

الإيجار Renting

We've reserved an apartment / cottage in the name of …	Hajaznaa shaqqa/shaalay bism … حجزنا شقة/شاليه باسم …
Where do we pick up the keys?	min ayn sa-nakhud al-mafaateeH من أين سنأخذ المفاتيح؟
Where is …?	ayn …؟ أين
the electricity meter	AHddaad al-kahrabaa عداد الكهرباء
the fuse box	AHilbat Sammaamaat al-kahrabaa' علبة صمامات الكهرباء
the valve [stopcock]	al-maHbas (aS-Samaam) المحبس (الصمام)
the water heater	sakh-khaan al-maa سخان الماء
Are there any spare …?	hal hunaak … iDaafeeya هل هناك … إضافية؟
fuses	Samaamaat al-kahrabaa صمامات الكهرباء
gas bottles	anaabeeb al-ghaaz أنابيب الغاز
sheets	milaayaat ملاءات
Which day does the maid come?	ayy yaum ya'tee AHmilat an-naZaafa أي يوم يأتي عاملة النظافة؟
Where/When do I put out the trash [rubbish]?	ayn/matta ukhrij az-zibaala أين/متى أخرج الزبالة؟

مشاكل؟ Problems?

Where can I contact you?	ayn attaSil bik أين اتصل بك؟
How does the stove / water heater work?	kayf yAHmal al-furn/sakh-khaan al-maa' كيف يعمل الفرن/سخان الماء؟
The … is/are dirty.	al-… wisikh/wiskha. الـ… وسخ/وسخة.
The … has broken down.	al-… tAHTal. الـ… تعطل.
We have accidentally broken/lost the …	bidoon qaSd kasarnaa/aDAHnaa al-… بدون قصد كسرنا/أضعنا الـ…
That was already damaged when we arrived.	kaan taalif AHandamaa waSalnaa كان تالفا عندما وصلنا.

Useful terms عبارات مفيدة

boiler	sakh-khaan	سخان
crockery	awaanee	أوانٍ
freezer	fireezir	فريزر
frying pan	miqlaa	مقلاة
kettle	ghallaaya	غلاية
lamp	miSbaH	مصباح
refrigerator	tallaaja	تلاجة
saucepan	inaa' Sahgeer	إناء صغير
stove [cooker]	furn	فرن
toilet paper	waraq al-Hammaam	ورق الحمام
washing machine	ghasaalat al-malaabis	غسالة الملابس

Rooms غرف

balcony	shurfa	شرفة
bathroom	Hammaam	حمام
bedroom	ghurfat naum	غرفة نوم
dining room	ghurfat TAHaam	غرفة طعام
kitchen	maTbakh	مطبخ
living room	ghurfat juloos	غرفة جلوس
toilet	marHaaD	مرحاض

Youth hostel بيت الشباب

Do you have any places left for tonight?	hal AHndakum amaakin li-layla	هل عندكم أماكن لليلة؟
Do you rent out bedding?	hal tu'ajjir aghTiyyat as-sareer	هل تؤجّر أغطية السرير؟
What time are the doors locked?	matta tuqfal al-abwaab	متى تقفل الأبواب؟
I have an International Student Card.	mAHaya baTaaqat Taalib AHlameeyya	معي بطاقة طالب عالمية.

التخييم Camping

Campsites are found throughout the Arab world and are often in attractive locations, close to the sea. Camping outside official sites is not recommended and can lead to fines and even arrest.

Reservations الحجز

Is there a campsite near here?	hal hunaak mukhayyam qareeb هل هناك مخيم قريب؟
Do you have space for a tent/ trailer [caravan]?	AHndak makaan li-khayma/ li-bayt mutanaqqil عندك مكان لخيمة/لبيت متنقل؟
What is the charge …?	maa huwa as-siAHr …؟ ما هو السعر
per day/week	li-yaum/li-usbooAH ليوم/لأسبوع
for a tent/a car	li-khayma/li-sayyaara لخيمة/لسيارة
for a trailer [caravan]	li-bayt mutanaqqil لبيت متنقل

Facilities خدمات

Are there cooking facilities on site?	hal hunaak lawaazim liT-Tabkh feel makaan هل هناك لوازم للطبخ في المكان؟
Are there any electric outlets [power points]?	hal hunaak mawaaqiAH li-akhd al-kahrabaa هل هناك مواقع لأخذ الكهرباء؟
Where is/are …?	ayn …؟ أين
the drinking water	maa' ash-shurb ماء الشرب
the trash can [dustbin]	Sundooq iz-zibaala صندوق الزبالة
the laundry facilities	al-maghsala المغسلة
the showers	ad-dush الدش
Where can I get some butane gas?	ayn astaTeeAH al-HuSool AHla ghaaz il-biyootaan أين أستطيع الحصول على غاز البيوتان؟

ممنوع التخييم	no camping
ماء الشرب	drinking water
ممنوع إشعال النار/الشواء	no fires/barbecues

Complaints شكاوى

It's too sunny/shady here.	*innahu mushmis/ muZallal jiddan hunaa* إنه مشمس/مظلل جدا هنا.
It's too crowded here.	*innahu muzdaHim jiddan hunaa* إنه مزدحم جدا هنا.
The ground's too hard/uneven.	*al-arD qaasya jiddan/ ghayr mustaweya* الأرض قاسية جدا/غير مستوية.
Do you have a more level spot?	*hal AHndak biqAHa mustaweya* هل عندك بقعة مستوية؟
You can't camp here.	*laa tastaTeeAH an tukhayyim hunaa* لا تستطيع أن تخيم هنا.

Camping equipment أدوات التخييم

butane gas	*ghaaz al-biyootaan* غاز البيوتان
campbed	*sareer safar* سرير سفر
charcoal	*faHm* فحم
flashlight [torch]	*baTaareeyat jayb* بطارية جيب
groundcloth [groundsheet]	*HaSeera* حصيرة
guy rope	*Habl il-khayma* حبل الخيمة
hammer	*miTraqa* مطرقة
kerosene [primus] stove	*mauqad il-bareemoos* موقد البريموس
knapsack	*Haqeebat iZ-Zahr* حقيبة الظهر
mallet	*miTraqa khashabeeya* مطرقة خشبية
matches	*kibreet* كبريت
mattress	*martaba* مرتبة
paraffin	*baaraafeen* بارافين
penknife	*miTwaa* مطواة
sleeping bag	*Haqeebat lil-naum* حقيبة للنوم
tent	*khayma* خيمة
tent pegs	*autaad il-khayma* أوتاد الخيمة
tent pole	*AHamood il-khayma* عامود الخيمة

Checking out المغادرة

What time do we need to vacate the room?	*matta nukhlee il-ghurfa* متى نخلي الغرفة؟
Could we leave our baggage here until ... p.m.?	*hal nastaTeeAH tark HaQaa'ibnaa hunaa Hatta as-sAHa ... bAHd aZ-Zuhr* هل نستطيع ترك حقائبنا هنا حتى الساعة ... بعد الظهر؟
I'm leaving now.	*ana mughaadir al-aan.* أنا مغادر الآن.
Could you order me a taxi, please?	*mumkin tuTlub lee taaksee, lau samaHt* ممكن تطلب لي تاكسي، لو سمحت؟
It's been a very enjoyable stay.	*kaanit iqaama mumtiAH.* كانت إقامة ممتعة.

Paying الدفع

Tipping is usual for most personal services in the Arab world, except perhaps Yemen where it is not customary. Hotel and restaurant staff, as well as taxi drivers, porters, parking lot/toilet attendants, etc., expect a tip at a level suitable to the service rendered. Tipping often supplements low basic wages and is an essential part of many people's income. Make sure you have the appropriate money easily accessible at all times.

May I have my bill, please?	*mumkin tAHTeenee al-Hisaab, lau samaHt* ممكن تعطيني الحساب، لو سمحت؟
I think there's a mistake in the bill.	*AHtaqid an hunaak khaTa feel Hisaab* أعتقد أن هناك خطأ في الحساب.
I've made ... telephone calls.	*itaSalt ... marra bit-tileefoon* اتصلت ... مرة بالتليفون.
I've taken ... from the mini-bar.	*akhadt ... min al-baar aS-Sagheer* أخذت ... من البار الصغير.
Can I have an itemized bill?	*mumkin taAHTeenee qaa'ima mufaSSala bil-Hisaab* ممكن تعطيني قائمة مفصلة بالحساب؟
Could I have a receipt, please?	*mumkin taAHTeenee al-waSl, lau samaHt* ممكن تعطيني الوصل، لو سمحت؟

Eating Out

Restaurants المطاعم

Food has always been one of the central features of the tradition of hospitality in the Arab world. For this reason, you will still find some of the best meals are home-cooked. However, there is also a large variety of restaurants, fast-food outlets, and stalls offering various snacks.

You may have difficulty finding restaurants that offer no-smoking areas, but as much of the seating is outside or in air-conditioned rooms you should not find this too much of a problem.

مطعم maTAHm
Restaurant. Ranging from the very expensive to the budget end of the market. Often offering a mixture of western and Middle-Eastern dishes.

قهوة qahwa
Coffee shop. Mainly for drinking coffee and tea, and smoking **sheesha** (water pipes ➤ 51), but you may be able to eat a sandwich or other snacks.

محل فول وفلافل maHall fool wa falaafil
Bean and falafel stall. One of the most popular snacks (➤ 40).

حلواني halawaanee
Shop selling desserts from rice pudding to sweet sticky cakes.

كأس عرق ومزة kaas AHraq wa mazza
Lebanese restaurant serving **mezza** (➤ 43) and the local aniseed drink, **araq.**

33

Meal times الوجبات أوقات

Generally meals are later than in North America or Northern Europe. However, whenever you get hungry you will generally find something open day or night.

al-futoor الفطور
Breakfast is served between 6 and 10 a.m. in most hotels.

al-ghada الغداء
Lunch is the main meal of the day, usually eaten between 1 and 3:30 p.m.

al-AHsha العشاء
Dinner is usually eaten between 8 and 11 p.m. (or even later) and can be a lighter version of lunch or a snack, such as **faTeer** (pancake ➤ 40).

Arabic cuisine المطبخ العربي

Middle-Eastern cooking is broadly Mediterranean in nature but displays a variety of influences. Lebanese cooking, itself influenced by Greek and Turkish cuisine, is popular throughout the region. A typical meal would consist of **mazza** (appetizers ➤ 43) with the local bread **khubz** (also known as **AHysh**, meaning "life"). This would be followed by the main course of fish or meat, accompanied by vegetables and/or salad. Dessert usually consists of fruit, sweet milk puddings, or small sticky cakes.

Ramadan رمضان

The month of Ramadan is the Muslim month of fasting and lasts for approximately 28 days. As the Muslim calendar is a lunar one, Ramadan moves through the seasons year by year. Your travel agent should be able to tell you the likely dates for a specific year.

During Ramadan many Muslims refrain from eating, drinking or smoking between sunrise and sunset as a communal display of religious faith. Eating habits and meal times change accordingly. The main meals of the day are **suHoor**, a pre-dawn snack, and **iftaar**, the sunset main meal which breaks the fast. There are specific drinks and dishes consumed during Ramadan. One of the most famous drinks is **qamar id-deen**, a type of thick juice made from dried apricot paste. You will find that many international hotels offer both **iftaar** at sunset and then dinner later during Ramadan. Generally cities come to life at night during Ramadan and people go out until the early hours of the morning. Shops are also often open very late. If you are visiting a Muslim country during Ramadan you will usually be able to find places to eat during the day that cater for tourists or non-Muslims. Out of courtesy, however, you should try to avoid eating or smoking in public places during daylight hours.

A table for ..., please.	maa'ida li ..., lau samaHt
	مائدة لـ...، لو سمحت.
1/2/3/4 (people)	shakhS/shakhSayn/talaat
	ashkhaaS/arbAH ashkhaaS
	شخص/شخصين/٣ أشخاص/٤ أشخاص
Thank you.	shukran شكراً
I'd like to pay.	ureed an adfAH
	أريد أن أدفع.

Finding a place to eat التفتيش عن مكان لنأكل

Can you recommend a good restaurant?	mumkin tinSaHnaa bi-maTAHm jayyid
	ممكن تنصحنا بمطعم جيد؟
Is there a ... restaurant near here?	hal hunaak maTAHm ... qareeb
	هل هناك مطعم ... قريب؟
traditional local restaurant	taqleedee maHallee تقليدي محلي
Lebanese	lubnaanee لبناني
Chinese	Seenee صيني
fish	samak سمك
Italian	eeTaalee إيطالي
inexpensive	rakheeS رخيص
vegetarian	nabaateeyeen نباتيين
Where can I find a(n) ... ?	ayn ajid ...
	أين أجد ...؟
burger stand	kushk "burger" كشك "burger"
café/restaurant	maqha/maTAHm مقهى/مطعم
fast food restaurant	maTAHm wajbaat sareeAHa
	مطعم وجبات سريعة
ice-cream parlor	maHall aayis kreem محل آيس كريم
pizzeria	maHall beetza محل بيتزا
steak house	maTAHm laHm steek مطعم لحم ستيك

حجز مائدة Reserving a table

I'd like to reserve a table for …	*ureed hajz maa'da li* أريد حجز مائدة لـ…
For this evening/ tomorrow at …	*li-haazihil layla/lil-ghad as-saAHa …* لهذه الليلة/للغد الساعة …
We'll come at 8.	*sa-na'tee as-saAHa tamaanya* سنأتي الساعة ٨.
A table for 2, please.	*maa'da li-shakhSayn, lau samaHt* مائدة لشخصين، لو سمحت.
We have a reservation.	*AHndina Hajz.* عندنا حجز.

ما هو الاسم، لو سمحت؟	What's the name, please?
آسف. المطعم مشغول/كامل العدد.	We're very busy/full up. I'm sorry.
ستتوفر مائدة بعد … دقائق.	We'll have a free table in … minutes.
رجاء عودوا بعد … دقائق.	Please come back in … minutes.

Where to sit أين نجلس

Could we sit …?	*mumkin najlis …؟* ممكن نجلس …؟
over there	*hunaak* هناك
outside	*feel khaarij* في الخارج
in a non-smoking area	*feel manTiqa mamnooAH feehaa at-tadkheen* في منطقة ممنوع فيها التدخين
by the window	*bi-qurb ash-shubaak* بقرب الشباك
Smoking or non-smoking?	*tadkheen au AHdam at-tadkheen* تدخين أو عدم التدخين؟

– ureed Hajz maa'da li-haazihil layla.
– *li-kam shakhS?*
– li-arbaAH ashkhaaS.
– *matta sa-ta'toon?*
– sa-na'tee as-sAHa at-tamaanya.
– *wa maa huwal ism, lau samaHt?*
– smith.
– Hasanan. ashoofkum.

Ordering الطلب

Waiter!/Waitress!	*yaa garsoon/yaa aanisa* ياجرسون!/يا آنسة!
Do you have a set menu?	*hal ladaykum Tabaq al-yaum* هل لديكم طبق اليوم؟
Can you recommend some typical local dishes?	*hal tinSaHnaa bi-aklaat taqleedeeya maHalleeya* هل تنصحنا بأكلات تقليدية محلية؟
Could you tell me what … is?	*mumkin tiqool lee maaza yakoon* ممكن تقول لي ماذا يكون …؟
What's in it?	*maaza bi-daakhiluh؟* ماذا بداخله؟
What kind of … do you have?	*ayy nauAH min … AHandak* أي نوع من … عندك؟
I'd like	*ureed …* أريد …
I'll have …	*sa-aakhud …* سآخذ …
a bottle/glass/carafe of …	*zujaajat/koob/ibreeq min* زجاجة/كوب/إبريق من …

جاهز لتطلب؟	Are you ready to order?
ماذا تحب؟	What would you like?
هل تفضل طلب المشروبات أولا؟	Would you like to order drinks first?
أنصحكم بـ…	I recommend …
لا يوجد عندنا …	We don't have …
هذا سيستغرق … دقائق.	That will take … minutes.
صحتين.	Enjoy your meal.

> – *jaahiz li taTlub?*
> – *hal tinSaHnaa bi-aklaat maHalleeya?*
> – *naAHm. anSaHkum bil-kufta.*
> – *muwaafiq, sa-aakhud haaza maAH salaTa, lau samaHt.*
> – *bit-ta'keed. wa maaza tureed an tishrab.*
> – *koob min AHSeer manga, lau samaHt.*
> – *bit-ta'keed.*

DRINKS ➤ 49; MENU READER ➤ 52

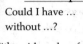

Accompaniments المتممات

| Could I have ... without ...? | mumkin tAHTeenee ... bidoon ...
ممكن تعطيني ... بدون ...؟ |
| With a side order of ... | mAHa Talb jaanibee min
مع طلب جانبي من ... |

Could I have salad instead of vegetables, please?
mumkin aakhud salaTa badal al-khuDaar, lau samaHt
ممكن آخذ سلطة بدل الخضار، لو سمحت؟

Does the meal come with vegetables/rice?
hal al-wajba ta'tee mAHa khuDaar/ruzz
هل الوجبة تأتي مع خضار/رز؟

Do you have any sauces?
AHndakum SalSa؟ عندكم صلصة؟

Would you like ... with that?
hal tureed ... mAHah
هل تريد ... معه؟

vegetables/salad	khuDaar/salaTa خضار/سلطة
potatoes/French fries	baTaaTis/baTaaTis maqleeya بطاطس/بطاطس مقلية
sauce	SalSa صلصة
ice	talj ثلج

May I have some ...?
mumkin aakhud ممكن آخذ ...؟

bread	khubz خبز
butter	zibda زبدة
chili	shaTTa شطة
lemon	leemoon ليمون
mustard	musTarda مسطردة
pepper	filfil فلفل
salt	malH ملح
sugar	sukkar سكر
artificial sweetener	sukkar SinaAH-ee سكر صناعي
vinaigrette [French dressing]	SalSat al-khall صلصة الخل

General questions أسئلة عامة

Could I have a clean ..., please?	mumkin taAHTeenee ... naDeef[a], lau samaHt
	ممكن تعطيني ... نظيف[ة]، لو سمحت؟
cup/glass	finjaan/koob فنجان/كوب
fork/knife	shauka/sikkeen شوكة/سكين
serviette [napkin]/ashtray	mindeel al-maa'ida/manfaDat sajaayir
	منديل المائدة/منفضة سجاير
plate/spoon	SaHn/malAHaqa صحن/ملعقة
I'd like some more ..., please.	ureed al-mazeed min ..., lau samaHt
	أريد المزيد من ...، لو سمحت
Nothing more, thanks.	haaza kifaaya, shukran. هذا كفاية، شكرا
Where are the bathrooms [toilets]?	ayn al-Hammaamaat أين الحمامات؟

Special requirements طلبات خاصة

I mustn't eat food containing ...	ana laa aakul TAHaam feeh
	أنا لا آكل طعاما فيه ...
flour/fat	TaHeen/duhn طحين/دهن
salt/sugar	milH/sukkar ملح/سكر
Do you have meals/drinks for diabetics?	AHndak wajbaat/mashroobaat li-marDa as-sukkaree
	عندك وجبات/مشروبات لمرضى السكري؟
Do you have vegetarian meals?	AHndak wajbaat lin-nabaatiyeen
	عندك وجبات للنباتيين؟

For the children للأطفال

Do you serve children's portions?	hal tuqaddimoo maqaadeer lil-aTfaal?
	هل تقدمون مقادير للأطفال؟
Could we have a child's seat, please?	mumkin taAHTeenee kursee lil-Tifl, lau samaHt
	ممكن تعطيني كرسي للطفل، لو سمحت؟
Where can I change the baby?	ayn ughayyeer al-fuwaT liT-Tifl
	أين أغيير الفوط للطفل؟

Fast food وجبات سريعة

Fast food is a Middle-Eastern specialty, with all sorts of stalls and small shops offering tasty and cheap meals. Arabic bread filled with **fool** (baked fava beans) or **falaafil** (fried crushed chickpeas) are particularly popular. It is best to stick to cooked vegetables or pickles rather than fresh salad if eating off the street. In addition, most major cities will also feature a large number of American-style fast food outlets.

Coffee/Tea, please.	*qahwa/shaay, min faDlak* قهوة/شاي، من فضلك.
with milk/black	*bil-Haleeb/saada* بالحليب/سادة
I'd like a glass of juice.	*ureed koob min al-AHSeer* أريد كوب من العصير.
I'd like two of those.	*ureed itnayn min haaza* أريد اثنين من هذا.
burger/fries	*"burger"/baTaaTis maqleeya* برغر/بطاطس مقلية
(bean/falafel) sandwich	*sandawitsh (fool/falaafil)* سندويتش (فول/فلافل)
(vanilla/chocolate/mango) ice cream	*aayis kreem (faneela/shokoolaata/manga)* آيس كريم (فنيلا/شكولاتة/منجا)
rice pudding	*ruzz bi-Haleeb/ruzz bi-laban* رز بحليب/رز بلبن
A ... portion, please.	*miqdaar ..., lau samaHt.* مقدار ...، لو سمحت.
small/large	*Sagheer/kabeer* صغير/كبير
It's to go [take away].	*sa-aakhuduh mAHaya.* سآخذه معي.
That's all, thanks.	*haaza kull maa ureed, shukran* هذا كل ما أريد، شكرا.

كشري *kosharee*
A mixture of pasta, lentils, fried onions, and rice with a garlic sauce.

شاورمة *shawaarma*
Spit-roasted meat, sliced and put into bread with salad, **humoos**, or **taheena**.

فطير *faTeer*
Thin, rolled savory or sweet pancakes. Watching the pancakes being made is an entertainment in itself.

– maaza tureed?
– itnayn qahwa, lau samaHt.
– bil-Haleeb au saada?
– bil-Haleeb, lau samaHt.
– ta'kul shay'?
– haaza kull maa ureed, shukran.

Complaints شكاوى

I have no knife/fork/spoon.	laysa AHndee sikkeen/shauka/milAHqa ليس عندي سكين/شوكة/ملعقة.
There must be some mistake.	AHtaqid an hunaak khaTa أعتقد أن هناك خطأ.
That's not what I ordered.	haaza laysa maa Talabtuh هذا ليس ما طلبته.
I asked for …	ana Talabt … أنا طلبت
I can't eat this.	laa astaTeeAH an aakul haaza لا أستطيع أن آكل هذا.
The meat is …	al-laHm … اللحم
overdone/underdone	kateer as-siwaa/qaleel as-siwaa كثير السوا/قليل السوا
too tough	AHseer al-maDgh عسير المضغ
This is too …	haaza … jiddan. هذا … جدا.
bitter/sour	murr/Haaziq مر/حادق
The food is cold.	aT-TAHaam baarid. الطعام بارد.
This isn't fresh/clean.	haaza ghayr Taazij/naZeef هذا غير طازج/نظيف.
How much longer will our food be?	kam min al-waqt yajib intiZaar aklinaa كم من الوقت يجب انتظار أكلنا؟
We can't wait any longer. We're leaving.	laa nastaTeeAH al-intiZaar aktar. sa-nughaadir لا نستطيع الانتظار أكثر. سنغادر.
I'd like to speak to the head waiter/manager.	ureed at-takallum mAHal mitr/mudeer أريد التكلم مع المتر/المدير.

الدفع Paying

Tipping is generally expected if you are happy with the service. ten percent is usually fine, although you might want to tip the main waiter and the assistants separately.

I'd like to pay.	ureed an adfAH. أريد أن أدفع.
The bill, please.	al-Hisaab, lau samaHt. الحساب، لو سمحت.
We'd like to pay separately.	nureed an nidfAH munfaSileen نريد أن ندفع منفصلين.
It's all together, please.	Hisaab waaHid, lau samaHt حساب واحد، لو سمحت.
I think there's a mistake in this bill.	AHtaqid an hunaak khaTa feel Hisaab اعتقد أن هناك خطأ في الحساب.
What is this amount for?	maa hazaal mablagh؟ ما هذا المبلغ؟
I didn't have that. I had …	maa akhadt haaza. akhadt ما أخذت هذا. أخذت …
Is service included?	hal al-khidma Dimn al-Hisaab هل الخدمة ضمن الحساب؟
Can I pay with this credit card?	mumkin adfAH bi-biTaaqat al-itimaan haazihi؟ ممكن أدفع ببطاقة الائتمان هذه؟
I've forgotten my wallet.	naseet maHfaZtee. نسيت محفظتي.
I don't have enough money.	laysa AHndee fuloos kifaaya ليس عندي فلوس كفاية.
Could I have a receipt, please?	mumkin taAHTeenee al-waSl, lau samaHt ممكن تعطيني الوصل، لو سمحت؟
That was a very good meal.	kaanat wajba mumtaaza. كانت وجبة ممتازة.

> – garsoon! mumkin tAHTeenee al-Hisaab, lau samaHt?
> – bit-ta'keed. tafaDDal.
> – hal il-khidma Dimn al-Hisaab?
> – naAHm.
> – mumkin adfAH bi-biTaaqat al-itimaan haazihi?
> – TabAHan.
> – shukran. kaanat wajba mumtaaza.

Course by course

Breakfast الفطور

A typical Arabic breakfast would consist of tea, **fool** and
falaafil (➤ 40), eggs, olives, cheese, and bread.
Many hotels will offer this and more Western-style dishes as well.

I'd like …	أريد … *ureed*
bread/butter	خبز/زبدة *khubz/zibda*
a boiled egg	بيضة مسلوقة *bayDa maslooqa*
fried/scrambled eggs	بيض مقلي/ممزوج *bayD maqlee/mamzooj*
fruit juice	عصير فواكه *AHseer fawaakih*
orange/grapefruit	برتقال/كريب فروت *burtuqaal/ greeb froot*
honey/jam	عسل/مربى *AHsal/murabba*
milk	حليب *Haleeb*
roll	خبز صغير *khubz sagheer*
toast	خبز محمص *khubz muHammaS*

Appetizers [Starters] المقبلات (المشهيات)

Appetizers, or **mazza,** are an important part of an Arabic meal. A mixture
of appetizers is usually placed in the middle of the table and shared by
everyone. Here are some of the most popular:

باباغنوج *babaghannooj*
A dip made with eggplant [aubergine] and tahini paste.

حمص بالطحينة *HumooS bi-TaHeena*
A dip made of ground chickpeas and sesame paste.

كفتة *kofta*
Fried or grilled balls/fingers of minced meat.

جبنة بيضاء بالطماطم *jibna bayDa biT-TamaaTim*
White, soft cheese (similar to Greek feta cheese) mashed with
tomatoes, and herbs.

طحينة *TaHeena*
A dip made of sesame paste with olive oil, lemon, and cumin.
Particularly popular in Egypt.

ورق عنب *waraq AHinab*
Rolled vine leaves stuffed with rice, sometimes mixed with minced meat.

بطارخ *baTaarikh*
Egyptian smoked grey mullet roe.

Soups شورية

Soups are popular in winter and tend to be rich. They are always accompanied by bread and sometimes include noodles. There is a huge variety of soups based on beans, vegetables, and meat. Here are some of the most popular:

شورية عدس	*shoorbit AHds*	lentil soup
شورية فراخ	*shoorbit firaakh*	chicken soup
شورية خضار	*shoorbit khuDaar*	vegetable soup
شورية لحم	*shoorbit laHm*	meat soup
شورية طماطم	*shoorbit TamaaTim*	tomato soup
شورية سمك	*shoorbit samak*	fish soup

ملوخية *mulookheeya*

Thick Egyptian soup made of finely chopped **mulookheeya** leaves (a green vegetable similar to spinach), cooked with rabbit, chicken, or meat. Often poured onto pieces of torn-up bread or rice.

شورية كوارع *shoorbit kawaariAH*

Thick gelatinous soup made from calves hoofs.

Egg dishes أطباق البيض

بيضة مسلوقة	*bayDa maslooqa*	boiled eggs
بيض مقلٍ	*bayD maqlee*	fried eggs
بيض ممزوج	*bayD mamzooj*	scrambled eggs
عجة	*AHjja*	omelet
بيض بالبسطرمة	*bayD bil-basTurma*	eggs with cured beef
بيض بالفول	*bayD bil-fool*	eggs with fava beans
بيض بالبلوبيف	*bayD bil-buloobeef*	eggs with corned beef

44

Pastries and pies الفطائر

Savory pastries and pies are a favorite in many parts of the Arab world, particularly North Africa. Here are a few you might want to sample in addition to the pancakes (**faTeer** ➤ 40):

سنبوسك sanboosak
Half-moon-shaped pastries filled with cheese or meat.

بريك breek
Fried Tunisian filo pastry parcels, with a variety of fillings.

بستلة bastilla
Moroccan pigeon pie, often baked for special occasions.

طاجن Taajin
Baked Tunisian meat pie with string [haricot] beans and cinnamon.

لحم بعجين laHm bi-AHjeen
Syrian baked, open-faced minced-meat pies.

Fish and seafood أسماك و مأكولات بحرية

In coastal areas, take advantage of the wonderful variety of fresh fish and seafood. You'll find the fish is often laid out fresh on ice or even alive in tanks for you to take your pick. You'll recognize **toona** and **sardeen**.

Other types of fish are regional and often have several different names, making it difficult to provide a comprehensive list.

Fish is usually eaten whole, either grilled (**mashwee**) or fried (**maqlee**), although fish kebabs (**kabaab samak**) are also popular.

كابوريا	kaaboorya	crab
استاكوزا	istaakooza	lobster
بوري/سلطان إبراهيم	booree/sulTaan ibraaheem	mullet
بلح البحر	balaH al-baHr	mussels
أخطبوط	akhTabooT	octopus
محار	maHHaar	oyster
جمبري/قريدس	jambaree/quraydis	shrimp [prawn]
سمك موسى	samak moosa	sole
سبيط	subbayT	squid

Meat and poultry اللحم والدواجن

Traditionally "meat" (**al-laHm**) in the Middle East meant lamb or mutton as cattle was not reared and pork is forbidden by Islamic law. Although lamb is still probably the most widely available meat, beef is now also popular and chicken, turkey, duck, pigeon, and some other small birds are also staples of Arabic cuisine. In some areas goat, rabbit, and camel meat are also eaten. However, pork (**laHm al-khinzeer**) is not generally available, except in some Christian areas.

I'd like some… أريد … *ureed*

لحم بقري	*laHm baqaree*	beef
ضاني	*Daanee*	lamb
بتلو	*bitilloo*	veal
أرانب	*araanib*	rabbit
دجاج	*dajaaj*	chicken
حمام	*Hamaam*	pigeon
ديك رومي	*deek roomee*	turkey
بط	*baTT*	duck
كبدة	*kibda*	liver
كلاوي	*kalaawee*	kidney
سجق	*sujuq*	sausage
فيليه	*feelayh*	steak
اسكالوب	*iskaaloob*	veal cutlet
كفتة	*kufta*	meatballs
مخ	*mukh*	brains

كبة نية *kibba nayya*
Raw minced meat with spices. A kind of Lebanese steak tartar.

طاجن *Taajin*
North African lamb stew baked in clay pots with fruit and honey.

فتة *fatta*
Boiled mutton with rice and bread soaked in broth, vinegar, and garlic.

كبيبة *kubayba*
Minced meat and cracked wheat, either in balls or flat in a tray.

سليق *saleeq*
Lamb cooked in spiced milk and served on rice. A Bedouin specialty.

حمام محشي *Hamaam maHshee*
Pigeon stuffed with cracked wheat or rice.

<u>Vegetables خضار</u>

Vegetables are more often found stuffed, stewed, or pickled than boiled. A wide range is generally available, and some vegetables, e.g., eggplant [aubergine], have seemingly endless variations.

باذنجان	*baazinjaan*	eggplant [aubergine]
كرنب/ملفوف	*kurunb/malfoof*	cabbage
بصل	*baSal*	onion
بسلة	*bisilla*	peas
فاصوليا خضراء	*faSoolya khaDra*	green beans
خس	*khass*	lettuce
بطاطس	*baTaaTis*	potatoes
فلفل أخضر	*filfil akhDar*	green pepper
بامية	*bamya*	okra [ladies' fingers]
كوسة	*koosa*	zucchini [courgette]
جزر	*jazar*	carrots
ذرة	*dura*	corn
خيار	*khiyaar*	cucumber
طماطم	*TamaaTim*	tomatoes

محشي *maHshee*
Vegetables stuffed with a mixture of rice, onion, minced meat, and herbs. Stuffed vine leaves (**waraq AHinab** ➤ 43) are one of the most popular **maHshee**. Others are stuffed eggplant [aubergine], cabbage, tomato, pepper, and zucchini [courgette]. They can be eaten hot or cold.

بامية بالموزة *bamya bil-mauza*
Okra [ladies' fingers] stewed with lamb knuckles.

تبولة *tabboola*
Lebanese salad made with cracked wheat and very finely chopped onion, tomato, parsley, mint, olive oil, and lemon.

طرشي *Torshee*
Pickled vegetables – carrots, cucumbers, etc. – which are sometimes a distinctive red color due to a red cabbage dye.

Cereals and beans الحبوب والبقول

Rice is the staple cereal but cracked wheat, lentils, beans and chickpeas are also popular. A specialty of North Africa is couscous (**kuskus**). This is steamed cracked wheat served hot with meat, vegetables, and the broth from the meat.

رز	*ruzz*	rice
عدس	*AHds*	lentils
مكرونة	*makaroona*	pasta
حمص	*HumuS*	chickpeas
فول	*fool*	brown (fava) beans
برغل	*burghul*	cracked wheat

Cheese جبنة

جبنة بيضاء	*jibna bayDa*	white (feta) cheese
جبنة رومي	*jibna roomee*	hard cheese, similar to Parmesan
لبنة	*labna*	curd cheese
جبنة مالحة	*jibna malHa*	salted curd cheese

Dessert الحلو

Most Arabs have a sweet tooth and tend to eat very sugary desserts, but in small portions, together with fruit (➤ 49). The most popular desserts are syrupy pastries or milk-based puddings.

مهلبية *maHallabeeya*
Smooth rice or corn-flour pudding.

أم علي *umm AHlee*
A type of sweet hot milk pudding with nuts and raisins.

قطايف *qaTaayif*
Pastry filled with nuts and soaked in syrup.

لقمة القاضي *luqmit al-QaaDee*
Small fried dough balls soaked in syrup. Literally means "the judge's morsel."

بسبوسة *basboosa*
Semolina cake soaked in syrup.

كعب الغزال *kAHb al-ghazaal*
North African speciality. Horn-shaped pastries filled with almonds and flavored with orange-flower water.

Fruit فواكه

برقوق	barqooq	plums
تين	teen	figs
فراولة	faraawla	strawberries
رمان	rummaan	pomegranates
أناناس	anaanaas	pineapples
بلح	balaH	dates
تفاح	tufaaH	apples
مشمش	mishmish	apricots
بطيخ	baTTeekh	watermelon
جوافة	jawaafa	guavas
خوخ	khookh	peaches
برتقال	burtuqaal	oranges
موز	mauz	bananas
منجا	manga	mangos
عنب	AHinab	grapes

Drinks مشروبات

Alcoholic drinks مشروبات كحولية

Alcohol is strictly forbidden to Muslims under Islamic law, and in some Arab countries, notably Saudi Arabia, it is illegal. However, in many other countries alcohol is relatively available in tourist areas and hotels. Lebanon and Egypt have a long history of wine and beer production, and local brews are worth sampling – and are much cheaper than imported brands. A local specialty of Lebanon and the Levant is **AHraq**, an aniseed drink similar to the Greek ouzo or the French pastis. Most other alcoholic drinks are known by their original names: **weeskee**, **rum**, **beera**, etc.

I'd like a bottle of …	*ureed zujaajit …*	أريد زجاجة …
local beer	*beera maHalleeya*	بيرة محلية
imported beer	*beera mustawrada*	بيرة مستوردة
white wine	*nabeet abyaD*	نبيذ أبيض
red wine	*nabeet aHmar*	نبيذ أحمر
I'd like a glass of araq.	*ureed koob AHraq.*	أريد كوب عرق.
with ice/without ice	*bi-talj/bidoon talj*	بثلج/بدون ثلج

Non-alcoholic drinks مشروبات بدون كحول

Freshly squeezed juices and bottles of international and local soft drinks are popular throughout the region. You will find juice bars serving a large variety of delicious fruit juices and cocktails squeezed in front of you. Soft drinks often have to be drunk on the spot and the bottles returned. Non-alcoholic beers and wines are also becoming widely available, and there are several international and local brands on the market.

You may also find **karkaday**, a drink made from the flowers of the fuchsia plant that can be drunk hot or cold, and tamarind or sugar-cane juice (see below).

I'd like a bottle of …	*ureed zujaajit* … أريد زجاجة
I'd like a/an …	*ureed* … أريد
apricot juice	*AHSeer mishmish* عصير مشمش
carrot juice	*AHSeer jazar* عصير جزر
grape juice	*AHSeer AHinab* عصير عنب
guava juice	*AHSeer jawaafa* عصير جوافة
lemon juice	*AHSeer laymoon* عصير ليمون
mango juice	*AHSeer manga* عصير منجا
orange juice	*AHSeer burTuqaal* عصير برتقال
pomegranate juice	*AHSeer rummaan* عصير رمان
strawberry juice	*AHSeer faraawla* عصير فراولة
sugar-cane juice	*AHSeer qaSab* عصير قصب
tamarind juice	*tamr hindee* تمر هندي
mineral water	*miyaah mAHdaneeya* مياه معدنية
non-alcoholic beer/wine	*beera/nabeet bidoon kuHool* بيرة/نبيذ بدون كحول

Tea and coffee شاي وقهوة

Tea and coffee are popular throughout the Middle East, drunk both in the traditional way – strong, sweet, and black – and increasingly also in the Western style. You can find Western-style cafés within hotels and in the larger towns, or you can try out a local coffee house (**al-qahwa**).

Going to an Arab coffee house is more than just refreshment. It's tradition. Inside or on the terrace you can entertain yourself by watching the local street life.

Tea is served in a glass, black with sugar and sometimes mint. Coffee is served in espresso-sized glasses or cups and is very strong and black. The coffee beans are roasted and cardamon is added for flavoring. You can order it regular, extra sweet, or without sugar.

You can also order a **sheesha** (or **naarjeela**), the famous Arab water pipe. You need to specify whether you want **tumbaak**, a natural coarse tobacco, or **maa AHsil**, a lighter tobacco mixed with molasses. You may also like to play backgammon or dominoes.

Unfortunately, it's almost exclusively men who patronize coffee houses, and if you go as an unaccompanied woman you could feel ill at ease.

I'd like a glass/cup of ...	*ureed koob/finjaan* ... أريد كوب/فنجان
tea	*shaay* ... شاي
mint tea	*shaay bi-nAHnAH* شاي بنعنع
(Arabic) coffee	*qahwa* قهوة
regular (Arabic) coffee	*qahwa maZbooT* قهوة مظبوط
extra-sweet (Arabic) coffee	*qahwa ziyaada* قهوة زيادة
(Arabic) coffee without sugar	*qahwa saada* قهوة سادة
instant coffee	*naskaafay* نسكافيه
I'd like a water pipe.	*ureed sheesha (naarjeela)* أريد شيشة (نارجيلة).
We'd like a backgammon board/some dominoes, please.	*nureed Taawlat az-zahr/doomeenoo, min faDlak* نريد طاولة الزهر/دومينو، من فضلك.

Menu Reader

This Menu Reader gives listings under main food headings. You will see that the Arabic script is shown in large type. This is to help you to identify, from a menu that has no English, at least the basic ingredients making up a dish.

Meat and poultry

لحم	laHm	meat (general)
بقري	baqaree	beef
ضاني	Daanee	lamb/mutton
دجاج	dajjaaj	chicken
بطّ	baTT	duck
ديك رومي	deek roomee	turkey
حمام	Hamaam	pigeon
كبدة	kibda	liver
سجق	sujuq	sausages
مخ	mukh	brain
شوربة	shoorba	soup

Fish and seafood

سمك	samak	fish (general)
كابوريا	kaaboorya	crab
استاكوزا	istaakooza/	lobster
بوري/ سلطان إبراهيم	booree/ sulTaan ibraheem	mullet
بلح البحر	balaH al-baHr	mussels
أخطبوط	akhTabooT	octopus
محار	maHHaar	oysters
جمبري/قريدس	jambaree/quraydis	shrimp [prawn]
سمك موسى	samak moosa	sole
سبيط	subbayT	squid
قاروس	qaaroos	sea bass
تونة	toona	tuna
قرش	qirsh	shark

<u>Vegetables</u>

خضار	khuDaar	vegetables (general)
ثوم	toom	garlic
سبانخ	sabaanikh	spinach
بطاطس	baTaaTis	potatoes
طماطم	TamaaTim	tomatoes
خس	khass	lettuce
خيار	khiyaar	cucumber
كوسة	koosa	zucchini [courgette]
بامية	bamya	okra [ladies' fingers]
جزر	jazar	carrots
بصل	baSal	onions
ذرة	dura	corn
باذنجان	baadinjaan	eggplant [aubergine]

Fruit

فواكه	*fawaakih*	fruit (general)
تفّاح	*tuffaaH*	apples
برتقال	*burtuqaal*	oranges
موز	*mauz*	bananas
عنب	*AHinab*	grapes
تين	*teen*	figs
منجا	*mangaa*	mangos
فراولة	*faraawla*	strawberries
بلح	*balaH*	dates
مشمش	*mishmish*	apricots
بطيخ	*batteekh*	watermelon
شمام	*shammaam*	cantaloupe
تين شوكي	*teen shaukee*	prickly pears

Staples: bread, rice, pasta, etc.

خبز	khubz	bread
رزّ	ruzz	rice
برغل	burghul	cracked wheat
مكرونة	makaroona	pasta
عدس	AHds	lentils
فول	fool	brown (fava) beans
حمص	HummuS	chickpeas

Basics

ملح	malH	salt
فلفل	filfil	pepper
خل	khall	vinegar
زيت زيتون	zayt zaytoon	olive oil

Herbs and spices

شطّة	shaTTa	chili
بقدونس	baqdoonis	parsley
زعتر	zAHtar	thyme
كرفس	karafs	celery
حب الهان	Habb al-haan	cardamon
قرفة	qirfa	cinnamon
كزبرة	kuzbara	coriander
كمون	kammoon	cumin
قرنفل	qurunfil	clove
حار	Haar	hot (chili)
طازج	Taazij	fresh
مجفف	mujaffaf	dried

محشٍ	maHshee	stuffed
مشوٍ	mashwee	grilled
مقلٍ	maqlee	fried
مدخّن	mudakhkhan	smoked
مسلوق	maslooq	boiled
متبّل	mutabbal	marinated
في الفرن	feel furn	baked
مهروس	mahroos	creamed
مكعّبات	mukAHabaat	diced
مخلّل	muKHallal	pickled
ني	nayy	raw
بالتقلية	bit-taqleeya	flavored with coriander and garlic

Classic dishes

كفتة	*kofta*	kofta *fried or grilled meat balls*
كباب	*kabaab*	shish kebab *grilled lamb chunks*
ورق عنب	*waraq AHinab*	stuffed vine leaves
طاجن	*Taajin*	*North African lamb stew*
كبيبة	*kubayba*	*balls of minced meat and cracked wheat*
فول مدمّس	*fool mudammis*	fava beans *slow baked fava beans*
فلافل	*falaafil*	falafel *fried crushed chick peas*
ملوخية	*mulookheeya*	*soup made of green-leaf plant*
كسكس	*kuskus*	couscous *steamed cracked wheat*
فطير	*faTeer*	*savory or sweet dough-based pancakes*
شاورمة	*shawarma*	*sliced, spit-roasted meat*

Drinks

مشروبات	*mashroobaat*	drinks (general)
ماء	*maa'*	water
حليب	*Haleeb*	milk
شاي	*shaay*	tea
شاي بنعناع	*shaay bi-nAHnaAH*	mint tea
قهوة	*qahwa*	(Arabic) coffee
نسكافيه	*naskaafayh*	instant coffee
كركديه	*karkadayh*	tea made from fuchsia flowers, *drunk hot or cold*
بيرة	*beera*	beer
نبيذ	*nabeet*	wine
مياه معدنية	*miyaah mAHdaneeya*	mineral water

Juices

عصير	*AHSeer*	juice
عصير برتقال	*AHSeer burtuqaal*	orange juice
عصير ليمون	*AHSeer laymoon*	lemon juice
تمر هندي	*tamr hindee*	tamarind juice
عصير قصب	*AHSeer qaSab*	sugar-cane juice
عصير منجا	*AHSeer manga*	mango juice
عصير جزر	*AHSeer jazar*	carrot juice
عصير مشمش	*AHSeer mishmish*	apricot juice
عصيرجوافة	*AHSeer jawaafa*	guava juice
عصير أناناس	*AHSeer anaanaas*	pineapple juice
عصير فراولة	*AHSeer faraawla*	strawberry juice

Snacks

بطاطس مقلية	*baTaaTis maqleeya*	French fries [chips]
برغر	*burghur*	burger
بسكوت	*baskoot*	cookies [biscuits]
كعكة	*kAHka*	cake
سندويتش	*sandwitsh*	sandwich
شبس	*shibs*	potato chips [crisps]
فول سوداني	*fool soodaanee*	peanuts
لبّ	*libb*	dried melon seeds
عين جمل	*AHyn jamal*	walnuts
فستق	*fuzduq*	pistachios
شوكولاتة	*shookoolaata*	chocolate
ذرة مشوية	*dura mashweeya*	grilled corn

Dairy products

جبنة	jibna	cheese
لبن زيادي	laban zabaadee	yogurt
قشطة	qishTa	cream
زبدة	zibda	butter
حليب	Haleeb	milk
لبنة	labna	curd cheese
جبنة قديمة	jibna qadeema	matured cheese
جبنة بيضاء	jibna bayDaa	feta cheese
بيض	bayD	eggs
سمنة	samna	ghee *clarified butter*
شنكليش	shankaleesh	curd cheese *with olive oil*

Desserts

رز بحليب	*ruzz bi-Haleeb*	rice pudding
آيس كريم	*aayis kreem*	ice cream
سلطة فواكه	*salaTat fawaakih*	fruit salad
كريم كرامل	*kreem karamil*	crème caramel
مهلبية	*muHallabeeya*	*smooth cold milk pudding*
بسبوسة	*basboosa*	semolina cake
قطايف	*qaTaayif*	*filled sweet pastries*
أمّ علي	*umm AHlee*	*sweet hot milk pudding*
كعب الغزال	*kAHb al-ghazaal*	North-African pastries
عجوة	*AHjwa*	dried dates
كنافة	*kunaafa*	vermicelli cake

Travel

ESSENTIAL

1/2/3 ticket(s) to …	waaHid/itnayn/talaata tazaakir ilaa
	١/٢/٣ تذاكر إلى …
To …, please.	ilaa …, lau samaHt.
	إلى … ، لو سمحت.
one-way [single]	zahaab ذهاب
round-trip [return]	zahaab wa eeyaab ذهاب وإياب
How much …?	bikam …؟ بكم

Safety السلامة

Would you accompany me to …?	mumkin turaafiqnee ilaa
	ممكن ترافقني إلى …؟
the bus stop	mauqaf il-ootoobees
	موقف الأوتوبيس
my hotel	al-funduq إلى الفندق
I don't want to … on my own.	laa ureed an … waHdee
	لا أريد أن … وحدي.
stay here	abqaa hunaa أبقى هنا
walk home	amshee lil-bayt أمشي للبيت
I don't feel safe here.	laa aHiss bil-amaan hunaa
	لا أحس بالأمان هنا.

الوصول Arrival

Visas are needed to enter most Middle-Eastern countries, but the cost and criteria vary. Sometimes visas can be bought at the point of entry, but you will need to check as this varies from country to country and from year to year. Check with your travel agent or with the relevant consulate. Usually it is better to obtain your visa from your own country prior to travel.

Generally it is easier to obtain visas to countries with a tradition of tourism – Egypt, Jordan, Morocco, Tunisia, etc. – than it is to Saudi Arabia or some of the Gulf states. You could experience difficulties obtaining a visa if you have evidence of a visit to Israel on your passport.

It is best generally to avoid bringing videotapes, camcorders, or electronic goods into the country as you could experience a delay, or could even have items confiscated, while the material is checked out by customs.

Saudi Arabia prohibits the import of alcohol or pork products.

مراقبة جوازات السفر Passport control

We have a joint passport.	mAHana jawaaz mushtarak معنا جواز مشترك.
The children are on this passport.	al-aulaad AHla hazal jawaaz الأولاد على هذا الجواز.
I'm here on vacation [holiday]/business.	ana huna fee ijaaza/fee riHlit AHmal أنا هنا في إجازة/في رحلة عمل.
I'm just passing through.	ana huna fee muroor أنا هنا في مرور.
I'm going to ...	ana zaahib ilaa أنا ذاهب إلى ...
I'm ...	ana ... أنا
on my own	waHdee وحدي
with my family	mAHa AHiltee مع عائلتي
with a group	mAHa majmooAH مع مجموعة

WHO ARE YOU WITH? ➤ 120

Customs الجمرك

I have only the normal allowances.	mAHaya al-mukhaSSaS al-AHdee faqaT معي المخصص العادي فقط.
It's a gift.	innahaa hadeeya. إنها هدية.
It's for my personal use.	haaza li-istiAHmaalee ash-shakhsee هذا لاستعمالي الشخصي.

هل عندك شيء للإعلان عنه؟	Do you have anything to declare?
يجب دفع رسوم على هذا.	You must pay duty on this.
أين اشتريت هذا؟	Where did you buy this?
من فضلك افتح هذه الحقيبة.	Please open this bag.
هل معك حقائب أخرى؟	Do you have any more baggage?

I would like to declare …	ureed al-iAHlaan AHn … أريد الإعلان عن …
I don't understand.	laa afham. لا أفهم.
Does anyone here speak English?	hunaaka aHad yitkallam injileezee هناك أحد يتكلم إنجليزي؟

مراقبة جوازات السفر	passport control
معبر الحدود	border crossing
الجمارك	customs
لاشيء للإعلان عنه	nothing to declare
بضائع للإعلان عنها	goods to declare
بضائع السوق الحرة	duty-free goods

Duty-free shopping مشتريات السوق الحرة

What currency is this in?	bi-ayy al-AHumlaat hazaa بأي العملات هذا؟
Can I pay in …	mumkin adfAH bil… ممكن أدفع بالـ…
dollars	dolaar دولار
marks	mark مارك
pounds (Sterling)	junayh (isterleenee) جنيه (إسترليني)

Plane الطائرة

Because of the distances involved and difficulties in traveling overland, flying is often the best option for moving around the region. Many countries have established airlines – EgyptAir, Saudia, Kuwait Air, etc. – and extensive internal networks. The services tend to be frequent and reliable.

Tickets and reservations التذاكر والحجز

When is the … flight to …?	matta ar-riHla … ilaa ؟	متى الرحلة ... إلى ...؟
first/next/last	al-oolaa/al-qaadima/al-akheera	الأولى/القادمة/الأخيرة
I'd like 2 … tickets.	ureed tazkaratayn	أريد تذكرتين ...
one-way [single]	zahaab (faqaT)	ذهاب (فقط)
round-trip [return]	zahaab wa eeyaab	ذهاب وإياب
first class	ad-daraja al-oolaa	الدرجة الأولى
business class	darajit rijaal al-AHmaal	درجة رجال الأعمال
economy class	ad-daraja as-siyaaHiyya	الدرجة السياحية
How much is a flight to …?	bikam ar-riHla ilaa … ؟	بكم الرحلة إلى ...؟
Are there any supplements/reductions?	hal hunaak ayy iDaafaat/takhfeeDaat	هل هناك أي إضافات/تخفيضات؟
I'd like to … my reservation for flight number 526.	ureed … al-Hajz lil-riHla raqm 526	أريد ... الحجز للرحلة رقم ٥٢٦.
cancel	ilhgaa'	إلغاء
change	tahgyeer	تغيير
confirm	ta'keed	تأكيد

Inquiries about the flight استعلامات عن الرحلة

What time does the plane leave?	matta tuqliAH aT-Taa'ira	متى تقلع الطائرة؟
What time will we arrive?	matta sa-naSil	متى سنصل؟
What time do I have to check in?	matta yajib an atsajjal feel maTaar	متى يجب أن أتسجل في المطار؟

Checking in التسجيل

Where is the check-in desk for flight ...?	*ayn maktab at-tasjeel lir-riHla* أين مكتب التسجيل للرحلة...؟
I have ...	*mAHaya* ... معي
3 cases to check in	*talat Haqaa'ib lit-tasjeel* ٣ حقائب للتسجيل
2 pieces of hand baggage	*Haqeebatayn lil-yad* حقيبتين لليد

تذكرتك/جواز سفرك، لو سمحت.	Your ticket/passport, please.
تريد مقعدا بجانب الشباك أم بقرب الممر؟	Would you like a window or an aisle seat?
للمدخنين أم لغير المدخنين؟	Smoking or non-smoking?
اذهب إلى قاعة الرحيل، لو سمحت.	Please go through to the departure lounge.
كم حقيبة معك؟	How many pieces of baggage do you have?
معك أمتعة زيادة.	You have excess baggage.
لازم تدفع مبلغ إضافي بقدر ... ريال.	You'll have to pay a supplement of ... Riyals
هذا ثقيل/كبير جدا لحقيبة يد.	That's too heavy/large for hand baggage.
هل حزمت هذه الحقائب بنفسك؟	Did you pack these bags yourself?
هل تحتوي على مواد حادة أو كهربائية؟	Do they contain any sharp or electronic items?

الوصول	arrivals
الرحيل	departures
الأمن	security check
لا تترك أمتعة وحدها.	Do not leave bags unattended.

BAGGAGE ➤ 71

Information المعلومات

Is there any delay on flight …?	hal hunaak ta'kheer AHla ar-riHla هل هناك تأخير على الرحلة …؟
How late will it be?	kam muddit at-ta'kheer? كم مدة التأخير؟
Has the flight from … landed?	hal waSalt ar-riHla min هل وصلت الرحلة من …؟
Which gate does flight … leave from?	min ayy bawwaaba tughaadir ar-riHla raqm من أي بوابة تغادر الرحلة رقم …؟

Boarding/In-flight الصعود/أثناء الطيران

Your boarding card, please.	baTaaqat aS-SuAHood, lau samaHt بطاقة الصعود، لو سمحت.
Could I have a drink/something to eat, please?	mumkin tAHTeenee mashroob/bAHD aT-TAHaam, lau samaHt ممكن تعطيني مشروبا/بعض الطعام، لو سمحت؟
Please wake me for the meal.	arjook ayqiZnee lil-wajba أرجوك أيقظني للوجبة.
What time will we arrive?	matta sa-naSil? متى سنصل؟

Arrival الوصول

Where is/are …?	ayn … ؟ أين
the currency exchange	maktab aS-Sarf مكتب الصرف
the buses	al-ootoobeesaat الأوتوبيسات
the car rental [hire]	sayyaara lil-isti'jaar سيارة للاستئجار
the exit	al-makhraj المخرج
the taxis	at-takseeyaat التكسيات
Is there a bus into town?	hal hunaak ootoobees ilaa wasT al-madeena هل هناك أوتوبيس إلى وسط المدينة؟
How do I get to the … Hotel?	kayf aSil ilaa funduq … كيف أصل إلى فندق …؟

Baggage أمتعة

Porters at airports and railway stations usually expect a tip
(➤ 32).

Porter! Excuse me!	shayyaal! lau samaHt شيال! لو سمحت!
Could you take my baggage to …?	mumkin tusaaAHidnee fee Haml Haqaa'ibee ilaa ممكن تساعدني في حمل حقائبي إلى …؟
the taxi/bus	at-taaksee/al-ootoobees التاكسي/الأوتوبيس
Where is/are the …?	ayn …؟ أين …؟
luggage carts [trolleys]	AHarabit al-Haqaa'ib عربة الحقائب
luggage lockers	khazaa'in al-Haqaa'ib خزائن الحقائب
luggage check [left-luggage office]	maktab al-amaanaat مكتب الأمانات
baggage reclaim	istirdaad al-Haqaa'ib استرداد الحقائب
Where is the baggage from flight …?	ayn al-Haqaa'ib min ar-riHla أين الحقائب من الرحلة …؟

Loss, damage, and theft فقدان، تلف وسرقة

I've lost my baggage.	faqadt Haqaa'ibee. فقدت حقائبي.
My baggage has been stolen.	suriqat Haqaa'ibee سرقت حقائبي.
My suitcase was damaged.	talifat Haqeebtee تلفت حقيبتي.
Our baggage has not arrived.	Haqaa'ibnaa lam taSil حقائبنا لم تصل.

ما شكل أمتعتك؟	What does your baggage look like?
هل معك بطاقة الاسترداد؟	Do you have the claim check [reclaim tag]?
أمتعتك …	Your baggage …
ربما بعثت إلى…	may have been sent to …
ربما تصل في أي وقت اليوم	may arrive later today
أرجوك أن تعود غدا.	Please come back tomorrow.
اتصل بهذا الرقم لمراجعة ما إذا كانت الأمتعة قد وصلت.	Call this number to check if your baggage has arrived.

قطار Train

In contrast to the airline network, the rail network in the
Middle East is patchy and sometimes decrepit. There are
virtually no international services in operation, a notable
exception being the Amman to Damascus route (part of the
famous Hijaaz railway line). In some tourist areas there are good quality
services running between cities, such as the Cairo to Luxor overnight
service which departs from Ramses station. Where such services exist,
they can be a relaxing alternative to traveling by bus or airplane and a
good way of seeing some of the countryside.

To the station إلى المحطة

How do I get to the (main) train station?	kayf aSil ilaa maHaTTat il-qiTaar (ar-ra'eeseeya)
	كيف أصل إلى محطة القطار (الرئيسية)؟
Does the train to Aswan leave from … Station?	hal al-qiTaar ilaa aswaan yaqoom min maHaTTat
	هل القطار إلى أسوان يقوم من محطة …؟
How far is it?	kam tabAHod كم تبعد؟
Can I leave my car there?	mumkin atruk sayyaartee hunaak
	ممكن أترك سيارتي هناك؟

At the station في المحطة

Where is/are …?	ayn …؟ أين
the information desk	maktab al-istiAHlaamaat مكتب الاستعلامات
the baggage check	maktab tasjeel al-amtiAHa
	مكتب تسجيل الأمتعة
the lost-and-found [lost property office]	maktab al-mafqoodaat
	مكتب المفقودات
the luggage lockers	khazaa'in al-amtiAHa خزائن الأمتعة
the platforms	al-arsifa الأرصفة
the snack bar	maTAHm snaak مطعم سناك
the ticket office	shibbaak at-tazaakir شباك التذاكر
the waiting room	Saalit il-intiZaar صالة الانتظار

مدخل	entrance
مخرج	exit
إلى الأرصفة	to the platforms
معلومات	information
الحجز	reservations
الوصول	arrivals
الرحيل	departures

Tickets and reservations التذاكر والحجز

Inter-rail passes, available for 30-day train travel in participating European countries, are also valid in Morocco. Student discounts are also often available if you have an International Student Card.

I'd like a … ticket to Cairo.	*ureed tazkara … ilaal qaaHira* أريد تذكرة ... إلى القاهرة.
one-way [single]	*zahaab (faqaT)* ذهاب (فقط)
round-trip [return]	*zahaab wa eeyaab* ذهاب وإياب
first/second class	*daraja oolaa/tanya* درجة أولى/ثانية
concessionary	*bi-takhfeeD* بتخفيض
I'd like to reserve a seat.	*ureed Hajz maqAHd* أريد حجز مقعد.
aisle seat	قرب الممر *qurb al-mamarr*
window seat	قرب الشباك *qurb ash-shibbaak*
Is there a sleeper car?	*hal hunaak AHarabit naum* هل هناك عربة نوم؟
I'd like a … berth.	*ureed sareer* أريد سرير ....
upper/lower	علوي/سفلى *AHlwee/sufla*

DIRECTIONS ➤ 94

73

ثمن Price

Be sure to check out ticket prices in advance at the station of departure. Finding out about and buying the correct tickets could take some time – and you don't want to do it five minutes before the train is due to leave!

How much is that?	*kam tamanuh* كم ثمنه؟
Are there discounts for …?	*hunaak takhfeeDaat lil* هناك تخفيضات للـ....؟
children / families	*aTfaal/AH'ilaat* أطفال/عائلات
senior citizens	*musinneen* مسنين
students	*Tullaab* طلاب
Do you offer a cheap same-day round-trip [return] fare?	*hunaak takhfeeDaat lil-AHauda fee nafs al-yaum* هناك تخفيضات للعودة في نفس اليوم؟

استفسارات Queries

Do I have to change trains?	*laazim ughayyir al-qiTaar* لازم أغير القطار؟
Is it a direct train?	*hal huwa qiTaar mubaashir* هل هو قطار مباشر؟
You have to change at …	*laazim tughayyir AHand …* لازم تغير عند …
How long is this ticket valid for?	*maa hiya muddit SalaaHeeyit hazihit tazkara* ما هي مدة صلاحية هذه التذكرة؟
Can I take my bicycle on to the train?	*mumkin aakhud ad-darraaja feel qiTaar* ممكن آخذ الدرّاجة في القطار؟
Can I return on the same ticket?	*mumkin arjAH bi-nafs at-tazkara* ممكن أرجع بنفس التذكرة؟
In which car [coach] is my seat?	*maqAHdee fee ayy maqToora* مقعدي في أي مقطورة؟
Is there a dining car on the train?	*hal hunaak ghurfit TAHaam feel qiTaar* هل هناك غرفة طعام في القطار؟

– ureed tazkara ilaa il-iskandareeya, lau samaHt.
– *zahaab faqaT au zahaab wa eeyaab?*
– zahaab wa eeyaab, lau samaHt.
– *haaza khamseen junayh.*
– hal yajib an ughayyir al-qiTaar?
– *nAHm, laazim tughayyir feel qahira.*
– shukran. mAHas salaama.

مواعيد القطارات Train times

Could I have a timetable, please?	mumkin tAHTeenee jadwal al-mawaaAHeed, lau samaHt ممكن تعطيني جدول المواعيد، لو سمحت؟
When is ... train to Luxor?	matta yaqoom al-qiTaar ... ilaal uqSur متى يقوم القطار ... إلى الأقصر؟
the first / next / last	al-awall / al-qaadim / al-akheer الأول / القادم / الأخير
How frequent are the trains to ...?	kam AHadad al-qiTaaraat ilaa كم عدد القطارات إلى...؟
once / twice a day	marra / marratayn feel yaum مرة / مرتين في اليوم
5 times a day	khamas marraat feel yaum ٥ مرات في اليوم
every hour	kull SaAHa كل ساعة
What time do they leave?	matta taqoom al-qiTaaraat متى تقوم القطارات؟
What time does the train stop at ...?	matta yaqif al-qiTar AHnd متى يقف القطار عند ...؟
What time does the train arrive in ...?	matta yaSil al-qiTar ilaa متى يصل القطار إلى ...؟
How long is the trip?	kam muddit ir-riHla كم مدة الرحلة؟
Is the train on time?	hal al-qiTaar fee mauAHiduh هل القطار في موعده؟

Departures رحيل

| Which platform does the train to … leave from? | min ayy raSeef yaqoom al-qiTaar ilaa
من أي رصيف يقوم القطار إلى …؟ |
| Where is platform 4? | ayn ar-raSeef raqm arbAHa
أين الرصيف رقم ٤؟ |

| over there | hunaak هناك |
| on the left/right | AHla al-yasaar/al-yameen
على اليسار/اليمين |

| Where do I change for …? | ayn ughayyir al-qiTaar li
أين أغير القطار لـ …؟ |
| How long will I have to wait for a connection? | kam Tool fatrat intiZaar al-muwaaSla
كم طول فترة انتظار المواصلة؟ |

Boarding الصعود

Is this the right platform for the train to …?	hal haaza huwa raSeef al-qiTaar ilaa هل هذا هو رصيف القطار إلى …؟
Is this the train to …?	hal haazal qiTaar ilaa هل هذا القطار إلى …؟
Is this seat taken?	hal haazal maqAHd maHjooz هل هذا المقعد محجوز؟
I think that's my seat.	aZunn an haaza makaanee أظن أن هذا مكاني.
Here's my reservation.	haaza Hajzee. هذا حجزي.
Are there any seats/berths available?	hal hunaak maqaaAHid/asirra farigha هل توجد مقاعد/أسرة فارغة؟
Do you mind if …?	hal AHndak maaniAH an هل عندك مانع أن …؟
I sit here	ajlis hunaa أجلس هنا
I open the window	aftaH ash-shibbaak أفتح الشباك

On the journey أثناء الرحلة

How long are we stopping here for?

kam sa-natwaqqaf hunaa

كم سنتوقف هنا؟

When do we get to ...?

matta naSil ilaa

متى نصل إلى ...؟

Have we passed ...?

hal futnaa

هل فتنا ... ؟

Where is the dining/ sleeper car?

ayn AHrabit aT-TAHaam/an-naum

أين عربة الطعام/النوم؟

Where is my berth?

ayn sareeree

أين سريري؟

I've lost my ticket.

faqadt tazkartee

فقدت تذكرتي.

فرامل الطوارئ	emergency brake
أداة الإنذار	alarm
باب أوتوماتيكي	automatic door

Long-distance bus [Coach] أوتوبيس رحلات

Long-distance buses are a popular means of transportation in the region and cover far more destinations than the rail network. They are usually cheap and fairly reliable, but can be crowded. You may have to book in advance to ensure you get a seat.

Where is the bus [coach] station?

ayn maHaTTit il-ootoobees

أين محطة الأوتوبيس؟

When's the next bus [coach] to ...?

matta yaqoom al-ootoobees al-qaadim ilaa

متى يقوم الأوتوبيس القادم إلى ...؟

Which bay does it leave from?

min ayy mawqaf sa-yantaliq

من أي موقف سينطلق؟

Where are the bus [coach] bays?

ayn mawaaqif al-ootoobees

أين مواقف الأوتوبيس؟

Does the bus [coach] stop at ...?

hal yaqif al-ootoobees AHnd

هل يقف الأوتوبيس عند ...؟

How long does the trip take?

kam min al-waqt ta'khud ar-riHla

كم من الوقت تأخذ الرحلة؟

تاكسي جماعي (سرفيس) Shared taxi

Another popular means of long-distance travel is the shared taxi or microbus (**servees**), which is the middle ground between long-distance buses and private taxis. These run between towns from known starting points and usually seat seven to ten people paying a fixed fare. Each **servees** will wait until it is full and then depart. If the wait is very long, it is possible for the existing passengers to agree to share the cost of the empty places.

From where does the shared taxi to ... leave?	min ayn yughaadir as-sarfees ilaa من أين يغادر السرفيس إلى ...؟
How much is the fare to ...?	kam al-ujra ilaa ... ؟ كم الأجرة إلى ...؟

أوتوبيس/ترام Bus/Tram

Buses and sometimes trams are a cheap way to travel around cities, but avoid them during the crowded rush hours. You might find the bus number in Western figures, but the destination is often written only in Arabic script, so you'll need to ask around to find the correct bus.

Where is the bus station/terminus?	ayn maHaTTit al-ootoobees/al-mawqaf أين محطة الأوتوبيس/الموقف؟
Where can I get a bus/tram to ...?	ayn mumkin aakhud al-ootoobees/ at-traam ilaa أين ممكن آخذ الأوتوبيس/الترام إلى ...؟
What time is the bus to ...?	matta yaqoom al-ootoobees ilaa متى يقوم الأوتوبيس إلى ...؟

تحتاج إلى هذا الموقف هناك/ في آخر الشارع.	You need that stop over there/ down the road.
تحتاج إلى الأوتوبيس رقم ...	You need bus number ...
لازم تغير الأوتوبيس عند ...	You must change buses at ...

موقف الأوتوبيس	bus stop
طلب التوقف	request stop
ممنوع التدخين	no smoking
مخرج (طوارئ)	(emergency) exit

Buying tickets شراء تذاكر

Where can I buy tickets?	ayn ashtaree at-tazaakir أين أشتري التذاكر؟
A … ticket, please.	tazkara …, lau samaHt تذكرة …، لو سمحت.
one-way [single]	zahaab (faqaT) ذهاب (فقط)
round-trip [return]	zahaab wa eeyaab ذهاب وإياب
one-day / weekly / monthly	yaumeeya/usbooAHeeya/shahreeya يومية/أسبوعية/شهرية
A booklet of tickets, please.	kutayb min at-tazaakir, lau samaHt كتيب من التذاكر، لو سمحت.
How much is the fare to …?	bikam at-tazkara ilaa بكم التذكرة إلى …؟

Traveling السفر

Is this the right bus/tram to …?	hal haaza huwa al-ootoobees/ at-traam ilaa هل هذا هو الأوتوبيس/الترام إلى …؟
Can you tell me when to get off?	mumkin taqool lee matta anzil, min faDlak؟ ممكن تقول لي متى أنزل، من فضلك؟
Do I have to change buses?	hal yajib an ughayyir al-ootoobees هل يجب أن أغير الأوتوبيس؟
How many stops are there to …?	kam maHaTTa qabl كم محطة قبل …؟
Next stop, please!	al-maHaTTa al-qaadima, lau samaHt المحطة القادمة، لو سمحت!

– lau samaHt. hal haaza huwa al-ootoobees
ilaa mabnal muHaafZa?
– naAHm, raqm tamanya.
– waHda ilaa mabnal muHaafZa, lau samaHt.
– haaza itnayn junayh.
– mumkin taqool lee matta anzil, min faDlak?
– arbaAH maHaTTaat min huna.

Subway [Metro] مترو (أنفاق)

Cairo has a modern subway [metro] which opened in the late 1980s. The single line runs for over 40 kilometers from the southern suburb of Helwan, through the center and out to the northeast suburbs. Further extensions are planned. It is an efficient, clean, and cheap way to travel.

General inquiries استعلامات عامة

Where's the nearest subway [metro] station?	ayn aqrab maHaTTit metro أين أقرب محطة مترو؟
Where can I buy a ticket?	ayn ashtaree tazkara أين أشتري تذكرة؟
Could I have a map of the subway [metro]?	mumkin tAHTeenee khareeTit al-metro ممكن تعطيني خريطة المترو؟

Traveling التنقل

Is this the right train for …?	hal haaza huwa al-qiTaar ilaa هل هذا هو القطار إلى…؟
Which stop is it for …?	ayy maHaTTa li أي محطة لـ…؟
How many stops is it to …?	kam maHaTTa qabl كم محطة قبل…؟
Is the next stop …?	hal al-maHaTTa al-qaadima hiya هل المحطة القادمة هي…؟
Where are we?	ayn naHnu؟ أين نحن؟
Where do I change for …?	ayn sa-ughayyir ilaa أين سأغير إلى…؟
What time is the last train to …?	matta aakhir qiTaar ilaa متى آخر قطار إلى…؟

إلى خطوط أخرى to other lines

المعدية Ferry

There are numerous ferries operating to and between Middle-Eastern countries, across the Mediterranean, the Red Sea, and the Persian Gulf. Taking a ferry is usually an economical choice, as well as being a good way of avoiding trouble spots on land.

A cruise down the Nile is a perennial favorite. Many ships operate between Luxor and Aswan. Check with your travel agent or the Egyptian tourist office for details about cruises currently available.

When is the ... car ferry?	matta mAHdeeyat as-sayyaaraat ... متى معدية السيارات ...؟
first/next/last	al-oolaa/al-qaadima/al-akheera الأولى/القادمة/الأخيرة
A round-trip [return] ticket for ...	tazkara zahaab wa eeyaab ilaa تذكرة ذهاب وإياب إلى ...
1 car and 1 trailer [caravan]	sayyaara wa bayt mutanaqqil سيارة وبيت متنقل
2 adults and 3 children	itnayn kubaar wa talaat aTfaal ٢ كبار و٣ أطفال
I want to reserve a ... cabin.	ureed Hajz kaabeena أريد حجز كابينة ...
single/double	li-shakhS/li-shakhSayn لشخص/لشخصين

life preserver [life belt]	حزام النجاة
lifeboat	مركب النجاة
muster station	محطة الاجتماع

Boat trips رحلات بالمركب

Is there a ...?	hal hunaak ...؟ هل هناك ...؟
boat trip	riHla bil-markib رحلة بالمركب
river cruise	jaula feen nahr جولة في النهر
What time does it leave/return?	matta tuqliAH/tAHood؟ متى تقلع/تعود؟
Where can I buy tickets?	min ayn ashtaree at-tazaakir من أين أشتري التذاكر؟

TIME ➤ 220; BUYING TICKETS ➤ 73, 79

1 brake pad *teel al-faraamil* تيل الفرامل
2 bicycle bag *Haqeebit ad-darraaja* حقيبة الدراجة
3 saddle *sarj* سرج
4 pump *maDakhkha* مضخة
5 water bottle *qaneenit maa* قنينة ماء
6 frame *iTaar* إطار
7 handlebars *maqwad ad-darraaja* مقود الدراجة
8 bell *jaras* جرس
9 brake cable *kabl al-faraamil* كبل الفرامل
10 gear shift [lever] *ziraAH al-musanninaat* ذراع المسننات
11 gear/control cable *musanninaat/* مسننات/ سلك التحكم
 silk at-taHakkum
12 inner tube *anbooba daakhileeya* أنبوبة داخلية
13 front/back wheel *doolaab (AHjala)* دولاب (عجلة) أمامي / خلفي
 amaamee/khalfee
14 axle *miHwar ad-doolaab* محور الدولاب
15 tire [tyre] *doolaab (AHjala)* دولاب (عجلة)
16 wheel *doolaab (AHjala)* دولاب (عجلة)
17 spokes *barmaq* برمق
18 bulb *lamba* لمبة
19 headlamp *noor AHalee* نور عال

20 pedal *dawaasa* دواسة
21 lock *qifl* قفل
22 generator [dynamo] *muwallid* مولّد
23 chain *silsila* سلسلة
24 rear light *noor khalfee* نور خلفي
25 rim *Hafa* حافة
26 reflectors *AHaakis* عاكس
27 fender [mudguard] *rafraf ad-doolaab (al-AHjala)* رفرف الدولاب (العجلة)
28 helmet *khooza* خوذة
29 visor *muqadimat al-khooza* مقدمة الخوذة
30 fuel tank *tank al-batrool* تنك البترول
31 clutch lever *dibriyaaj* دبرياج
32 mirror *miraaya* مرآة
33 ignition switch *miftaH al-muHarrik* مفتاح المحرك
34 turn switch [indicator] *mu'ashshir* مؤشر
35 horn *aalat at-tanbeeh* آلة التنبيه
36 engine *muHarrik* محرك
37 gear stick [shift] *mubaddil as-surAHa* مبدل السرعة
38 kick [main] stand *sannaada wuqoof* سنادة وقوف
39 exhaust pipe *maasoorat al-AHdim* ماسورة العادم
40 chain guard *ghaTaa as-silsila* غطاء السلسلة

82

Bicycle/Motorbike دراجة/دراجة نارية

Bicycles can be rented in many tourist resorts and are often a fun and cheap alternative to taxis. Look for rental places in the street or ask your guide or at your hotel.

I'd like to rent a …	*ureed isti'jaar* … أريد استئجار
3-/10-speed bicycle	*darraaja bi-talaat/ bi-AHshar musanninaat* دراجة بثلاثة/بعشرة مسننات
moped/motorbike	*darraaja naareeya Sahgeera/darraaja naareeya* دراجة نارية صغيرة/دراجة نارية
How much does it cost per day/week?	*kam tukallif bil-yaum/bil-usbooAH* كم تكلف باليوم/بالأسبوع؟
Do you require a deposit?	*hal taHtaaj ilaa AHrboon* هل تحتاج إلى عربون؟
The brakes don't work.	*al-faraamil laa tAHmil.* الفرامل لا تعمل.
There is/are no lights.	*laa yoojad anwaar.* لا يوجد أنوار.
The front/rear tire [tyre] has a flat [puncture].	*al-AHjala al-amaameeya/ al-khalfeeya feehaa thuqb.* العجلة الأمامية/الخلفية فيها ثقب.

Hitchhiking طلب توصيل

People do hitchhike around the region but it is not recommended, particulary for women. Often the truck or car providing the lift will expect to be paid anyway, in which case you might as well have taken a bus or a shared taxi (➤ 78).

Where are you heading?	*ilaa ayn tazhab* إلى أين تذهب؟
I'm heading for …	*azhab ilaa* … أذهب إلى
Could you drop me off …?	*mumkin tunazzilnee* …؟ ممكن تنزلني
here	*hunaa* هنا
at the next exit	*AHnd al-makhraj al-qaadim* عند المخرج القادم
downtown	*fee wasT al-balad* في وسط البلد
Thanks for the lift.	*shukran AHla tawSeelee.* شكرا على توصيلي.

تاكسي Cab [Taxi]

Where can I get a taxi?	ayn mumkin aakhud taaksee أين ممكن آخذ تاكسي؟
Do you have the number for a taxi?	AHndak nimrit tileefoon taaksee عندك نمرة تليفون تاكسي؟
I'd like a taxi …	ureed taaksee … أريد تاكسي …
now	al-aan الآن
in an hour	bAHd saAHa بعد ساعة
for tomorrow at 9:00	ghadan as-saAHa at-taasiAHa غدا الساعة التاسعة
The address is … .	al-AHunwaan huwa العنوان هو… .
I'm going to … .	azhab ilaa … . أذهب إلى… .

● للتأجير for hire ●

Please take me to …	min faDlak, waSSilnee ilaa من فضلك، وصلني إلى …
the airport	al-maTaar المطار
the train station	maHaTTat al-qiTaar محطة القطار
this address	hazaal AHunwaan هذا العنوان
How much will it cost?	kam sa-tukallif؟ كم ستكلف؟
How much is that?	bikam hazaa؟ بكم هذا؟
You said … pounds.	anta qult … junayh أنت قلت … جنيه.
On the meter it's … .	inaahaa … AHlal AHdaad إنها … على العداد.
Keep the change.	iHtafiZ bil-baaqee احتفظ بالباقي.

> – mumkin tuwaSSilnee ilaal maHaTTa, lau samaHt?
> – bit-ta'keed.
> – shukran … kam sa-tukallif?
> – AHshara junayh.
> – tafaDDal. iHtafiz bil-baaqee

Car / Automobile سيارة

Having your own car can be an advantage in some parts of the Middle East, for example Saudi Arabia and the Gulf states, but driving presents several problems, and you might find it easier to use other available means of transportation.

Driving between towns is reasonable by day, but obtaining permits and finding a feasible route may not be – especially if this involves crossing borders.

You will need an International Driver's license for all countries in the region. Minimum driving ages vary, and regulations can be difficult to fathom or non-existent. Unless you have sufficient time to get used to the local driving conditions, you might want to opt for a local driver.

One general feature of driving in the area is the frequent use of the horn, which Western visitors should try to understand. This is often interpreted as impatience – and sometimes it is – but it is also the most usual way of alerting a car in front to your presence when, for example, passing. Many vehicles do not make use of rearview mirrors and will expect you to give a couple of short blasts on the horn when you are about to pass. They will probably also move over to give you more room.

Conversion chart

Kilometers are the standard measure of distance in the Arab world. Here is a conversion chart to convert distance and speed:

km	1	10	20	30	40	50	60	70	80	90	100	110	120	130
miles	0.62	6	12	19	25	31	37	44	50	56	62	68	74	81

Road network

Main roads in Arab countries, often desert roads, are generally reliable, and you will sometimes find signs in both English and Arabic. However, these roads can be dangerous at night as they have no barriers and other vehicles can be traveling at high speeds.

Finding your way within towns, especially the older cities, can be a major problem. Streets may not have names, and many traffic signs are written only in Arabic. It is therefore easy to get completely lost. You will be more comfortable with a driver.

Car rental تأجير سيارة

Renting a car is possible in most towns, but it is often expensive. It may be possible to rent a car with an English-speaking driver, either through your hotel or a travel agent.

Where can I rent a car?	*ayn astaTeeAH isti'jaar sayyaara* أين أستطيع استئجار سيارة؟
I'd like to rent ...	*ureed isti'jaar ...* أريد استئجار ...
a 2-/4-door car	*sayyaara bi-baabayn/bi-arbAHa abwaab* سيارة ببابين/بأربع أبواب
an automatic	*otomateek* أوتوماتيك
a car with 4-wheel drive	*sayyaara bid-dafAH ar-rubaaAHee* سيارة بالدفع الرباعي
a car with air conditioning	*sayyaara bit-takyeef*. سيارة بالتكييف.
I'd like it for a day/week.	*ureedha li-muddit yaum/usbooAH* أريدها لمدة يوم/أسبوع.
How much does it cost per day/week?	*kam sa-tukallif bil-yaum/bil-usbooAH* كم ستكلف باليوم/بالأسبوع؟
Is mileage/insurance included?	*hal al-massafa/at-ta'meen mashmool* هل المسافة/التأمين مشمول؟
Are there special weekend rates?	*hunaak asAHaar khaaSSa bi-nihaayat al-usbooAH* هناك أسعار خاصة بنهاية الأسبوع؟
Can I return the car at ...?	*mumkin urajjiAH as-sayyaara AHnd ...* ممكن أرجّع السيارة عند ...؟
What sort of fuel does it take?	*maa nauAH al-wuqood alazee tatazawwad bih* ما نوع الوقود الذي تتزود به؟
Where is the high [full]/ low [dipped] beam?	*ayn aD-Dau' al-AHalee/al-munkhafiD* أين الضوء العالي/المنخفض؟
Could I have full insurance?	*mumkin aakhud ta'meen shaamil* ممكن آخذ تأمين شامل؟

Gas [Petrol] station محطة البنزين

Where's the next gas [petrol] station, please?	*ayn maHaTTa al-banzeen at-taaleeya, lau samaHt* أين محطة البنزين التالية، لو سمحت؟
Is it self-service?	*hal hiya khidma zaateeya* هل هي خدمة ذاتية؟
Fill it up, please.	*imlaa'haa, lau samaHt* املأها، لو سمحت.
... liters of gasoline [petrol], please.	*... litraat banzeen, lau samaHt* ... لترات بنزين، لو سمحت.
premium [super]/regular	*mumtaaz/AHadee* ممتاز/عادِ
lead-free/diesel	*doon raSaaS/deezil* دون رصاص/ديزل
Pump number ...	*al-maDakhkha raqm ...* المضخة رقم ...
Where is the air pump/water?	*ayn maDakhkhat al-hawaa/al-maa'* أين مضخة الهواء/الماء؟

• price per liter ثمن اللتر •

Parking الركن

Parking is usually a question of survival of the fittest and double parking is common – although most town centers do have restrictions. Often you can find people in the street who, for a modest tip, will find you a parking place and look after your car while you're gone. Many of the larger hotels will have their own parking lots [car parks] for the use of the guests.

Is there a parking lot [car park] nearby?	*hal hunaak makaan rakn sayyaaraat qareeb* هل هناك مكان ركن سيارات قريب؟
What's the charge per hour/ per day?	*kam al-Hisaab fees saAHa/feel yaum* كم الحساب في الساعة/في اليوم؟
Do you have some change for the parking meter?	*AHndak Sarraafa li-AHdaad ar-rakn* عندك صرافة لعداد الركن؟
My car has been booted [clamped]. Who do I call?	*sayyaaratee rubiTat bi-mulzim. bi-man attaSil* سيارتي رُبطت بملزم. بمن أتصل؟

NUMBERS ➤ 216; DIRECTIONS ➤ 94

Breakdown تعطل

If you break down in a populated area, you can usually find a local mechanic who can at least temporarily repair your car. Otherwise you will have to flag down a passing car or truck to take you to a garage. In more remote areas you should try to travel in a convoy with at least one more vehicle. The various international recovery services do not cover most of the region.

Where is the nearest garage?	ayn aqrab garaaj	أين أقرب كراج؟
My car broke down.	AHndee AHTl	عندي عطل.
Can you send a mechanic/ tow [breakdown] truck?	mumkin tibAHat meekaaneekee/al-winsh	ممكن تبعث ميكانيكي/الونش؟
I belong to ... recovery service.	ana antamee ilaa ... li-khidmaat al-AHTaal	أنا أنتمي إلى ... لخدمات الأعطال.
My registration number is ...	raqm as-sayyaara huwa ...	رقم السيارة هو ...
The car is ...	as-sayyaara ...	السيارة ...
on the main highway	AHlaaT Tareeq ar-ra'eesee	على الطريق الرئيسي
2 km from ...	itnayn keeloo min ...	٢ كم من ...
How long will you be?	kam sa-tastaghriq	كم ستستغرق؟

What is wrong? ما هي المشكلة؟

My car won't start.	sayyaaratee laa tureed an tabdaa	سيارتي لا تريد أن تبدأ.
The battery is dead.	al-baTaareeya faargha.	البطارية فارغة.
I've run out of gas [petrol].	nafaz minee al-banzeen.	نفذ مني البنزين.
I have a flat [puncture].	AHndee thuqb.	عندي ثقب.
There is something wrong with ...	hunaak shay khaTa fee ...	هناك شيء خطأ في ...
I've locked the keys in the car.	qafalt AHlal miftaaH daakhil as-sayyaara	قفلت على المفتاح داخل السيارة.

Repairs تصليح

Do you do repairs?	hal tuSalliH	هل تصلح؟
Can you repair it (temporarily)?	hal mumkin tuSalliHhaa (mu'aqqatan)	هل ممكن تصلحها (مؤقتا)؟
Please make only essential repairs.	ar-rajaa taSleeH aD-Darooreeyaat faqaT	الرجاء تصليح الضروريات فقط.
Can I wait for it?	mumkin antaZirhaa	ممكن أنتظرها؟
Can you repair it today?	mumkin tuSalliHhaa al-yaum	ممكن تصلحها اليوم؟
When will it be ready?	matta sa-takoon jaahiza	متى ستكون جاهزة؟
How much will it cost?	kam sa-tukallif	كم ستكلف؟
That's outrageous!	haaza junoonee	هذا جنوني!
Can I have a receipt for my insurance?	mumkin aakhuz al-waSl li-ajl sharikat at-ta'meen	ممكن آخذ الوصل لأجل شركة التأمين؟

English	Arabic
The ... isn't working.	الـ ... لا يعمل.
I don't have the necessary parts.	ما عندي قطع الغيار المطلوبة.
I will have to order the parts.	لازم أطلب قطع الغيار.
I can only repair it temporarily.	ممكن أصلحها مؤقتا.
Your car is beyond repair.	لا يوجد أمل من تصليح سيارتك.
It can't be repaired.	لا يمكن تصليحها.
It will be ready ...	ستكون جاهزة ...
later today	بعدين
tomorrow	غدا
in ... days	بعد ... أيام

1 taillights [back lights] *aDwaa' khalfeeya*
أضواء خلفية

2 brakelights *aDwaa' al-faraamil* أضواء الفرامل

3 trunk [boot] *Sundooq as-sayyaara*
صندوق السيارة

4 gas tank door [petrol cap] *ghaTaa baab (Haud)
al-banzeen* غطاء باب (حوض) البنزين

5 window *shibbaak* شباك

6 seat belt *Hazaam al-amaan* حزام الأمان

7 sunroof *saqf munzaliq* سقف منزلق

8 steering wheel *AHjalat al-qiyaada* عجلة القيادة

9 ignition *mushaghghil* مشغل

10 ignition key *miftaaH mushaghghil* مفتاح مشغل الأمامي

11 windshield [windscreen] *az-zujaaj
al-amaamee* الزجاج الأمامي

12 windshield [windscreen] wipers
massaaHat az-zujaaj مساحات الزجاج

13 windshield [windscreen] washer
maghsalt az-zujaaj مغسلة الزجاج

14 hood [bonnet] *ghaTaa al-muHarrik* غطاء المحرك

15 headlights *al-aDwaa' al-amaameeya*
الأضواء الأمامية

16 license [number] plate *lauHat raqm
as-sayyaara* لوحة رقم السيارة

17 fog lamp *Dav' aD-Dabaab* ضوء الضباب

18 turn signal [indicator] *al-mu'ashshir* المؤشر

19 bumper *maSadd (mukhaffif aS-Sadma)*
مصد (مخفف الصدمة)

20 tires [tyres] *iTaaraat* إطارات

21 hubcap *ghaTaa al-AHjala* غطاء العجلة

22 valve *Sammaam* صمام

23 wheels *AHjalaat* عجلات

24 outside [wing] mirror *al-miraya al-jaanibeeya*
المرأة الجانبية

25 central locking *qafl markazee* قفل مركزي

26 lock *qifl* قفل

27 wheel rim *iTaar mAHdanee* إطار معدني

28 exhaust pipe *anboob al-AHdim* أنبوب العادم

29 odometer [milometre] *AHdaad al-masaafa*
عداد المسافات

30 warning light *Dau' al-inzaar* ضوء الإنذار
31 fuel gauge/pump *mu'ashshir/miDakhkhat al-banzeen* مؤشر/مضخة البنزين
32 speedometer *AHdaad as-surAHa* عداد السرعة
33 oil gauge *mu'ashshir az-zayt* مؤشر الزيت
34 back-up [reversing] lights *Dau ar-rujooAH* ضوء الرجوع
35 spare wheel *AHjala iHtiyaaTeeya* عجلة احتياطية
36 choke *sharaaqa* شراقة
37 heater *sakhkhaan* سخان
38 steering column *AHmood al-qiyaada* عامود القيادة
39 accelerator *dawaasat al-banzeen* دواسة البنزين
40 pedal *dawaasa* دواسة
41 clutch *dibriyaaj* دبرياج
42 carburetor *mukarbin* مكربن
43 battery *baTaareeya* بطارية
44 alternator *munauba* منوبة
45 camshaft *AHmood al-Hudbaat* عمود الحدبات
47 distributor *muwazziAH* موزع
48 points *ru'oos* رؤوس

49 radiator hose *kharToom khazaan al-maa'* خرطوم خزان الماء
50 radiator *khazaan al-maa'* خزان الماء
51 fan *marwaHa* مروحة
52 engine *muHarrik* محرك
53 oil filter *miSfaat az-zayt* مصفاة الزيت
54 starter motor *mushaghghil al-muHarrik* مشغل المحرك
55 fan belt *Hizaam al-marwaHa* حزام المروحة
56 horn *aalat at-tanbeeh* آلة التنبيه
57 brake pads *teel al-faraamil* تيل الفرامل
58 transmission [gearbox] *AHulbat at-turoos* علبة التروس
59 brakes *faraamil* فرامل
60 shock absorbers *mumtaSS aS-Sadamaat* ممتص الصدمات
61 fuses *Sammaamaat kahrabaa'eeya* صمامات كهربائية
62 gear shift [lever] *ziraaAH at-turoos* ذراع التروس
63 handbrake *faraamil al-yad* فرامل اليد
64 muffler [silencer] *mukhammid aS-Saut* مخمد الصوت

Accidents حوادث

If you have an accident, you should go to the nearest police station and report it rather than wait for the police to come to you. Try not to get into a dispute about blame as this could end you up in an argument with more people than you had bargained for. If the car is rented, contact the rental company as soon as you can with the details. They can give you further instructions.

There has been an accident.	hunaak Haadis. هناك حادث
It's ...	innahu ... إنه
on the highway [main road]	AHlaT Tareeq ar-ra'eesee على الطريق الرئيسي
near ...	qareeb min ... قريب من
Where's the nearest telephone?	ayn aqrab tilifoon? أين أقرب تلفون؟
Call ...	ittaSil bi ... اتصل بـ
the police	ash-shurTa الشرطة
an ambulance	sayyaarat isAHaaf سيارة إسعاف
a doctor	doktoor دكتور
the fire department [brigade]	al-maTaafi' المطافئ
Can you help me, please?	mumkin tusaAHidnee, lau samaHt ممكن تساعدني، لو سمحت؟

Injuries إصابات

There are people injured.	hunaak naas muSaaboon هناك ناس مصابون.
No one is hurt.	lam yu'azza aHad. لم يؤذى أحد
He is seriously injured.	AHnduh iSaabaat khaTeera عنده إصابات خطيرة.
She's unconscious.	hiya faaqidat al-wAHee. هي فاقدة الوعي
He can't breathe/move.	huwa laa yastaTeeAH at-tanaffus/ al-Haraka. هو لا يستطيع التنفس/الحركة.
Don't move him.	laa tuHarrikuh. لا تحركه

ACCIDENT/INJURY ➤ 162; DIRECTIONS ➤ 94

Legal matters أمور قانونية

What's your insurance company?	maa hiya sharikat ta'meenak?	ما هي شركة تأمينك؟
What's your name and address?	maa huwa ismak wa AHunwaanak	ما هو اسمك وعنوانك؟
He ran into me.	huwa Sadamnee.	هو صدمني.
She was driving too fast/ too close.	kaanat tasooq bi-surAHa/qareeb jiddan minnee.	كانت تسوق بسرعة/قريبة جدا مني.
I had the right of way.	kaan AHndee Haqq al-muroor	كان عندي حق المرور.
I was only driving at … km/h.	kunt asooq AHlaa … kiloo fess-saAHa	كنت أسوق على … ك م في الساعة.
I'd like an interpreter.	ureed mutarjim.	أريد مترجم.
I didn't see the sign.	lam ara al-laafita.	لم أرى اللافتة.
He/She saw it happen.	huwa shaahid/hiya shaahdat al-Haadis	هو شاهد/هي شاهدت الحادث.
The registration number was …	raqm as-sayyaara kaan …	رقم السيارة كان …

ممكن أرى … رجاءً؟	Can I see your …, please.
شهادة السواقة	driver's license
شهادة التأمين.	insurance card
أوراق السيارة	vehicle registration document
متى حدثت؟	What time did it happen?
أين حدثت؟	Where did it happen?
في شخص ثاني متورط؟	Was anyone else involved?
هناك أي شهود؟	Are there any witnesses?
كنت تسوق بسرعة.	You were speeding.
الأضواء لا تعمل.	Your lights aren't working.
لازم تدفع غرامة (فورا).	You'll have to pay a fine (on the spot).
نريدك أن نأخذ أقوالك في المركز.	We need you to make a statement at the station.

TIME ➤ 220

Asking directions
أسئلة عن الاتجاهات

Excuse me, please.	*lau samaHt.*	لو سمحت.
How do I get to …?	*kayf aSil ilaa …?*	كيف أصل إلى …؟
Where is …?	*ayn …?*	أين …؟
Can you show me on the map where I am?	*mumkin tareenee ayn ana AHlaal khareeTa?*	ممكن تريني أين أنا على الخريطة؟
I've lost my way.	*ana tuht.*	أنا تهت.
Can you repeat that, please?	*mumkin tukarir maa qultuh lau samaHt*	ممكن تكرّر ما قلته، لو سمحت؟
More slowly, please.	*bi-buT', lau samaHt.*	ببطء، لو سمحت.
Thanks for your help.	*shukran AHlaal musaaAHda*	شكرا على المساعدة.

Traveling by car التنقل بالسيارة

Is this the right road for …?	*hal haaza aT-Tareeq aS-SaHeeH ilaa*	هل هذا الطريق الصحيح إلى …؟
How far is it to … from here?	*kam al-masaafa ilaa … min hunaa*	كم المسافة إلى … من هنا؟
Where does this road lead?	*ilaa ayn yu'addee haazaT Tareeq*	إلى أين يؤدي هذا الطريق؟
What's the next town called?	*maa ism al-madeena at-taaleeya*	ما اسم المدينة التالية؟
How long does it take by car?	*kam ta'khud bis-sayyaara?*	كم تأخذ بالسيارة؟

– lau samaHt, kayf aSil ilaa maHattat al-qiTaar?
– khud ash-sharriAH at-taalit AHlaal yasaar, wa min hunaak AHlaa Tool.
at-taalit AHlaal yasaar. hal huwa bAHeed?
– AHshara daqaa'iq – masheeyan.
– shukran AHlaal musaaAHda.
– AHfwan.

موقع Location

إنه ...	It's ...
على طول	straight ahead
على اليسار	on the left
على اليمين	on the right
في آخر الطريق	at the end of the street
على الزاوية	on the corner
حول الزاوية	around the corner
باتجاه ...	in the direction of ...
خلف ... /مقابل ...	behind .... / opposite ...
بعد ... /بجانب ...	after ... / next to ...
اذهب إلى ...	Go down the ...
الطريق الجانبي/الطريق الرئيسي.	side street / main street
اعبر ...	Cross the ...
الميدان/الجسر	square / bridge
خذ المنعطف الثالث إلى اليمين.	Take the third right.
انعطف إلى اليسار ...	Turn left ...
بعد أول إشارة مرور	after the first traffic lights
عند نقطة التقاطع الثانية	at the second intersection [crossroad]

بالسيارة By car

إنها ... من هنا.	It's ... of here.
شمال/جنوب	north / south
شرق/غرب	east / west
خذ الطريق إلى ...	Take the road for ...
أنت على طريق خاطئ.	You're on the wrong road.
لازم ترجع إلى ...	You'll have to go back to ...
اتبع اللافتات إلى ...	Follow the signs for ...

كم تبعد؟ How far?

إنها ...	It's ...
قريبة/بعيدة جدا	close / a long way
خمس دقائق ماشيا	5 minutes on foot
١٠ دقائق بالسيارة	10 minutes by car
قرابة ١٠٠متر على هذا الطريق	about 100 meters down the road
تبعد ١٠ كيلو مترات تقريبا	about 10 kilometers away

TIME ➤ 220; NUMBERS ➤ 216

Road signs علامات الطريق

للدخول فقط	access only
طريق مؤقت	alternate route
تحويل	detour [diversion]
أبقى في الممر	stay in lane
أعطي الأولوية	yield [give way]
جسر منخفض	low bridge
طريق باتجاه واحد	one-way street
طريق مسدود	road closed
مدرسة	school
استعمل الأضواء الأمامية	use headlights

Town plans خريطة المدينة

مطار	airport
مسلك الأوتوبيس	bus route
موقف الأوتوبيس	bus stop
كنيسة	church
مكتب الاستعلامات	information office
الشارع الرئيسي	main [high] street
جامع	mosque
سينما	movie theater [cinema]
مدينة قديمة	old town
حديقة عامة	park
موقف السيارات	parking lot [car park]
ممر المشاة	pedestrian crossing
منطقة المشاة	pedestrian zone [precinct]
أرض الملعب	playing field [sports ground]
مركز الشرطة	police station
مكتب البريد	post office
بناء للعامة	public building
محطة	station
مدرج	stadium
نفق	underpass
موقف تاكسي	taxi stand [rank]
مسرح	theater
أنت هنا	you are here

Sightseeing

Tourist information office مكتب السياحة

In major tourist areas you will probably find tourist offices downtown
with information about attractions, special events, etc. You may also be
able to find special tours, for example of pharaonic sites or crusader
castles, with English-speaking guides.

Where's the tourist office?	*ayn maktab as-siyyaaHa* أين مكتب السياحة؟
What are the main points of interest?	*maa hiya al-mAHaalim al-athreeya al-muhimma* ما هي المعالم الأثرية المهمة؟
We're here for ...	*naHnu hunaa li-muddat* نحن هنا لمدة ...
only a few hours	*saAHaat faqaT* ساعات فقط
a day	*yaum waaHid* يوم واحد
a week	*usbooAH waaHid* أسبوع واحد
Can you recommend ...?	*hal tastaTeeAH an tinSaHnaa bi* هل تستطيع أن تنصحنا بـ ...؟
a sightseeing tour	*jaula li-ziyaarat al-mAHaalim* جولة لزيارة المعالم
an excursion	*jaula siyyaaHeeya munaZZama* جولة سياحية منظمة
a boat trip	*riHla bil-markib* رحلة بالمركب
Do you have any information on ...?	*AHndak ayy mAHloomaat AHn* عندك أي معلومات عن ...؟
Are there any trips to ...?	*hal hunaak riHlaat ilaa* هل هناك رحلات إلى ...؟

Excursions جولات سياحية

English	Transliteration / Arabic
How much does the tour cost?	kam tukallif ar-riHla
	كم تكلف الرحلة؟
Is lunch included?	hal al-ghadaa mashmool
	هل الغداء مشمول؟
Where do we leave from?	min ayn sa-nughaadir
	من أين سنغادر؟
What time does the tour start?	matta tabda' ar-riHla
	متى تبدأ الرحلة؟
What time do we get back?	matta sa-narjAH متى سنرجع؟
Do we have free time in ...?	hal AHndanaa waqt Hurr fee
	هل عندنا وقت حر في ...؟
Is there an English-speaking guide?	hal hunaak murshid yatkallam injileezee
	هل هناك مرشد يتكلم إنجليزي؟

On tour خلال الجولة

English	Transliteration / Arabic
Are we going to see ...?	hal sa-nushaahid ...؟ هل سنشاهد
We'd like to have a look at the ...	nureed ilqaa' naZra AHlaa
	نريد إلقاء نظرة على ...
Can we stop here ...?	mumkin naqif huna
	ممكن نقف هنا ...؟
to take photographs	liltiqaaT Suwar لالتقاط صور
to buy souvenirs	li-shiraa' tizkaar لشراء تذكار
to use the bathrooms [toilets]	lil-Hammaamaat للحمامات
Would you take a photo of us, please?	mumkin ta'khud linaa Soora, lau samaHt
	ممكن تأخذ لنا صورة، لو سمحت؟
How long do we have here/in ...?	kam mAHnaa min al-waqt huna/fee
	كم معنا من الوقت هنا/في ...؟
Wait! ... isn't back yet	intaZir! ... lam yAHud bAHd
	انتظر! ... لم يعد بعد.

Sights معالم

Where is the ...?	ayn ...?	أين ...؟
art gallery	mAHraD al-funoon	معرض الفنون
battle site	mawqiAH al-mAHraka	موقع المعركة
botanical garden	Hadeeqat an-nabaat	حديقة النبات
castle	al-qalAHa	القلعة
cemetery	al-maqbara	المقبرة
church	al-kaneesa	الكنيسة
downtown area	wasT al-madeena	وسط المدينة
fountain	an-naafoora	النافورة
market	as-sooq	السوق
monastery	ad-dayr	الدير
mosque	al-jaamiAH	الجامع
museum	al-matHaf	المتحف
old town	al-madeena al-qadeema	المدينة القديمة
opera house	darr al-oobraa	دار الأوبرا
palace	al-qaSr	القصر
park	al-Hadeeqa al-AHama	الحديقة العامة
parliament building	mabnaa al-barlamaan	مبنى البرلمان
ruins	al-aTlaal	الأطلال
statue	at-timthaal	التمثال
theater	al-masraH	المسرح
temple	al-mAHbad	المعبد
tower	al-burj	البرج
town hall	daar al-baladeeya	دار البلدية
viewpoint	makaan murtafiAH lil-mushaahada	مكان مرتفع للمشاهدة
Can you show me on the map?	mumkin tureenee AHlal khareeTa	ممكن تريني على الخريطة؟

Admission الدخول

Museums are usually closed on Fridays and on important
holidays (➤ 219). Check in advance for individual opening
times.

Can we look around?	ممكن نلقي نظرة؟ *mumkin nalqee naZra*
What are the opening hours?	*maa hiya al-muwaaAHeed* ما هي المواعيد؟
When does it close?	متى تغلق؟ *matta tughliq*
Is ... open on Fridays?	*hal ... maftooH yaum al-jumAha* هل ... مفتوح يوم الجمعة؟
When's the next guided tour?	*matta al-jaula at-taaleeya mAHal murshid* متى الجولة التالية مع المرشد؟
Do you have you a guide book (in English)?	*hal mAHak daleel (bil-injileezee)* هل معك دليل (بالإنجليزي)؟
Can I take photos?	*mumkin uSawwir* ممكن أصوّر؟
Is there access for the disabled?	*hal hunaak madkhal lil-muAHaaqeen* هل هناك مدخل للمعاقين؟

Paying/Tickets الدفع/التذاكر

How much is the entrance fee?	*bi-kam ad-dukhool* بكم الدخول؟
Are there any discounts for ...?	*hal hunaak takhfeeD lil-...* هل هناك تخفيض لل ...؟
children	أطفال *ATfaal*
the disabled	معاقين *muAHaaqeen*
senior citizens	كبار السن *kubaar as-sinn*
students	طلاب *Tullaab*
1 adult ticket and 3 children, please.	*tazkara wa talaat aTfaal, lau samaHt* تذكرة و٣ أطفال، لو سمحت.
I've lost my ticket.	*faqadt tazkartee* فقدت تذكرتي.

– arbAHa tazaakir, lau samaHt.
AHndak takhfeeDaat?
– naAHm. khamsa junayh lil-aTfaal
wal-kubaar fees-seen.
– tazkirtayn wa talaata aTfaal, lau samaHt.
– khamsa wa talaateen junayh, lau samaHt.

الدخول مجاني	admission free
مغلق	closed
محل هدايا	gift shop
آخر موعد للدخول الساعة ٥ مساء.	latest entry at 5 p.m.
الجولة القادمة الساعة ...	next tour at ...
ممنوع الدخول	no entry
ممنوع التصوير	no flash photography
مفتوح	open
مواعيد الزيارة	visiting hours

Impressions انطباعات

It's ...	إنه ... *innahu*
amazing	مدهش *mudhish*
awful	مرعب *murAHib*
beautiful	جميل *jameel*
boring	ممل *mumill*
great fun	ممتع جدا *mumtiAH jiddan*
incredible	رائع *raa'iAH*
interesting	*mutheer lil-ihtimaam* مثير للاهتمام
magnificent	جميل جدا *jameel jiddan*
strange	غريب *ghareeb*
stunning	مذهل *muzhil*
superb	ممتاز *mumtaaz*
terrible	فظيع *faZeeAH*
ugly	بشع *bashiAH*
I like it.	أحبه. *uHibbuh*
I don't like it.	لا أحبه. *laa uHibbuh*

قائمة للسائح Tourist glossary

قلعة	qalAHa	castle / citadel
كنيسة	kaneesa	church
مسجد	masjid	mosque
متحف	matHaf	museum
واحة	waaHa	oasis
مدينة قديمة	madeena qadeema	old city
قصر	qaSr	palace
هرم	haram	pyramid
معبد	mAHbad	temple
مقبرة	maqbara	tomb
برج	burj	tower
أطلال	aTlaal	ruins
شاطئ	shaaTi'	beach
حديقة	Hadeeqa	park

دراسة الآثار	*diraasat al-aathaar*	archaeology
فن العمارة	*fann al-Ahimaara*	architecture
الفن	*al-fann*	art
الخط	*al-khaTT*	calligraphy
الخزف	*al-khazaf*	ceramics/pottery
الصناعات اليدوية	*aS-SinaaAHaat al-yadaweeya*	handicrafts
الهيروغليفية	*al-heerooghleefeeya*	hieroglyphics
التاريخ	*at-taareekh*	history
الفن الإسلامي	*al-fann al-islaamee*	Islamic art
الرسم	*ar-rasm*	painting
الدين	*ad-deen*	religion
النحت	*an-naHt*	sculpture

من/ماذا/متى؟ Who/What/When?

What's that building?	*maa hazaal binaa* ما هذا البناء؟
When was it built?	*matta buniya* متى بني؟
Who was the artist/architect?	*man kaan al-fanaan/ al-muhandis al-mAHmaaree* من كان الفنان/المهندس المعماري؟

Some of the sightseeing highlights of a region rich in history and architecture:

Egypt
Pyramids at Giza; Islamic Cairo; Coptic Christian Cairo; Egyptian Museum; pharaonic temples and tombs at Luxor, Aswan, and Abu Simbel; Mount Sinai and St. Catherine's Monastery.

Lebanon
Ruined Roman temple at Baalbek; Saladin's restored palace at Ash-shouf; Biblical cedar tree forests near Bsherri.

Jordan
Ruined Nabataean capital at Petra; Roman ampitheater in Amman.

Syria
Medieval crusader castles; Islamic architecture of Damascus and Aleppo; Roman ruins at Palmyra.

Saudi Arabia
Ancient Islamic cities of Mecca and Medina (only accessible to Muslims); Nabataean ruins of Mada'in Salih in the north of the country; ruins of original Saud capital city of ad-Dir'iyah near Riyadh.

Other countries
Old walled city of San'a, Yemen; medieval forts built by local rulers and Portuguese occupiers in Oman and Bahrain; "Queen of Sheeba's palace" – ancient ruins and fortifications at Ras al-Khaima in the United Arab Emirates.

Places of worship دور العبادة

The Arab world is predominantly Muslim. However, other religions are represented as well – there are large Christian populations in Lebanon and Egypt. Muslims pray five times a day and gather in the mosques for Friday prayers. In some areas, non-Muslims may not be able to enter mosques, and you should ask for permission first. If allowed, you should remove your shoes, cover your legs and arms, and women should cover their hair.

church	kaneesa كنيسة
mosque	jaamiAH جامع
What time is/are prayers/mass?	ayy saAHa aS-Salaat/ al-qaddaas
	أي ساعة الصلاة/القداس ...

History التاريخ

Early civilizations (5000–30 B.C.)

Details are sketchy about the very earliest civilizations. In 3100 B.C., Menes united Upper and Lower Egypt to form a kingdom that lasted over 2000 years. From the eighth century B.C. Egypt went through periods of rule by the Nubians, Assyrians, Persians and Greeks until it's final conquest in 30 B.C. by the Roman Emperor Augustus. About 500 B.C. the Nabataeans also established themselves in present-day Jordan.

Eastern Roman (Byzantine) Empire (400 B.C.–700 A.D.)

By the time Augustus conquered Egypt, the Romans were dominant in most of Asia Minor, the Levant, and Egypt. A Persian dynasty, the Sassanians, ruled further to the East. The Byzantine Empire gradually declined through the Middle Ages until its final demise in 1453.

Early Islam (610–932)

The prophet Mohammed lived from 570–632 in western Arabia. In the 100 years after his death his followers conquered a huge area from Spain to India. Early Islamic history is dominated by two dynasties: the Umayyads, based in Damascus, and the later Abbasids, based in Baghdad.

The Middle Ages (932–1520)

The early medieval period was dominated by the Papal Crusades and the Mogul invasions of Genghis Khan. For nearly 300 years, beginning in 1250, much of the region was ruled by the Mamelukes, self-styled soldier monarchs.

Ottoman Empire (1520–1914)

In 1453, the Islamic Ottomans took Constantinople, ending Byzantine rule. They then expanded their empire to include most of the Middle East. In the nineteenth century the empire declined in the face of the European powers. The Ottoman sultan finally sealed the fate of the empire by siding with Germany in the First World War.

The Twentieth Century

For the period between the wars, most of the Middle East was under the direct or indirect control of the European colonial powers. After the Second World War this influence gradually declined and the different countries of the region followed their own separate courses.

In the countryside / desert
في الريف/الصحراء

I'd like a map of …	ureed khareeTa li …	أريد خريطة لـ …
this region	haazihil minTaqa	هذه المنطقة
walking routes	Turuq as-sayr	طرق السير
desert tracks	Turuq aS-SaHraa'	طرق الصحراء
How far is it to …?	kam al-masaafa ilaa	كم المسافة إلى …؟
Is there a right of way?	hal AHndanaa Haqq al-muroor	هل عندنا حق المرور؟
Is there a desert route to …	hal hunaak Tareeq SaHraawee ilaa	هل هناك طريق صحراوي إلى …؟
Can you show me on the map?	mumkin tureenee AHlal khareeTa	ممكن تريني على الخريطة؟
I'm lost.	ana tuht.	أنا تهت.

Organized treks رحلات السير منظمة

When does the trek start?	matta tabda' ar-riHla	متى تبدأ الرحلة؟
When will we return?	matta sa-narjAH	متى سنرجع؟
What is the trek like?	kayf kaanat ar-riHla	ما هي طبيعة الرحلة؟
gentle/medium/tough	sahla/mutwassiTa/SaAHba jiddan	سهلة/متوسطة/صعبة جدا
I'm exhausted.	ana munhak.	أنا منهك.
How long are we resting here?	maa hiya muddat al-istiraaHa hunaa	ما هي مدة الاستراحة هنا؟
What kind of … is that?	min ayy nauAH hazaa	من أي نوع هذا …؟
animal/bird	al-Hayawaan/aT-Tayr	الحيوان/الطير
flower/tree	az-zahra/ash-shajara	الزهرة/الشجرة

Geographic features معالم جغرافية

bridge	*jisr*	جسر
cave	*kahf*	كهف
cliff	*munHadar*	منحدر
coast	*saaHil*	ساحل
date palms	*nakheel*	نخيل
desert	*SaHraa'*	صحراء
farm	*mazrAHa*	مزرعة
field	*Haql*	حقل
forest / wood	*ghaaba*	غابة
hill	*tall*	تل
lake	*buhayra*	بحيرة
mountain	*jabal*	جبل
mountain pass	*mamarr jabalee*	ممر جبلي
mountain range	*silsila jabaleeya*	سلسلة جبلية
oasis	*waaHa*	واحة
park	*Hadeeqa AHama*	حديقة عامة
peak	*qimma*	قمة
pond	*birka*	بركة
river	*nahr*	نهر
sand dune	*kuthayb ramlee*	كثيب رملي
sea	*baHr*	بحر
stream	*jadwal*	جدول
swamp	*mustanqAH*	مستنقع
valley	*waadee*	وادٍ
village	*qarya*	قرية
waterfall	*shallaal*	شلال

Leisure

Events الأنشطة

At your hotel or in the tourist information centers you'll often find publications listing local attractions, or you can consult the English-language newspapers.

Television programs are mostly in Arabic, but news and foreign films are also broadcast in English – and some countries have a separate English-language channel.

Most major hotels have English-language cable and satellite TV.

Do you have a program of events?	hal AHandak barnaamij al-anshiTa هل عندك برنامج الأنشطة؟
Can you recommend a good ...?	mumkin tinSaHnaa bi ... jayyid ممكن تنصحنا بـ ... جيد؟
ballet/concert	baaleyh/Hafla mooseeqeeya باليه/حفلة موسيقية
movie [film]	feelm seenamaa'ee فيلم سينمائي
opera	oobraa أوبرا

Availability التوفر

When does it start?	matta yabda' متى يبدأ؟
When does it end?	matta yantahee متى ينتهي؟
Are there any seats for tonight?	hal hunaak amaakin li-haazihil layla هل هناك أماكن لهذه الليلة؟
Where can I get tickets?	ayn ashtaree at-tazaakir أين أشتري التذاكر؟

تذاكر Tickets

How much are the tickets?	bikam at-tazaakir
	بكم التذاكر؟
Do you have anything cheaper?	AHndak shay' arkhaS
	عندك شيء أرخص؟
I'd like to reserve …	ureed Hajz … أريد حجز
for Sunday evening	li-yaum al-aHad masaa'an
	ليوم الأحد مساءً

What's your credit card …?	ما … بطاقة الائتمان؟
number	رقم
type	نوع
expiration [expiry] date	تاريخ الانتهاء
Please pick up the tickets …	الرجاء أخذ التذاكر …
by … p.m.	قبل الساعة … بعد الظهر.
at the reservations desk	عند مكتب الحجز

May I have a program, please?	mumkin aakhud al-barnaamij, lau samaHt
	ممكن آخذ البرنامج، لو سمحت؟
Where's the coatcheck [cloakroom]?	ayn Hujrat al-mAHaaTif
	أين حجرة المعاطف؟

– mumkin usaAHidak?
– ureed talaat tazaakir li-Haflat al-layla.
– bit-ta'keed.
– mumkin adfAH bi-biTaaqat al-itimaan?
– naAHm, yaa seedee.
– izaa, sa-astAHmil "VISA".
– shukran … tauqeeAHak huna, lau samaHt.

Advance reservations	حجز مسبق
Sold out	العدد كامل
Tickets for today	تذاكر لليوم

NUMBERS ➤ 216

109

Movies [Cinema] سينما

Foreign films are usually shown in their original language
with Arabic subtitling. However, some popular films may be
dubbed, so check in advance.

Is there a movie theater [cinema] near here?	*hal hunaak seenimaa qareeba* هل هناك سينما قريبة؟
What's playing at the movies [on at the cinema] tonight?	*maaza tAHraD as-seenimaa al-layla* ماذا تعرض السينما الليلة؟
Is the film dubbed / subtitled?	*hal al feelm madablaj/mutarjam* هل الفيلم مدبلج /مترجم؟
Is the film in the original English?	*hal al feelm naaTiq bil-injileezeeya* هل الفيلم ناطق بالإنجليزية؟
A ... please.	*ureed ... lau samaHt* أريد ... لو سمحت.
packet of roasted seeds	*kees lubb* كيس لب
chocolate ice cream [choc-ice]	*ayes kreem shookoolaata* آيس كريم شوكولاتة
hot dog	*sandwitsh sujuq* ساندويتش سجق
juice / soft drink	*AHSeer/kaazooza* عصير/كازوزة
small / regular / large	*Sahgeer/mutawassiT/kabeer* صغير/متوسط/كبير

Theater مسرح

What's the play at the ... Theater?	*maa al-masraHeeya fee masraH ...* ما المسرحية في مسرح ...؟
Who's the playwright?	*man kaatib al-masraHeeya* من كاتب المسرحية؟
Do you think I'd enjoy it? I don't know much Arabic.	*taZunn annanee sa-AHjab bihaa. ana laa ujeed al-AHrabeeya* تظن أنني سأعجب بها؟ أنا لا أجيد العربية.

Opera/Ballet/Dance أوبرا/باليه/رقص

Where's the opera house?	ayn daar al-oobraa أين دار الأوبرا؟
Who is the composer/soloist?	man huwal mu'allif/ al-AHazif al-munfarid من هو المؤلف/العازف المنفرد؟
Who's dancing?	man ar-raaqiS من الراقص؟

Music/Concerts موسيقى/حفلات موسيقية

Where's the concert hall?	ayn qaAHat al-Hafla al-mooseeqeeya أين قاعة الحفلة الموسيقية؟
Which orchestra/band is playing?	ayy oorkistraa/firqa sa-tAHzif أي أوركسترا/فرقة ستعزف؟
What are they playing?	maaza sa-yAHzifoon ماذا سيعزفون؟
Who is the conductor/soloist?	man huwa qaa'id al-firqa/ al-aazif al-munfarid من هو قائد الفرقة/العازف المنفرد؟
Who is the singer?	man al-mughannee؟ من المغني؟
I really like ...	ana uHibb ... kateeran أنا أحب ... كثيراً
Arabic music	al-mooseeqaa al-AHrabeeya الموسيقى العربية
jazz	al-jaaz الجاز
rock/pop music	mooseeqaa ar-rook/al-boob موسيقى الروك/البوب
Have you ever heard of her/him?	hal samiAHt bihaa/bih هل سمعت بها/به؟
Are they popular?	hal hum mash-hooroon هل هم مشهورون؟

الحياة الليلية Nightlife

What is there to do in the evenings?	maaza yumkinana an nafAHal feel masaa	ماذا يمكننا أن نفعل في المساء؟
Can you recommend a ...	mumkin tinSaHnaa bi ...	ممكن تنصحنا بـ ...؟
Is there a ... in town?	hal hunaak ... feel madeena	هل هناك ... في المدينة؟
bar/restaurant	baar/maTAHm	بار/مطعم
casino	Saalat al-qumaar	صالة القمار
discotheque	deeskoo	ديسكو
nightclub	naadee laylee	نادٍ ليلي
What type of music do they play?	maa nauAH al-mooseeqaa hunaak	ما نوع الموسيقى هناك؟
How do I get there?	kayf aSil hunaak	كيف أصل هناك؟

Admission الدخول

What time does the show start?	matta yabda al-AHrD	متى يبدأ العرض؟
Is evening dress required?	hal malaabis as-sahra maTlooba	هل ملابس السهرة مطلوبة؟
Is there a cover charge?	hunaak Hisaab AHlal khidma	هناك حساب على الخدمة؟
Is a reservation necessary?	yajib an naHjiz	يجب أن نحجز؟
Do we need to be members?	yajib an nakoon AHDaa	يجب أن نكون أعضاءً؟
Is it customary to dine there?	hal min al-ma'loof an na'kul hunaak	هل من المألوف أن نأكل هناك؟
How long will we have to stand in line [queue]?	kam min al-waqt yajib an naSTaff	كم من الوقت يجب أن نصطف؟
I'd like a good table.	ureed maa'ida jayyida.	أريد مائدة جيدة.

112

Children الأطفال

Can you recommend something for the children?	mumkin tinSaHna bi-shay' lil-aTfaal
	ممكن تنصحنا بشيء للاطفال؟

Are there changing facilities here for babies?	hal hunaak tas-heelaat li-tahgyeer fuwaT aT-Tifl hunaa
	هل هناك تسهيلات لتغيير فوط الطفل هنا؟

| Where are the bathrooms [toilets]? | ayn al-maraaHeeD؟ أين المراحيض |

amusement arcade	qaAHat tasleeya قاعة تسلية
fairground	madeenat al-malaahee مدينة الملاهي
kiddie [paddling] pool	masbaH lil-aTfaal مسبح للأطفال
playground	malAHb ملعب
play group	majmooAHat lAHb
	مجموعة لعب
zoo	Hadeeqat al-Hayawaanaat
	حديقة الحيوانات

Babysitting الحضن

Can you recommend a reliable babysitter?	mumkin tinSaHnaa bi-HaaDina mausooq bihaa
	ممكن تنصحنا بحاضنة موثوق بها؟

Is there constant supervision?	hal hunaak ishraaf daa'im
	هل هناك إشراف دائم؟

Is the staff properly trained?	hal al-musaaAHideen mudarraboon jayyidan?
	هل المساعدون مدرَّبون جيدا؟

When can I drop them off?	matta astaTeeAH eeSaalhum
	متى أستطيع إيصالهم.

I'll pick them up at …	sa-akhudhum as-saAHa
	سآخذهم الساعة …

| We'll be back by … | sa-narjAH qabl … سنعود قبل … |

She's 3 and he's 18 months.	AHumrahaa talaata wa AHumruh tamantashar shahr
	عمرها ٣ وعمره ١٨ شهر.

الرياضة Sports

The Arab world is mad about soccer. Going to watch a local game can be an experience and is something you can enjoy as a tourist without needing to know the language. Games are usually held on Fridays.

Basketball, volleyball, squash and horseback riding are also popular. Some countries, such as the United Arab Emirates, offer a huge variety of land and water-based sports as well as local specialties such as camel racing and falconry. Many of these you can take part in as well as being a spectator.

المشاهدة Spectating

Is there a soccer [football] game this Friday?	*hal hunaak maatsh kurrat qadam hazaal jumAHa* هل هناك ماتش كرة قدم هذا الجمعة؟
Which teams are playing?	*ayy al-firaq sa-talAHb* أي الفرق ستلعب؟
Can you get me a ticket?	*mumkin taHSul lee AHla tazkara* ممكن تحصل لي على تذكرة؟
What's the admission charge?	*maa huwa rasm ad-dukhool* ما هو رسم الدخول؟
Where's the racetrack [racecourse]?	*ayn miDmaar as-sibaaq* أين مضمار السباق؟
Is there camel racing near here?	*hal hunaak sibaaq lil-jimaal qurayb min hunaa* هل هناك سباق للجمال قريب من هنا؟
Are there any falconry expeditions?	*hal hunaak riHlaat Sayd biS-Suqoor* هل هناك رحلات صيد بالصقور؟
aerobics	*tamreenaat riyaaDeeya* تمرينات رياضية
angling	*Sayd as-samak* صيد السمك
athletics	*alAHaab al-quwa* ألعاب القوى
badminton	*tanis ar-reesha* تنس الريشة
baseball	*al-baayisbool* البايسبول
basketball	*kurat as-salla* كرة السلة
boxing	*al-mulaakma* الملاكمة

114

cycling	*rukoob ad-darraajaat*
	ركوب الدراجات
falconry	*SayD biS-Suqoor*
	صيد بالصقور
field hockey	*al-hookee* الهوكي
golf	*al-goolf* الجولف
horseracing	*sibaaq al-khayl* سباق الخيل
horseback riding	*rukoob al-khayl* ركوب الخيل
judo	*al-joodoo* الجودو
mountaineering	*tasalluq al-jibaal* تسلق الجبال
rowing	*at-tajdeef* التجديف
skiing	*at-tazaHluq AHlaal jaleed*
	التزحلق على الجليد
soccer [football]	*kurat al-qadam* كرة القدم
squash	*al-iskwaash* الإسكواش
swimming	*as-sibaaHa* السباحة
table tennis	*tanis aT-Taawla* تنس الطاولة
tennis	*at-tanis* التنس
volleyball	*al-kura aT-Taa'ira* الكرة الطائرة

Playing لعب

Where's the nearest ...?	*ayn aqrab ...?* أين أقرب ...؟
golf course	*arD al-goolf* أرض الجولف
sports club	*nadee riyaaDee* نادٍ رياضي
Where are the tennis courts?	*ayn malaaAHib at-tanis*
	أين ملاعب التنس؟
What's the charge per ...?	*kam al-Hisaab li ...?* كم الحساب لـ ...؟
day/round/hour	*yaum/jaula/saAHa* يوم/جولة/ساعة

115

Where can I rent ...?	min ayn asta'jir	من أين أستأجر ...؟
boots	Hizaa	حذاء
clubs	maDaarib (goolf)	مضارب (جولف)
equipment	muAHiddaat	معدات
a racket	miDrab	مضرب
Do I need to be a member?	hal yajib an akoon AHDoo	هل يجب أن أكون عضوا؟
Can I get lessons?	mumkin aakhud duroos	ممكن آخذ دروسا؟
Do you have a fitness room?	hal AHandakum ghurfa lil-yaaqa al-badaneeya	هل عندكم غرفة للياقة البدنية؟
Can I join in?	mumkin ashtarik	ممكن أشترك؟

Arabic	English
آسف، كل شيء محجوز.	I'm sorry. We're booked up.
هناك عربون بمبلغ...	There is a deposit of ...
قياسك كم؟	What size are you?
تحتاج لصورة بحجم جواز السفر.	You need a passport-size photo.
تغيير الملابس	changing rooms
ممنوع صيد السمك	no fishing
لحاملي التصاريح فقط	permit holders only

Horseback riding ركوب الخيل

Arab horses are famous the world over, and the desert is the ideal place to ride as long as you avoid the hottest part of the day. You will find stables all over over the Middle East where you can rent horses by the hour or day.

English	Transliteration / Arabic
I'm an experienced rider.	ana faaris mumtaaz. أنا فارس ممتاز.
I'm a beginner.	ana mubtadi'. أنا مبتدئ.
Do you have a Western [American]/English saddle?	hal AHandak sarj amreekee/ooroobee هل عندك سرج أمريكي/أوروبي؟

116

At the beach على الشاطئ

Some resort beaches are supervised, but many are not – and you should take care to assess conditions before bathing, particularly where children are concerned.

In coral reef areas (the Red Sea, for example), wear plastic shoes to protect your feet when swimming – and be careful not to deliberately or accidently break off any of the coral, which is protected by law.

Is the beach pebbly / sandy?	*hal as-saaHil Sakhree/ramlee* هل الساحل صخري/رملي؟
Is there a … here?	*hal hunaak … hunaa* هل هناك … هنا؟
children's pool	*misbaH lil-aTfaal* مسبح للأطفال
swimming pool	*Hammaam sibaaHa* حمام سباحة
indoor / open-air	*masqoof/makshoof* مسقوف/مكشوف
Is it safe to swim / dive here?	*hal hazza aamin lis-sibaaHa/lil-ghaTs* هل هذا آمن للسباحة/للغطس ؟
Is it safe for children?	*hal huwa aamin lil-aTfaal* هل هو آمن للأطفال؟
Is there a lifeguard?	*hal hunaak munqiz* هل هناك منقذ؟
I want to rent a / some …	*ureed isti'jaar …* أريد استئجار …
deck chair	*kursee ash-shaaTi'* كرسي الشاطئ
jetski	*darraaja maa'eeya* دراجة مائية
motorboat	*zauraq bukhaaree* زورق بخاري
scuba [skin-diving] equipment	*mAHiddaat al-ghaTs* معدات الغطس
umbrella [sunshade]	*maZalla (shamseeya)* مظلة (شمسية)
surfboard	*lauH rukoob al-mauj* لوح ركوب الموج
water skis	*lauh at-tazaHluq AHlaal maa'* لوح التزحلق على الماء
For … hours.	*li-muddit … SaAHaat* لمدة … ساعات.

Making Friends

Introductions التعارف

Arabic speakers usually have three names. These are their own first name, their father's first name, and their family name. For example, the son of Mohammed Yousef Shaheen would be Ashraf Mohammed Shaheen. If they are being less formal, they will drop the middle name: Mohammed Shaheen/Ashraf Shaheen. Note that this also applies to women, who retain their family name after marriage rather than adopting their husband's. So the daughter of Mohammed Yousef Shaheen would be Mona Mohammed Shaheen.

There are many different greetings and replies in Arabic depending on the situation. From the point of view of the tourist it is better to stick to one of the general greetings, such as **marHaban** (hello) or **ahlan** (Hi!). It's also usual to shake hands when you meet someone.

Hello.	marHaban.	مرحبا.
My name is …	ismee …	اسمي …
May I introduce …?	mumkin uqaddim lak …؟	ممكن أقدم لك …؟
Pleased to meet you.	tasharrafnaa.	تشرفنا.
What's your name?	maa ismak؟	ما اسمك؟
How are you?	kayf Haalak؟	كيف حالك؟
Fine, thanks. And you?	bi-khayr, al-Hamdu lilaah. wa-anta	بخير، الحمد لله. وأنت؟

– marHaban. kayf Haalak?
– bi-khayr, shukran. wa-anta?
– bi-khayr, al-Hamdu lilaah.

Where are you from? من أين أنت؟

Where are you from?	min ayn anta	من أين أنت؟
Where were you born?	ayn wulidt	أين ولدت؟
I'm from ...	ana min ...	أنا من ...
Australia	ostraalyaa	استراليا
Britain	bireeTaanya	بريطانيا
Canada	Kanadaa	كندا
England	injilteraa	إنجلترا
Ireland	irlandaa	إرلندا
Scotland	iskootlandaa	اسكوتلندا
U.S.	amreekaa	أمريكا
Wales	waylz	ويلز
Where do you live?	ayn taskun	أين تسكن؟
What part of ... are you from?	anta min ayy manTiqa fee	أنت من أي منطقة في ... ؟
Egypt	muSr	مصر
Morrocco	al-maghrib	المغرب
the (Persian) Gulf	al-khaleej	الخليج
We come here every year.	najee hunaa kull sana	نجيء هنا كل سنة.
It's my/our first visit.	innahaa awwal ziyaara lee/linaa	إنها أول زيارة لي/لنا.
Have you ever been to ...	zurt ... bi-Hayaatak	زرت ... بحياتك؟
Britain/the U.S.	bireeTaanya/amreekaa	بريطانيا/أمريكا
Do you like it here?	hal anta sAHeed hunaa	هل أنت سعيد هنا؟
What do you think of ...	maa ra'yak fee	ما رأيك في ... ؟
I love ... here.	uHibb ... huna	أحب ... هنا.
I don't really like ... here.	laa uHibb ... hunaa	لا أحب ... هنا.
the food/people	al-akl/an-naas	الأكل/الناس

Who are you with? / Family
من معك؟/ عائلة

Who are you with?	man mAHak	من معك؟
I'm on my own.	ana waHdee	أنا وحدي.
I'm with a friend.	ana mAHa Sadeeq	أنا مع صديق.
I'm with ...	ana mAHa ...	أنا مع ...
my husband / wife	zaujee/zaujatee	زوجي/زوجتي
my family	AH'iltee	عائلتي
my children / parents	aulaadee/waalidayya	أولادي/والديّ
my boyfriend / girlfriend	SaaHbee/SaaHbatee	صاحبي/صاحبتي
my father / son	abee/ibnee	أبي/ابني
my mother / daughter	ummee/ibnatee	أمي/ابنتي
my brother / uncle	akhee/AHmee (khaalee)	أخي/عمي (خالي)
my sister / aunt	ukhtee/AHmatee (khaaltee)	أختي/عمتي (خالتي)
What's your son's / wife's name?	maa ism ibnak/zaujatak	ما اسم ابنك/زوجتك؟
Are you married?	hal anta mutzawwij	هل أنت متزوج؟
I'm ...	ana ...	أنا ...
married / single	mutzawwij/AHaazib	متزوج/عازب
divorced / separated	muTallaq/munfaSil	مطلق/منفصل
engaged	khaaTib	خاطب
We live together.	naskun mAHa bAHD	نسكن مع بعض.
Do you have any children?	AHandak aulaad	عندك أولاد؟
a boy and a girl	walad wa bint	ولد وبنت.
How old are they?	AHmaarhum kam?	أعمارهم كم؟
10 and 12 years old	AHshara wa itnaAHshar sana	عشرة واثنا عشر سنة.

What do you do? بماذا تعمل؟

What do you do?	*bi-maaza tAHmal* بماذا تعمل؟
What line are you in?	*fee ayy majaal tAHmal* في أي مجال تعمل؟
What are you studying?	*mazaa tadrus* ماذا تدرس؟
I'm studying ...	*adrus* ... أدرس
I'm in ...	*ana fee* ... أنا في
business	*tijaara* تجارة
engineering	*handasa* هندسة
retail	*baa'iAH tajzi'a* بائع تجزئة
sales	*mabeeAHaat* مبيعات
Who do you work for?	*li-Hisaab man tAHmil؟* لحساب من تعمل؟
I work for ...	*AHmil li-Hisaab* ... أعمل لحساب
I'm a/an ...	*ana* ... أنا
accountant	*muHaasib* محاسب
housewife	*rabbat manzil* ربة منزل
student	*Taalib* طالب
retired	*mutaqaAHid* متقاعد
self-employed	*SaaHib mihna Hurra* صاحب مهنة حرة
between jobs	*bayn waZeeftayn* بين وظيفتين
What are your interests/hobbies?	*maa hiya hiwaayaatak؟* ما هي هواياتك؟
I like ...	*uHibb* ... أحب
music	*al-mooseeqa* الموسيقى
reading	*al-qiraa'a* القراءة
sports	*ar-riyaaDa* الرياضة
I play ...	*alAHb* ... ألعب
Would you like to play ...?	*tuHibb talAHb؟* ... تحب تلعب
cards	*kootsheena* كوتشينة
chess	*shaTranj* شطرنج

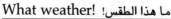

What weather! ما هذا الطقس!

What a lovely day!	al-jau mumtaaz al-yaum	الجو ممتاز اليوم!
What awful weather!	al-jau shaneeAH al-yaum	الجو شنيع اليوم!
Isn't it cold/hot today!	alaysa al-jau baarid/Harr al-yaum	أليس الجو بارداً/حاراً اليوم!
Is it usually this warm?	hal al-jau AHadatan Harr li-haazihid daraja	هل الجو عادةً حار لهذه الدرجة؟
Do you think it's going to ... tomorrow ?	hal tAHtaqid innahaa ... ghadan	هل تعتقد أنها ... غداً؟
be a fine day	sa-yakoon yaum jameela	سيكون يوما جميلا
rain	sa-tumTir	ستمطر
What is the weather forecast?	maa hiya tanabu'aat al-jau	ما هي تنبؤات الجو؟
It's ...	innahu ...	إنه ...
cloudy	ghaa'im	غائم
sunny	mushmis	مشمس
stormy	raAHid	راعد
windy	mazroo bir-riyaaH	مذرو بالرياح
Has the weather been like this for long?	hal al-jau AHlaa haazihil Haal min mudda Taweela	هل الجو على هذه الحال من مدة طويلة؟
What's the pollen count?	maa hiya nisbat ghubaar aT-TalAH	ما هي نسبة غبار الطلع؟
high/medium/low	murtafiAH/mutwassiTa/munkhafiDa	مرتفعة/متوسطة/منخفضة

---

weather forecast   تنبؤات الجو

122

Enjoying your trip? مستمتع بالرحلة؟

أنت في عطلة؟	Are you on vacation?
كيف وصلت إلى هنا؟	How did you get/ travel here?
أين تقيم؟	Where are you staying?
منذ متى وأنت هنا؟	How long have you been here?
كم ستبقى؟	How long are you staying?
ماذا فعلت حتى الآن؟	What have you done so far?
أين ستذهب من بعد هنا؟	Where are you going next?
مستمتع بالعطلة؟	Are you enjoying your vacation [holiday]?

I'm here on ...	ana hunaa fee ...	أنا هنا في ...
a business trip	riHlat AHmal	رحلة عمل
vacation [holiday]	ijaaza	إجازة
We came ...	waSalnaa ...	وصلنا ...
by train/by bus/by plane	bil-qiTaar/bil-ootoobees/biT-Taa'ira	بالقطار/بالأوتوبيس/بالطائرة
by car/by ferry	bis-sayyaara/bil-mAHdeeya	بالسيارة/بالمعدية
I have a rental [hire] car.	mAHaya sayyaara mu'ajjara	معي سيارة مؤجرة.
We're staying in ...	nuqeem fee ...	نقيم في ...
an apartment	shaqqa	شقة
a hotel/campsite	funduq/mukhayyam	في فندق/مخيّم
with friends	mAHa aSdiqaa	مع أصدقاء
Can you suggest ...?	mumkin taqtariH ...?	ممكن تقترح ...؟
things to do	ashyaa' nAHmilhaa	أشياء نعملها
places to eat	amaakin lil-akl	أماكن للأكل
places to visit	amaakin liz-ziyaara	أماكن للزيارة
We're having a great/awful time.	naqDee waqt raa'iAH/shaneeAH	نقضي وقتاً رائعاً/شنيعاً.

Invitations دعوى

Would you like to have dinner with us on …?	tuHibb tatAHshshaa mAHaana yaum تحب تتعشى معنا يوم …؟
May I invite you to lunch?	mumkin adAHook lil-ghadaa ممكن أدعوك للغداء؟
We are having a party. Can you come?	AHndanaa Hafla. taqdar taHDar عندنا حفلة. تقدر تحضر؟
May we join you?	mumkin nushaarik-kum ممكن نشاركم؟
Would you like to join us?	tuHibb tushaarik-naa تحب تشاركنا؟

Going out الخروج

What are your plans for …?	mazza sa-tafAHal fee ماذا ستفعل في …؟
today / tonight	al-yaum / al-layla اليوم / الليلة
tomorrow	al-ghad الغد
Are you free this evening?	hal anta faaDee al-layla هل أنت فاضٍ الليلة؟
Would you like to …?	tuHibb تحب …؟
go dancing	nurqus نرقص
go out for a meal	na'kul feel-khaarij نأكل في الخارج
go for a walk	natmashshaa نتمشى
go shopping	natsawwaq نتسوق
I'd like to go to …	uHibb an azhab ilaa أحب أن أذهب إلى …
I'd like to see …	uHibb an ushaahid أحب أن أشاهد …
Do you enjoy …?	hal tastamtiAH bi هل تستمتع بـ…؟

Accepting/Declining قبول/رفض

Thank you. I'd love to.	mumtaaz. sa-yusharrifnee
	ممتاز. سيشرفني.
Thank you, but I'm busy.	shukran, laakinee mashghool
	شكرا، لكني مشغول.
May I bring a friend?	mumkin uHDir Sadeeq? ممكن أحضر صديقاً؟
Where shall we meet?	ayn sa-naltaqee? أين سنلتقي؟
I'll meet you ...	sa-ulaaqeek ... سألاقيك ...
in front of your hotel	amaam funduqak أمام فندقك
I'll call for you at 8.	sa-aatee li-aakhudak as-saAHa tamanya
	سآتي لآخذك الساعة ٨.
Could we make it a bit later/earlier?	mumkin badree/mutakhkhar aktar
	ممكن بدري/متأخر أكثر؟
That will be fine.	hazaa mumtaaz. هذا ممتاز.

Dining out/in الأكل خارج البيت/في البيت

Hospitality is taken very seriously in the Middle East. If you are invited out to a meal in a restaurant you would not be expected to pay, nor should you try! If you are invited to a meal in someone's home you should take a gift – a cake, chocolates, or something for the house.

Expect to have your plate piled high and to be bombarded with constant encouragements to have more. A polite way of refusing is to say **dayman** or "always," which roughly means "may you always be in a position to provide such a sumptuous meal."

Let me buy you a drink.	dAHnee ashtaree lak mashroob
	دعني أشتري لك مشروبا.
Do you like ...?	hal tuHibb ...? هل تحب ...؟
What are you going to have?	mazaa sa-ta'khud? ماذا ستأخذ؟
That was a lovely meal.	kaanat wajba raa'iAHa
	كانت وجبة رائعة.

لقاءات بالصدفة Encounters

Do you mind if …?	AHandak maaniAH izaa عندك مانع إذا ...؟
I sit here / I smoke	ajlis hunaa/udakhkhin أجلس هنا/أدخن
Can I get you a drink?	mumkin ajeeb lak mashroob ممكن أجيب لك مشروباً؟
I'd love to have some company.	yasAHadnee muraafaqtak يسعدني مرافقتك.
Why are you laughing?	li-mazaa taDHak لماذا تضحك؟
Is my Arabic that bad?	hal lughatee al-AHrabeeya sayy'ia li-hazihid daraja هل لغتي العربية سيئة لهذه الدرجة؟
Shall we go somewhere quieter?	tuHibb nazhab ilaa makaan ahda تحب نذهب إلى مكان أهدأ؟
Leave me alone, please!	utruknee waHdee, lau samaHt اتركني وحدي، لو سمحت!
You look great!	shaklak Hilw شكلك حلو!
Would you like to come back with me?	tuHibb tirjAH mAHaya تحب ترجع معي؟
I'm not ready for that.	ana lastu jaahiz li-kull haaza أنا لست جاهزا لكل هذا.
Unfortunately we've got to leave now.	lil-asaf yajib an nimshee al-aan للأسف يجب أن نمشي الآن.
Thanks for the evening.	shukran AHlas sahra شكرا على السهرة.
It was great.	kaanat AHZeema كانت عظيمة.
Can I see you again tomorrow?	mumkin ashoofak marra taanya ghadan ممكن أشوفك مرة ثانية غدا؟
See you soon.	ilaal liqaa إلى اللقاء.
May I have your address?	mumkin tAHTeenee AHunwaanak ممكن تعطيني عنوانك؟

Telephoning الاتصالات بالتلفون

The major cities of the Arab World are rapidly becoming part of the international telephone network. You can often call home direct or use international calling cards. Outside the major cities, however, you may still have to go to a post office or telephone bureau to make international calls. You will be directed to a booth and connected by an operator. Find out the rates per minute in advance.

Telephone cards for use in public phones are still not common, although some Gulf states have introduced them on a limited basis.

Can I have your telephone number?	*mumkin aakhud raqm tilifoonak* ممكن آخذ رقم تلفونك؟
Here's my number.	*hazaa raqmee.* هذا رقمي.
Please call me.	*ittaSil bee lau samaHt.* اتصل بي لو سمحت.
I'll give you a call.	*sa-attaSil bik.* سأتصل بك.
Where's the nearest telephone booth?	*ayn aqrab tilifoon AHamm* أين أقرب تلفون عام؟
May I use your phone?	*mumkin astAHmil tilifoonak* ممكن أستعمل تلفونك؟
It's an emergency.	*Haala Taari'a.* حالة طارئة.
I'd like to call someone in England.	*ureed an attaSil bi-shakhS fee injiltaraa* أريد أن أتصل بشخص في إنجلترا.
What's the area [dialling] code for …?	*maa raqm an-nidaa' ad-daulee li* ما رقم النداء الدولي لـ …؟
Which booth shall I use?	*sa-astAHmil ayy kushk* سأستعمل أي كشك؟
What's the number for Information [Directory Enquiries]?	*maa huwa raqm daleel at-tilifoonaat* ما هو رقم دليل التلفونات؟
What's the number for …	*maa ar-raqm li …* ما الرقم لـ …؟
I'd like the number for …	*ureed ar-raqm li …* أريد الرقم لـ …
I'd like to reverse the charges / call collect.	*ureed taHweel ujrat al-mukaalma AHlal mustalim* أريد تحويل أجرة المكالمة على المستلم.

التكلم Speaking

Hello. This is …	aloo. ana …	ألو. أنا …
I'd like to speak to …	ureed at-takallum mAHa …	أريد التكلم مع …
extension …	imtidaad …	امتداد …
Speak louder / speak more slowly, please.	irfAH Sautak/takallam bi-buT', lau samaHt	ارفع صوتك/تكلم ببطء، لو سمحت.
Could you repeat that, please?	mumkin tukarrir hazaa, lau samaHt	ممكن تكرر هذا، لو سمحت؟
Can you hear me clearly?	hal tasmAHnee bi-wuDooH	هل تسمعني بوضوح؟
I'm afraid he's not in / she's not in.	mutassif. huwa ghayr maujood/ hiya ghayr maujooda	متأسف. هو غير موجود/هي غير موجودة.
You have the wrong number.	ar-raqm ghalaT	الرقم غلط.
Just a moment.	intaZir laHZa	انتظر لحظة.
Hold on, please.	laHZa, lau samaHt	لحظة، لو سمحت.
We were cut off!	al-khaTT inqaTAH!	الخط انقطع!
When will he/she be back?	matta sa-yaAHood/sa-tAHood	متى سيعود/ستعود؟
Will you tell him/her that I called?	mumkin taqool luh/lahaa annanee attaSalt	ممكن تقول له/لها أنني اتصلت؟
My name is …	ismee …	اسمي …
Would you ask him/her to call me?	mumkin taTlub minuh/minhaa an yattaSil/tattaSil bee	ممكن تطلب منه/منها أن يتصل/تتصل بي؟
I'll be in touch.	sa-attaSil qareeban	سأتصل قريباً.
Bye.	mAHas salaama	مع السلامة.

Stores & Services

Although there are large shopping malls and supermarkets in the region, the most interesting way to shop is still in the many local markets (**sooq**). These sell everything from perfumes and spices to gold and carpets. You will be expected to bargain (▶ 156), but make sure you don't overdo it and end up making an insulting offer.

ESSENTIAL

I'd like ...	*ureed* ...	أريد ...
Do you have ...?	*hal AHndak* ؟...	هل عندك ؟...
How much is that?	*bikam haaza* ؟بكم هذا	بكم هذا؟
Thank you.	*shukran* .شكرا	شكرا.

مفتوح	open
مغلق	closed
تخفيضات	sale

Stores and services محلات وخدمات

Where is ...? ؟... الـ أين

Where's the nearest ...?	أين أقرب ...؟ ayn aqrab
Where's there a good ...?	ayn yoojad ... jayyid أين يوجد ... جيد؟
Where's the main shopping mall [centre]?	ayn al-markaz at-tijaaree ar-ra'eesee أين المركز التجاري الرئيسي؟
Is it far from here?	hal huwa bAHeed min hunaa هل هو بعيد من هنا؟
How do I get there?	kayf aSil hunaak كيف أصل هناك؟

Stores محلات

antique store	maHall anteekaat محل أنتيكات
bakery	makhbaz مخبز
bank	bank بنك
bookstore	maktaba مكتبة
butcher	jazzaar جزار
camera store	maHall kaameeraat محل كاميرات
cigarette kiosk [tobacconist]	kushk sajaa'ir كشك سجائر
clothing store [clothes shop]	maHall malaabis محل ملابس
delicatessen	maHall aTAHima mutanawiAHa محل أطعمة متنوعة
department store	maHall tijaaree محل تجاري
drugstore	Saydaleeya صيدلية
fish store [fishmonger]	maHall samak محل سمك
florist	maHall zuhoor محل زهور
gift store	mahall hadaayaa محل هدايا
greengrocer	maHall khuDaar محل خضار
health food store	maHall aTAHima SiHHeeya محل أطعمة صحية
jeweler	maHall mujauharaat محل مجوهرات

market	سوق *sooq*
newsstand	كشك جرائد *kushk jaraa'id*
pastry store	*maHall Halawiyaat* محل حلويات
pharmacy [chemist]	*ajzakhaana/Saydaleeya* أجزخانة/صيدلية
produce store	بقالة *baqaala*
record/music store	*maHall kaaseetaat* محل كاسيتات
shoe store	*maHall aHzeeya* محل أحذية
shopping mall [centre]	*markaz tijaaree* مركز تجاري
souvenir store	*maHall hadaayaa tizkaareeya* محل هدايا تذكارية
sporting goods store	*maHall adawaat riyaaDeeya* محل أدوات رياضية
supermarket	*soobarmaarkit* سوبرماركت
toy store	*maHall luAHb* محل لعب

Services خدمات

dentist	طبيب أسنان *Tabeeb asnaan*
doctor	*duktoor/Tabeeb* دكتور/طبيب
dry cleaner	*maHall tanZeef malaabis* محل تنظيف ملابس
hairdresser (ladies'/men's)	*Saaloon Hilaaqa (lin-nisaa/lir-rijaal)* صالون حلاقة (للنساء/للرجال)
hospital	*mustashfaa* مستشفى
laundromat	*maghsala (khidma zaateeya)* مغسلة (خدمة ذاتية)
optician	*naZaaraatee* نظاراتي
police station	*qism boolees* قسم بوليس
post office	*maktab al-bareed* مكتب البريد
travel agency	*maktab safar* مكتب سفر

Opening hours أوقات العمل

Opening hours for stores and banks vary from country to country. Often stores will close in the middle of the day and re-open in the afternoon. Times also vary seasonally and during Ramadan (▶ 34).

Friday is usually the official closing day, but in some areas this can extend to Saturday as well.

Stores and offices will be closed on Sundays in predominantly Christian areas.

When does the … open/shut?	*matta yaftaH/yaqfil* متى يفتح/يقفل ...؟
Are you open in the evening?	*hal taftaH feel masaa* هل تفتح في المساء؟
Do you close for lunch?	*hal tuqfil li-fitrat al-ghadaa* هل تقفل لفترة الغداء؟
Where is the …?	*ayn* ...؟ أين
cashier [cash desk]	*al-khazeena* الخزينة
escalator	*as-silim al-kahrabaa'ee* السلم الكهربائي
elevator [lift]	*al-maSAHd* المصعد
store guide	*daleel al-maHall* دليل المحل
first [ground (Brit.)] floor	*aT-Taabiq al-arDee* الطابق الأرضي
second [first (Brit.)] floor	*aT-Taabiq al-awwal* الطابق الأول
Where's the … department?	*ayn qism al* ...؟ أين قسم الـ

مواعيد العمل الرسمية	business hours
مغلق لفترة الغداء	closed for lunch
مفتوح طوال اليوم	open all day
المدخل	entrance
سلم كهربائي	escalator
المخرج	exit
طوارئ/مخرج طوارئ	emergency/fire exit
مصعد	elevator [lift]
سلم	stairs

132

Service خدمة

Can you help me?	mumkin tusaAHidnee
	ممكن تساعدني؟
I'm looking for …	ana abHas AHn
	أنا أبحث عن …
I'm just browsing.	ana atfarraj faqaT
	أنا أتفرج فقط.
It's my turn.	dooree. دوري
Do you have any …?	hal AHndak ayy
	هل عندك أي …؟
I'd like to buy …	ureed shiraa … أريد شراء …
Could you show me …?	mumkin tureenee
	ممكن تريني …؟
How much is this/that?	bikam haaza/zaalik
	بكم هذا/ذلك؟
That's all, thanks.	hazaa kulluh, shukran
	هذا كله، شكرا.

صباح الخير/نهارك سعيد، سيدي/سيدتي.	Good morning/afternoon, madam/sir.
هل خدمك أحد؟	Are you being served?
ماذا تحب؟	What would you like?
هل هذا كل شيء؟	Is that everything?
أي شيء آخر؟	Anything else?

– mumkin usaAHidak?
– laa, shukran. ana atfarraj faqaT.
– hasanan …
–lau samaHt.
–nAHm, mumkin usaAHidak?
–bikam haaza?
–dAHnee at'akkad … haaza bi-AHishreen junayh.

خدمة الزبائن	customer service
خدمة ذاتية	self-service
عرض خاص	clearance

133

المفاضلة Preference

I want something ...	ureed shay ...	أريد شيئا ...
It must be ...	yajib an yakoon ...	يجب أن يكون ...
big / small	kabeer/Sagheer	كبير/صغير
cheap / expensive	rakheeS/ghaalee	رخيص/غال
dark / light	ghaamiq/faatiH	غامق/فاتح
genuine / imitation	aSlee/taqleed	أصلي/تقليد
light / heavy	khafeef/thaqeel	خفيف/ثقيل
oval / round / square	bayDaawee/mustadeer/murabbAH	بيضاوي/مستدير/مربع

I don't want anything too expensive.
laa ureed ashyaa ghaalya jiddan
لا أريد أشياء غالية جدا.

In the region of ... pounds.
fee Hudood ... junayh
في حدود ... جنيه.

Arabic	English
أي ... تحب؟	What ... would you like?
لون/شكل	color/shape
نوع/كمية	quality/quantity
ما هو الصنف الذي تحبه؟	What sort would you like?
ما المبلغ التقريبي الذي تفكر به؟	What price range are you thinking of?

Do you have anything ...?
hal AHndak ayy shay ...?
هل عندك أي شيء ...؟

larger / smaller	akbar/aSghar	أكبر/أصغر
better quality / cheaper	afDal/arkhaS	أفضل/أرخص

Can you show me ...?
mumkin tureenee
ممكن تريني ...؟

| that / this one | zaalik/haaza | ذلك/هذا |
| these / those ones | haazihi/tilka | هذه/تلك |

the one in the window / display case
allazee feesh-shibbaak/ feeS-Sundooq al-AHrD
الذي في الشباك/صندوق العرض

some others
bAHD al-ashyaa al-ukhraa
بعض الأشياء الأخرى

Conditions of purchase شروط الشراء

| Is there a guarantee? | *hal hunaak Damaan* هل هناك ضمان؟ |
| Are there any instructions with it? | *hal mAHuh daleel* هل معه دليل؟ |

Out of stock نفاذ البضاعة

أنا آسف، ليس موجودا عندنا.	I'm sorry, we haven't any.
البضاعة نفذت.	We're out of stock.
هل أستطيع أن أريك شيء آخر/ صنف مختلف؟	Can I show you something else/ a different type?
هل تريدنا أن نطلبه لك؟	Shall we order it for you?

Can you order it for me?	*mumkin taTlubuh lee* ممكن تطلبه لي؟
How long will it take?	*kam sa-tastaghriq* كم ستستغرق؟
Where else can I get ...?	*wa ayn aHSul AHlaa* وأين أحصل على ...؟

Decision القرار

That's not quite what I want.	*haaza laysa maa ureed biD-DabT* هذا ليس ما أريد بالضبط.
No, I don't like it.	*laa, laa yuAHjibnee* لا، لا يعجبني.
That's too expensive.	*haaza ghaalee jiddan* هذا غال جدا.
I'd like to think about it.	*ureed at-tafkeer feel amr* أريد التفكير في الأمر.
I'll take it.	*sa-aakhuduh* سآخذه.

– SabaaH al-khayr. ureed sweet sheert.
– bit-ta'keed. ayy laun?
– laun burtuqaalee, lau samaHt. wa ureed qiyaas kabeer.
– tafaDDal. at-taman khamseen junayh.
– haaza laysa maa ureeduh biD-DabT. shukran.

الدفع Paying

Where do I pay?	*ayn adfAH* أين أدفع؟
How much is that?	*bikam haaza* بكم هذا؟
Could you write it down, please?	*hal mumkin taktubuh, lau samaHt* هل ممكن تكتبه، لو سمحت؟
Do you accept traveler's checks [cheques]?	*hal taqbal sheekaat siyaaHeeya* هل تقبل شيكات سياحية؟
I'll pay ...	*sa-adfAH ...* سأدفع ...
by cash	*naqdan* نقدا
by credit card	*bi-biTaaqat itimaan* ببطاقة ائتمان
I don't have any smaller change.	*laysa mAHaya Sarf aSghar* ليس معي صرف أصغر.
Sorry, I don't have enough money.	*aasif. laa yoojad mAHaya nuqood kifaaya* آسف، لا يوجد معي نقود كفاية.

كيف ستدفع؟	How are you paying?
هذه الحوالة المصرفية رفضت.	This transaction has not been approved / accepted.
هذا الكرت غير ساري المفعول.	This card is not valid.
هل معك إثبات آخر لشخصيتك؟	May I have further identification?
هل عندك صرف أصغر؟	Do you have any smaller change?

Could I have a receipt, please?	*mumkin aakhud al-waSl, lau samaHt* ممكن آخذ الوصل، لو سمحت؟
I think you've given me the wrong change.	*AHtaqid an hunaak khaTa feel-baaqee* أعتقد أن هناك خطأ في الباقي.

الرجاء الدفع هنا	please pay here
سارق المعروضات سيقدم إلى المحاكمة	shoplifters will be prosecuted

Complaints شكاوى

This doesn't work.	haaza laa yAHmal هذا لا يعمل.
Can you exchange this, please?	mumkin tughayyir haaza, lau samaHt ممكن تغير هذا، لو سمحت؟
I'd like a refund.	ureed istirjaAH nuqoodee أريد استرجاع نقودي.
Here's the receipt.	haaza huwa al-eeSaal هذا هو الإيصال.
I don't have the receipt.	al-eeSaal laysa mAHaya الإيصال ليس معي.
I'd like to see the manager.	ureed an uqaabil al-mudeer أريد أن أقابل المدير.

Repairs/Cleaning تصليح/تنظيف

Many towns in Egypt have ironing shops (**maqwagee**). For a modest price you can get your clothes expertly ironed. Some combine this with a cleaning service which works out at a fraction of what you would pay in an international hotel.

This is broken. Can you repair it?	haaza maksoor. hal mumkin taSleeHuh هذا مكسور. هل ممكن تصليحه؟
Do you have ... for this?	hal AHndak ... li-haaza؟ هل عندك ... لهذا؟
a battery	baTaareeya بطارية
replacement parts	qiTAH ghiyaar قطع غيار
There's something wrong with ...	hunaak khalal fee ... هناك خلل في ...
Can you ... this?	hal mumkin ... haaza؟ هل ممكن ... هذا؟
clean	tunaZZif تنظّف
press	takwee تكوي
patch	turaqqiAH ترقّع
alter	tuAHddil تعدّل
When will it be ready?	matta sa-takoon jaahza متى ستكون جاهزة؟
This isn't mine.	haazihi laysat milkee هذه ليست ملكي.
There's ... missing.	hunaak ... mafqood. هناك ... مفقود.

Bank/Currency exchange office
البنك/مكتب الصرافة

Most of the larger banks in Saudi Arabia and throughout the Gulf have ATMs [cash machines], but they are not common in the rest of the region, although some are starting to appear in big cities and international hotels. However, you can usually find a bank or a currency exchange office that will allow you to withdraw money on an international credit card.

Traveler's checks [cheques] from well-known companies are also usually accepted. If you carry a combination of cash and cards/checks you will be able to keep your options open.

Note: It is better to avoid any black market in currency exchange as it can be risky, and the difference in rates is often not significant.

Where's the nearest …?	*ayn aqrab* …؟ أين أقرب
bank	*bank* بنك
currency exchange office [bureau de change]	*maktab taHweel al-AHumlaat* مكتب تحويل العملات

جميع المعاملات	all transactions
مكتب الصرف	currency exchange office
مفتوح/مغلق	open/closed
صرافون	cashiers

Changing money تبديل عملات

Can I exchange foreign currency here?	*hal mumkin ughayyir AHumlaat ajnabeeya huna* هل ممكن أغيّر عملات أجنبية هنا؟
I'd like to change some dollars/ sterling into riyal.	*ureed taghyeer doolaaraat/ junayhaat istarleeneeya ilaa riyaal* أريد تغيير دولارات/جنيهات إسترلينية إلى ريال.
I want to cash some traveler's checks [cheques].	*ureed Sarf sheekaat siyaaHaeeya* أريد صرف شيكات سياحية.
What's the exchange rate?	*maa huwa siAHr aS-Sarf* ما هو سعر الصرف؟
How much commission do you charge?	*kam takhud ka-AHmoola* كم تأخذ كعمولة؟
I've lost my traveler's checks. These are the numbers.	*faqadt sheekaatee as-siyaaHeeya. haazihi hiya arqaamhaa* فقدت شيكاتي السياحية. هذه هي أرقامها.

Security أمن

ممكن أرى ...؟	Could I see ...?
جواز سفرك	your passport
بعض الإثباتات الشخصية	some identification
كرت البنك	your bank card
ما هو عنوانك؟	What's your address?
أين تقيم؟	Where are you staying?
إملاء هذه الاستمارة، لو سمحت.	Fill in this form, please.
وقع هنا، لو سمحت.	Please sign here.

ATMs [Cash machines] آلة سحب نقود من الحساب

Can I withdraw money on my credit card here?	hal astaTeeAH saHb nuqood bi-biTaaqat i'timaan huna
	هل أستطيع سحب نقود ببطاقة ائتمان هنا؟
Where are the ATMs [cash machines]?	ayn aalaat saHb an-nuqood
	أين آلات سحب النقود؟
Can I use my ... card in the cash machine?	hal astaTeeAH istiAHmaal biTaaqat ... fee aalat saHb an-nuqood haazihi
	هل أستطيع استعمال بطاقة ... في آلة سحب النقود هذه؟
The cash machine has eaten my card.	aalat saHb an-nuqood akalat baTaaqtee
	آلة سحب النقود أكلت بطاقتي.

automated teller [cash machine]	آلة سحب النقود

Currency	Countries using currency
dinar	Algeria, Bahrain, Iraq, Jordan, Kuwait, Libya, Tunisia
pound (junayh)	Egypt, Sudan
pound (leera)	Lebanon, Syria
dirham	Morocco, United Arab Emirates
riyal	Oman, Qatar, Saudi Arabia, Yemen

(Note: although the currency in different countries may have the same name, the value will vary enormously.)

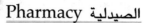

الصيدلية Pharmacy

Pharmacies increasingly offer a wide range of imported toiletries and medicines, although the local alternatives will still be much cheaper.

You may find you can obtain drugs over the counter that would be prescription only back home, e.g., antibiotics or strong sedatives. The pharmacist will be able to advise you and even sometimes administer. If in doubt, get a second opinion before deciding what to take.

Where's the nearest (all-night) pharmacy?	*ayn aqrab Saydaleeya munaawaba (Tawaal al-layl)* أين أقرب صيدلية مناوبة (طوال الليل)؟
What time does the pharmacy open/close?	*ayy SaAHa taftaH/tughliq aS-Saydaleeya* أي ساعة تفتح/تغلق الصيدلية؟
Can you make up this prescription for me?	*hal yumkinak tarkeeb haazihil waSfa aT-Tibbeeya lee* هل يمكنك تركيب هذه الوصفة الطبية لي؟
Shall I wait?	*hal antaZir* هل أنتظر؟
I'll come back for it.	*sa-AHood li-akhd-haa* سأعود لأخذها.

تعليمات الجرعة Dosage instructions

How much should I take?	*kam yajib an aakhud* كم يجب أن آخذ؟
How often should I take it?	*kam marra yajib an aakhud-haa* كم مرة يجب أن آخذها؟

خذ ... أقراص/... ملاعق صغيرة	Take ... tablets/... teaspoons
قبل/بعد الوجبات	before/after meals
مع ماء	with water
كاملة	whole
في الصباح/في المساء	in the morning/at night
لمدة ... أيام	for ... days

Asking advice طلب نصيحة

What would you recommend for …?	bi-maazaa tinSaHnaa min ajl بماذا تنصحنا من أجل …
a cold / a cough	bard/suAHaal برد/سعال
diarrhea	ishaal إسهال
hay fever	Huma al-qash حمى القش
insect bites	ladgh al-Hasharaat لدغ الحشرات
a sore throat	alam feel Hanjara ألم في الحنجرة
sunburn	Harqat ash-shams حرقة الشمس
motion [travel] sickness	dawwaar as-safar دوار السفر
an upset stomach	alam feel baTn ألم في البطن
Can I get it without a prescription?	mumkin ashtareehaa bidoon waSfa Tibbeeya ممكن أشتريها بدون وصفة طبية؟
Is it suitable for children?	hal huwa munaasib lil-aTfaal هل هو مناسب للأطفال؟

Over-the-counter treatment

علاج دون إرشادات الطبيب

Can I have …?	mumkin aakhud ممكن آخذ…؟
antihistamine	muDaad lil-Hassaaseeya مضاد للحساسية
antiseptic cream	kreem muTTahir كريم مطهر
aspirin	asbareen أسبرين
condoms	ghishaa Tibbee غشاء طبي
cotton [cotton wool]	qutn Tibbee قطن طبي
eye drops	nuqaT li-tanZeef al-AHuyoon نقط لتنظيف العيون
gauze [bandages]	Damaad ضماد
insect repellent	Taarid lil-Hasharaat طارد للحشرات
pain killers	musakkin al-alam مسكن الألم
vitamin tablets	aqraaS feetaameen أقراص فيتامين

مستحضرات تجميل Toiletries

I'd like ...	ureed ... أريد
after shave	AHiTr bAHd al-Hilaaqa عطر بعد الحلاقة
after-sun lotion	loosiyoon li-bAHd ash-shams لوسيون لبعد الشمس
deodorant	muzeel li-raa'iHat al-AHraq مزيل لرائحة العرق
razor blades	shafrat al-Hilaaqa شفرة الحلاقة
sanitary napkins [towels]	fuwaT SiHHeeya (lis-sayyidaat) فوط صحية (للسيدات)
soap	Saaboon صابون
suntan cream	kreem ash-shams كريم الشمس
factor ...	darajat quwa ... درجة قوة
tampons	Samaamaat quTneeya lis-sayyiddaat صمامات قطنية للسيدات
tissues	manaadeel waraq مناديل ورق
toilet paper	waraq twaaleet ورق تواليت
toothpaste	mAHjoon asnaan معجون أسنان

Haircare العناية بالشعر

brush/comb	fursha/mishT فرشاة/مشط
conditioner	mukayyif ash-shAHr مكيّف الشعر
hair mousse/gel	muthabbit ash-shAHr/jal مثبت الشعر/جل
hair spray	isbraay lish-shAHr اسبراي للشعر
shampoo	shamboo شامبو

For the baby للرضيع

baby food	TAHaam al-aTfaal طعام الأطفال
baby wipes	massaaHaat al-aTfaal مساحات الأطفال
diapers [nappies]	HafaaDaat حفاضات
sterilizing solution	saa'il maAHqqim سائل معقم

Clothing ملابس

The markets are a good place to buy traditional items such as robes and headscarfs. Many countries also have a good range of locallymade western-style clothes. Alternatively, you could buy the material and have your clothes made-to-measure or copied from another item by one of the many tailors in the region.

General بشكل عام

I'd like ...	*ureed* ... أريد
Do you have any ...?	*hal AHndak ayy* هل عندك أي ...؟

ملابس نسائية	ladieswear
ملابس رجالية	menswear
ملابس للأطفال	childrenswear

Color لون

I'm looking for something in ...	*abHas AHn shay bil-laun al* أبحث عن شيء باللون الـ...
beige	*bayj* بيج
black/white	*aswad/abyaD* أسود/أبيض
blue/green	*azraq/akhDar* أزرق/أخضر
brown	*bunnee* بني
gray	*ramaadee* رمادي
orange	*burtuqaalee* برتقالي
purple	*banafsijee* بنفسجي
red/pink	*aHmar/wardee* أحمر/وردي
yellow	*aSfar* أصفر
light (blue)	*(azraq) faatiH* (أزرق) فاتح
dark (blue)	*(azraq) ghaamiq* (أزرق) غامق
I want a darker/lighter shade.	*ureed nafs al-laun laakin bi-daraja aghmaq/afatH* أريد نفس اللون لكن بدرجة أغمق/أفتح.
Do you have the same in ...?	*AHndak nafs ash-shay bil-laun al ...* عندك نفس الشيء باللون الـ...؟

Clothes and accessories ملابس وكماليات

	belt	Hizaam	حزام
	bikini	bikeenee	بكيني
	blouse	bilooza	بلوزة
	bra	Hammaalat Sidr	حمالة صدر
briefs		sirwaal taHtaanee	سروال تحتاني
cap		kaab	كاب
coat		miAHTaf	معطف
dress		fustaan	فستان
hat		qubaAHa	قبعة
jacket		jaakeet	جاكيت
jeans		jeenz	جينز
pants (U.S.)		banTaloon	بنطلون
panty hose [tights]		shuraab Hareemee Taweel	شراب حريمي طويل
raincoat		miAHTaf lil-maTar	معطف للمطر
scarf		lifaaH	لفاح
shirt		qameeS	قميص
shorts		shoort	شورت
skirt		tannoora	تنورة
socks		shuraab	شراب
stockings		jawaarib Hareemee	جوارب حريمي
suit		badla	بدلة
sweater		kanza	كنزة
sweatshirt		sweet sheert	سويت شيرت
swimming trunks		maayoo rijaalee	مايوه رجالي
swimsuit		maayoo nisaa'ee	مايوه نسائي
T-shirt		tee-sheert	تي-شيرت
tie		krafatta	كرفتة
trousers		banTaloon	بنطلون
underpants		libaas daakhilee	لباس داخلي
with long/short sleeves		bi-akmaam Taweela/qaSeera	بأكمام طويلة/قصيرة
with a V-/round neck		bi-yaaqa sabAHa/mustadeera	بياقة سبعة/مستديرة

Shoes أحذية

boots	*boot* بوت
flip-flops	*shibshib Hammaam* شبشب حمام
running shoes [trainers]	*Hizaa riyaaDa* حذاء رياضة
sandals	*Sandal* صندل
shoes	*Hizaa* حذاء
slippers	*shibshib* شبشب

Walking/Hiking gear أمتعة السير/التنزه مشيا

knapsack	*Haqeebat aZ-Zahr* حقيبة الظهر
hiking boots	*boot lil-mashy* بوت للمشي
waterproof jacket	*jaakeet waaqeeya min al-maa'* جاكيت واقية من الماء

Fabric قماش

I want something in …	*ureed shay min* أريد شيئا من …
cotton	*al-quTn* القطن
denim	*al-jeenz* الجينز
leather	*al-jild* الجلد
linen	*al-kittaan* الكتان
wool	*aS-Soof* الصوف
Is this …?	*hal haaza* هل هذا …؟
pure cotton	*quTn khaaliS* قطن خالص
synthetic	*iSTinaAHee* اصطناعي
Is it hand/machine washable?	*hal huwa qaabil lil-ghaseel al-yadawee/bil-ghasaala* هل هو قابل للغسيل اليدوي/بالغسالة؟

dry clean only	للتنظيف الجاف فقط
handwash only	غسيل يدوي فقط
do not iron	لا يكوى

Does it fit? هل تلائمك؟

Can I try this on?	hal astaTeeAH an ujarrib haaza هل أستطيع أن أجرّب هذا؟
Where's the fitting room?	ayn ghurfat al-qiyaas أين غرفة القياس؟
It fits well. I'll take it.	innuh yulaa'imnee jiddan. sa-aakhuduh إنه يلائمني جدا. سآخذه.
It doesn't fit.	laa yulaa'imnee لا يلائمني.
It's too …	innuh … kateer إنه … كثيرا.
short/long	qaSeer/Taweel قصير/طويل
tight/loose	Dayyiq/waasiAH ضيق/واسع
Do you have this in size …?	AHndak hazaa qiyaas …؟ عندك هذا قياس …؟
What size is this?	maa huwa qiyaas haaza ما هو قياس هذا؟
Could you measure me, please?	mumkin takhud qiyaasee, lau samaHt ممكن تأخذ قياسي، لو سمحت؟

Size قياس

The Middle East generally uses continental sizes and metric measures.

	Dresses/Suits						Women's shoes			
American	8	10	12	14	16	18	6	7	8	9
British	10	12	14	16	18	20	$4^{1/2}$	$5^{1/2}$	$6^{1/2}$	$7^{1/2}$
Continental	36	38	40	42	44	46	37	38	40	41

	Shirts				Men's shoes							
American) British)	15	16	17	18	5	6	7	8	$8^{1/2}$ 9	$9^{1/2}$	10	11
Continental	38	41	43	45	38	39	41	42	43	43	44	45

كبير جدا	extra large (XL)
كبير	large (L)
وسط	medium (M)
صغير	small (S)

1 centimeter (cm.) = 0.39 in.	1 inch = 2.54 cm.
1 meter (m.) = 39.37 in.	1 foot = 30.5 cm.
10 meters = 32.81 ft.	1 yard = 0.91 m.

Health and beauty الصحة و الجمال

I'd like a ...	*ureed* ... ... أريد
facial	*tanZeef lil-wajh* تنظيف للوجه
manicure	*tajmeel al-aZaafir* تجميل الأظافر
massage	تدليك *tadleek*
waxing	*izaalat ash-shAHr bish-shamAH* إزالة الشعر بالشمع

Hairdresser / Hairstylist (الحلاق) المزين

It is usual to tip approximately 10% if you are happy with the service.

I'd like to make an appointment for ...	*ureed AHmal mawAHid li* أريد عمل موعد لـ ...
Can you make it a bit earlier / later?	*mumkin tAHmil al-mauAHid abkar/* *mutakhkhar* ؟ممكن تعمل الموعد أبكر/متأخر
I'd like a ...	*ureed* أريد...
cut and blow-dry	*qaSS wa tansheef* قص وتنشيف
shampoo and set	*shamboo wa taSfeef* شامبو وتصفيف
trim	*taqleem* تقليم
I'd like my hair ...	*ureed shAHree* ... أريد شعري
highlighted	*mumayyash* مميش
permed	*mumawwaj* مموج
Don't cut it too short.	*laa taqaSSuh aktar mimaa yanbaghee* لا تقصه أكثر مما ينبغي.
A little more off the ...	*aktar qaleel min* ... أكثر قليلا من
back / front	*al-khalf/al-amaam* الخلف/الأمام
neck / sides	*ar-raqaba/al-jawaanib* الرقبة/الجوانب
top	*al-qimma* القمة
That's fine, thanks.	*haaza mumtaaz, shukran* هذا ممتاز، شكرا.

Household articles أدوات منزلية

I'd like a/an …	*ureed* … أريد
adapter	*muHawwil* محول
alumin(i)um foil	*raqaa'iq aluminyoom* رقائق ألمنيوم
bottle-opener	*fattaaHat zujaajaat* فتاحة زجاجات
can [tin] opener	*fattaaHat muAHlabaat* فتاحة معلبات
clothes pins [pegs]	*milqaT malaabis* ملقط ملابس
corkscrew	*fattaaHat nabeet* فتاحة نبيذ
light bulb	*lamba* لمبة
matches	*kibreet* كبريت
paper napkins	*manaadeel waraq* مناديل ورق
plug	*saddaada* سدادة
scissors	*miqaSS* مقص
screwdriver	*mifakk* مفك

Cleaning items مواد تنظيف

bleach	*bleetsh* بليتش
dish cloth	*minshafat SuHoon* منشفة صحون
dishwashing [washing-up] liquid	*saa'il li-ghaseel aS-SuHoon* سائل لغسيل الصحون
garbage [refuse] bags	*akyaas qimmaama* أكياس قمامة
detergent [washing powder]	*mas-Hooq ghaseel al-malaabis* مسحوق غسيل الملابس
sponge	*isfinj* إسفنج

Crockery / Cutlery الأواني/ملاعق، سكاكين، شوك

cups / glasses	*fanaajeen/akwaab* فناجين/أكواب
knives / forks	*sakaakeen/shuwak* سكاكين/شوك
spoons	*malaAHiq* ملاعق
mugs	*akwaaz* أكواز
plates	*SuHoon* صحون
bowls	*sulTaaneeyaat* سلطانيات

Jeweler جواهرجي

Could I see ...?	mumkin araa
	ممكن أرى ...؟
this/that	haaza/zaalik هذا/ذلك.
It's in the window/	innaha feesh-shibbaak/
display cabinet.	fee-khazaanat al-AHrD
	إنها في شباك/خزانة العرض.
alarm clock	munabbih منبه
battery	baTaareeya بطارية
bracelet	sawaar سوار
brooch	broosh بروش
chain	silsila سلسلة
clock	saAHat Haa'iT ساعة حائط
earrings	Halaq حلق
necklace	AHuqd عقد
ring	khaatim خاتم
watch	saAHa ساعة

Materials مواد

Is this real silver/real gold?	hal haazihi faDDa Haqeeqeeya/
	dahab Haqeeqee
	هل هذه فضة حقيقية/ذهب حقيقي؟
Is there a certificate for it?	hal mAHahu shahaada هل معه شهادة؟
Do you have anything in ...?	hal AHndak ayy shay min
	هل عندك أي شيء من ...؟
copper	an-naHHaas النحاس
crystal	al-baloor البلور
diamond	al-maas الماس
gold	ad-dahab الذهب
gold plate	qishrat dahab قشرة ذهب
pearl	al-lu'lu' اللؤلؤ
pewter	al-qaSdeer القصدير
platinum	al-balaateen البلاتين
silver	al-faDDa الفضة
silver plate	qishrat faDDa قشرة فضة
wood	al-khashab الخشب

Newsstand [Newsagent]/
Tobacconist. بائع الجرائد/الدخان

Larger newsstands usually carry English-language newspapers and magazines, although they may be expensive and a few days old. You may also be able to find local English-language papers which will give you news and details about events.

Do you sell English-language books/newspapers?	*hal tabeeAH kutub/jaraa'id bi-lugha al-injileezeeya* هل تبيع كتب/جرائد باللغة الإنجليزية؟
I'd like a/an/some ...	*ureed ...* أريد
book	*kitaab* كتاب
candy [sweets]	*sakaakir* سكاكر
chewing gum	*libaan* لبان
chocolate bar	*lauH shookalaata* لوح شوكلاتة
(packet of) cigarettes	*(AHulbat) sajaa'ir* (علبة) سجائر
cigars	*siijaar* سيجار
dictionary	*qaamoos* قاموس
Arabic–English	*AHrabee-injileezee* عربي–إنجليزي
envelopes	*aZruf* أظرف
guidebook of ...	*daleel siyaaHee AHn ...* دليل سياحي عن ...
lighter	*walaAHa* ولاعة
magazine	*majalla* مجلة
map	*khareeTa* خريطة
map of the town	*khareeTat al-madeena* خريطة المدينة
road map of ...	*khareeTat ash-shawaariAH fee ...* خريطة الشوارع في ...
matches	*kibreet* كبريت
newspaper	*jareeda* جريدة
American/English	*amreekeeya/injileezeeya* أمريكية/إنجليزية
paper	*waraq* ورق
pen	*qalam* قلم
stamps	*TawaabiAH* طوابع
tobacco	*tabgh* تبغ

Photography تصوير

I'm looking for a ... camera.	abHas AHn kaameeraa	
	أبحث عن كاميرا ...	
automatic	ootoomaateek	أوتوماتيك
compact	muSaghghara	مصغرة
disposable	tustAHmal marra waaHda	
	تستعمل مرة واحدة	
I'd like a/an ...	ureed	أريد ...
battery	baTaareeya	بطارية
camera case	AHulba lil-kaameeraa	علبة للكاميرا
flash (electronic)	flaash (iliktroonee)	فلاش (إلكتروني)
filter	filtir	فلتر
lens	AHdasa	عدسة
lens cap	ghiTaa' lil-AHdasa	غطاء للعدسة

Film/Processing فيلم/تحميض

I'd like a ... film for this camera.	ureed feelm ... li-haazihil kaameeraa	
	أريد فيلم ... لهذه الكاميرا.	
black and white	aswad wa abyaD	أسود وأبيض
color	alwaan	ألوان
24/36 exposures	arbAHa wa AHishreen/sitta wa talaateen Soora	٣٦/٢٤ صورة
I'd like this film developed, please.	ureed taHmeeD hazaal feelm, lau samaHt	
	أريد تحميض هذا الفيلم، لو سمحت.	
Would you enlarge this, please?	mumkin takbeer haazihi, lau samaHt	
	ممكن تكبير هذه، لو سمحت؟	
How much do ... exposures cost?	kam hiya ujrat taHmeeD ... Soora	
	كم هي أجرة تحميض ... صورة؟	
When will the photos be ready?	matta sa-takoon aS-Suwar jaahza	
	متى ستكون الصور جاهزة؟	
I'd like to collect my photos.	ureed an aakhud Suwaree	
	أريد أن آخذ صوري.	
Here's the receipt.	haazaa huwa al-waSl	
	هذا هو الوصل.	

شرطة Police

!

You will need to report crimes, thefts or accidents to the police. Emergency numbers vary from country to country, but if you need to make an emergency call you can ask someone for the **an-najda** ("help") telephone number.

Where's the nearest police station?	ayn aqrab markaz shurTa أين أقرب مركز شرطة؟
Does anyone here speak English?	hunaak aHad yatKallam al-injileezeeya huna هناك أحد يتكلم الإنجليزية هنا؟
I want to report a(n) ...	ureed an uballigh AHn أريد أن أبلّغ عن...
accident/attack	Haadis/iAHtidaa حادث/اعتداء
mugging/rape	salb/ightiSaab سلب/اغتصاب
My child is missing.	Tiflee mafqood. طفلي مفقود.
Here's his photo/her photo.	haazihi Sooratuh/Soorathaa هذه صورته/صورتها.
Someone's following me.	shakhS ma yatbAHnee. شخص ما يتبعني.
I need an English-speaking lawyer.	ureed muHamee yatkallam al-injileezeeya. أريد محام يتكلم الإنجليزية.
I need to make a phone call.	aHtaaj an atkallam AHlaal tilifoon أحتاج أن أتكلم على التلفون.
I need to contact the ... Consulate.	aHtaaj ilaal ittiSaal bil-qunSuleeya ... أحتاج إلى الاتصال بالقنصلية ...
American/British	al-amreekeeya/al-bireeTaaneeya الأمريكية/البريطانية

هل يمكنك وصفه/وصفها؟	Can you describe him/her?
ذكر/أنثى	male/female
شعر أشقر/بني غامق/أحمر.	blond/brunette/red-headed
شيب (أبيض)	gray-haired
بشعر طويل/قصير/بدون شعر (أصلع)	long/short hair/balding
الطول تقريبا ...	approximate height ...
السن تقريبا ...	aged approximately ...
كان/كانت يرتدي/ترتدي ...	He/She was wearing ...

CLOTHES ➤ 144; COLORS ➤ 143

Lost property / Theft المفقودات/السرقة

I want to report a theft/break-in.	ureed at-tableegh AHn saraqa/iqtiHaam أريد التبليغ عن سرقة/اقتحام.
My car has been broken into.	HaSal iqtiHaam li-sayyaartee حصل اقتحام لسيارتي.
I've been robbed/mugged.	laqad suriqt/sulibt. لقد سرقت/سلبت.
I've lost a …	faqadt … فقدت
A/an … has been stolen from me.	laqad suriqat minnee … لقد سرقت مني …
bicycle	darraaja دراجة
camera	kaameeraa كاميرا
(rental) car	sayyaara (mu'ajjara) سيارة (مؤجرة)
credit cards	baTaaqaat aD-Damaan بطاقات الضمان
handbag	Haqeebat yad حقيبة يد
money	naqood نقود
passport	jawaaz as-safar جواز السفر
purse [wallet]	maHfaZa محفظة
ticket	tazkara تذكرة
watch	saAHa ساعة
What shall I do?	mazaa afAHl؟ ماذا أفعل؟
I need a police report for my insurance claim.	ureed shihaadat ash-shurTa li-uqaddimhaa li-sharikat at-ta'meen أريد شهادة الشرطة لأقدمها لشركة التأمين.

ما الذي ضاع؟	What's missing?
ما الذي أخذ؟	What's been taken?
متى سرقت؟	When was it stolen?
متى حصل الحادث؟	When did it happen?
أين تقيم؟	Where are you staying?
من أين أخذت؟	Where was it taken from?
أين كنت وقتها؟	Where were you at the time?
سنحضر لك مترجم.	We're getting an interpreter for you.
سننظر في الأمر.	We'll look into the matter.
الرجاء تعبئة هذه الاستمارة.	Please fill out this form.

Post office مكتب البريد

Mailboxes vary in color and shape from country to country. However, it is best to mail material at a post office. Sometimes hotels have their own mailboxes for postcards and letters, and these are also usually reliable.

General queries أسئلة عامة

Where is the nearest (main) post office?	*ayn aqrab maktab bareed (ra'eesee)* أين أقرب مكتب بريد (رئيسي)؟
What time does the post office open/close?	*matta yaftaH/yughliq maktab al-bareed* متى يفتح/يغلق مكتب البريد ؟
Does it close for lunch?	*hal yughliq waqt al-ghadaa* هل يغلق وقت الغداء؟
Where's the mailbox [postbox]?	*ayn Sundooq al-bareed* أين صندوق البريد؟
Is there any mail for me?	*hal hunaak rasaa'il lee* هل هناك رسائل لي؟

Buying stamps شراء طوابع

A stamp for this postcard, please.	*TaabiAH li-haazal kaart, lau samaHt* طابع لهذا الكارت، لو سمحت.
What's the postage for a letter to ...	*maa hiya ujrat al-bareed li-risaala ilaa ...* ما هي أجرة البريد لرسالة إلى ...؟
Is there a stamp machine here?	*hal hunaak aalat TawaabiAH huna* هل هناك آلة طوابع هنا؟

الطرود	parcels
موعد جمع البريد ...	next collection ...
صندوق البريد	general delivery [poste restante]
الطوابع	stamps

– *ureed irsall haazihil kuroot ilaa amreekaa.*
– *kam kart?*
– *tisAHa, lau samaHt.*
– *al-majmooAH arbAHa dinaar.*

Sending parcels إرسال طرود بريدية

I want to send this package by …	ureed irsaal haazaT Tard bi …
	… ـب الطرد هذا إرسال أريد
airmail	al-bareed al-jauee البريد الجوي
special delivery [express]	al-bareed as-sareeAH
	البريد السريع
registered mail	bareed musajjal بريد مسجل
It contains …	yaHtawee AHlaa … على يحتوي

إملاء شهادة الجمارك، لو سمحت.	Please fill in the customs declaration.
ما هي القيمة؟	What's the value?
ماذا في الداخل؟	What's inside?

Telecommunications الاتصالات السلكية و اللاسلكية

The major towns of the Arab world are rapidly becoming part of the international telephone network (► 127). In addition, hotels and office service bureaus in major cities often offer photocopying, word-processing and fax services, sometimes with translation facilities.

E-mail and Internet access in the Middle East is sporadic and ISPs (Internet Service Providers) may be limited to one or two approved companies.

Do you have a photocopier?	hal AHndak aalat naskh
	هل عندك آلة نسخ؟
I'd like to send a message …	ureed an abAHs risaala
	… رسالة أبعث أن أريد
by e-mail/fax	bi-waasiTat al-eemayl/al-faaks
	بواسطة الإي–ميل/الفاكس
What's your e-mail address?	maa huwa AHunwaanak feel eemayl?
	ما هو عنوانك في الإي–ميل؟
Can I access the Internet here?	hal mumkin istiAHmaal al-intarnat huna
	هل ممكن استعمال الإنترنت هنا؟
What are the charges per hour?	maa huwal Hisaab fees saAHa
	ما هو الحساب في الساعة؟
How do I log on?	kayf abda' كيف أبدأ؟

Souvenirs تذكارات

Here are some suggestions for souvenirs to take home. Many of these items can be found at the local markets (**sooq**), which offer a huge range of interesting articles. You will need to bargain, but try to find out price ranges before you go so you have some idea of what you should be paying.

How much is this?	*bikam haaza* بكم هذا؟
That's too much. I'll pay …	*haaza kateer. sa-adfAH* هذا كثير. سأدفع …
That's my last offer.	*haaza aakhir kalaam* هذا آخر كلام.
long Egyptian robe	*gallaabeya* جلابية
carpets	*sijaad* سجاد
pottery	*awaanee fukhaareeya* أوانٍ فخارية
water pipe	*sheesha (naarjeela)* شيشة (نارجيلة)
jewelry	*mujauharaat* مجوهرات
backgammon board	*Taawlat zahr* طاولة زهر
woodwork	*maSnooAHaat khashabeeya* مصنوعات خشبية
leather goods	*maSnooAHaat jildeeya* مصنوعات جلدية
sandals	*Sandal* صندل
electrical goods	*baDaa'iAH kahrabaa'eeya* بضائع كهربائية

Gifts هدايا

box of chocolates	*AHulbat shookaalaata* علبة شوكولاتة
calendar	*raznaama* رزنامة
key ring	*silsilat mafaateeH* سلسلة مفاتيح
postcard	*kart boostaal* كرت بوستال
tea towel	*fooTat maTbakh* فوطة مطبخ
T-shirt	*tee-sheert* تي-شيرت

موسيقى Music

I'd like a...	ureed ... أريد
cassette	shareeT kaaseet شريط كاسيت
compact disc	usTuwaana koombaakt أسطوانة كومباكت
record	usTuwaana أسطوانة
videocassette	shareeT feedyoo شريط فيديو
Who are the popular local singers/bands?	man hum ash-har al-mughaneeyeen/ al-firaq al-maHalleeya من هم أشهر المغنين/الفرق المحلية؟

Toys and games لعب وألعاب

I'd like a toy/game ...	ureed lAHba ... أريد لعبة
for a boy	li-walad لولد
for a 5-year-old girl	li-bint AHumrahaa khamas sanawaat لبنت عمرها خمس سنوات
ball	kura كرة
pail and shovel [bucket and spade]	dilw wa jaaroof دلو وجاروف
chess set	shaTranj شطرنج
doll	dumya دمية
electronic game	lAHba ileektrooneeya لعبة إليكترونية
teddy bear	dumya bi-shakl dubb دمية بشكل دب

Antiques أنتيكات

How old is this?	kam AHumr haaza؟ كم عمر هذا؟
Do you have anything from the ... era?	AHndak ayy shay min AHhd عندك أي شيء من عهد ...؟
Can you send it to me?	hal tastaTeeAH irsaaluh lee هل تستطيع إرساله لي؟
Will I have problems with customs?	hal sa-takoon AHndee mushkila mAHal jamaarik هل ستكون عندي مشكلة مع الجمارك؟
Is there a certificate of authenticity?	hal hunaak shihaada annahaa aSleeya هل هناك شهادة أنها أصلية؟

Supermarket / Minimart
سوبرماركت / بقالة

In Saudi Arabia and throughout the Gulf you will find huge hypermarkets, some local and some branches of international chains such as **Safeway** and **Spinnies**. In other parts of the region there are supermarkets, but generally on a smaller scale.

Most supermarkets offer a mix of imported / Western-style goods and locally produced goods.

At the supermarket. في السوبرماركت

Excuse me. Where can I find a …?	lau samaHt. ayn ajid لو سمحت. أين أجد ...؟
Do I pay for this here or at the checkout?	hal adfAH huna am AHndal mughaadra هل أدفع هنا أم عند المغادرة؟
Where are the carts [trolleys] / baskets?	ayn al-AHrabaat / as-silaal أين العربات / السلال؟
Is there a pharmacy here?	hal hunaak Saydaleeya huna هل هناك صيدلية هنا؟

نقدا فقط	cash only
مواد تنظيف	cleaning products
ألبان	dairy products
سمك طازج	fresh fish
لحم طازج	fresh meat
خضروات طازج	fresh produce
طعام مجمد	frozen foods
بضائع منزلية	household goods
دواجن	poultry
فواكه / خضار	fruit / vegetables
خبز وكيك	bread and cakes

Weights and measures
- **1 kilogram** or kilo (kg.) = **1000 grams** (g.); **100 g.** = 3.5 oz.; **1 kg.** = 2.2 lb 1 oz. = **28.35 g.**; 1 lb. = **453.60 g.**
- **1 liter** (l.) = 0.88 imp. quart or 1.06 U.S. quart; 1 imp. quart = **1.14 l.**; 1 U.S. quart = **0.951 l.**; 1 imp. gallon = **4.55 l.**; 1 U.S. gallon = **3.8 l.**

Food hygiene نظافة الطعام

يوكل خلال ... أيام من فتحه	eat within ... days of opening
يحفظ بالثلاجة	keep refrigerated
يمكن طبخه في الميكرويف	microwavable
سخنه قبل الأكل	reheat before eating
مناسب للنباتيين	suitable for vegetarians
يستخدم قبل ...	use by ...

At the minimart عند محل البقالة

I'd like some of that/those.	*ureed bAHD min haaza/haazihi*	أريد بعضا من هذا/هذه.
This one/those.	*haaza/haazihi*.	هذا/هذه.
To the left/right.	*ilaal yasaar/yameen*.	إلى اليسار/اليمين.
Over there/Here.	*hunaak/huna*.	هناك/هنا.
Which one(s)?	*ayy minhaa?*	أي منها؟
That's all thanks.	*hazaa kulluh, shukran*.	هذا كله، شكرا.
I'd like a ...	*ureed ...*	أريد ...
kilo of apples	*keeloo tufaaH*	كيلو تفاح
half-kilo of tomatoes	*niSf keeloo TamaaTim*	نصف كيلو طماطم
100 grams of cheese	*meet graam jibna*	١٠٠ غرام جبنة
liter of milk	*leetr Haleeb*	ليتر حليب
half-dozen eggs	*nuSf dastat bayD*	نصف دستة بيض
piece of cake	*qiTAHt kayk*	قطعة كيك
carton of juice	*kartoonat AHSeer*	كرتونة عصير
carton of milk	*kartoonat Haleeb*	كرتونة حليب
jar of jam	*barTumaan murabba*	برطمان مربى
bag of potato chips [crisps]	*baakeet shibs (baTaaTis maqleeya)*	باكيت شبس (بطاطس مقلية)
can of cola	*AHulbat koolaa*	علبة كولا

lau samaHt.
– ureed niSf keeloo min haazihil jibna,
– *haazihi?*
– naAHm, jibna bayDa, lau samaHt.
bit-ta'keed … hal haaza kulluh?
– naAHm, haaza kulluh.
– tafaDDal.

Provisions/Picnic مؤونة/نزهة

butter	*zibda*	زبدة
cheese	*jibna*	جبنة
cookies [biscuits]	*baskaweet*	بسكويت
eggs	*bayD*	بيض
grapes	*AHinab*	عنب
ice cream	*aayis kreem*	آيس كريم
loaf of bread	*ragheef khubz*	رغيف خبز
milk	*Haleeb*	حليب
rolls	*khubz mudawwar*	خبز مدور
sausages	*sujuq*	سجق
soft drinks	*kaazooza*	كازوزة
tea bags	*akyaas shay*	أكياس شاي

Bread (**khubz**) is very important to the Arabs and is eaten with every meal. It is often called **AHysh**, which literally means "life." It is considered disrespectful to throw away bread or drop it on the floor.

خبز (عيش شامي) **khubz (AHysh shaamee)**: Traditional Arabic bread is round, flat, and only slightly leavened.

عيش بلدي **AHysh baladee**: A wholemeal version of khubz.

خبز محمّص **khubz muHammas**: Bread crisped in the oven.

خبز مبسّس **khubz mubassis**: Tunisian semolina bread.

سميط **semiT**: Egyptian bread rings covered in sesame seeds.

Health

Before you leave, make sure your health insurance policy covers illness and accidents while away from home. There is only a very basic system of state health care in most Arab countries, and you will be expected to pay doctors and dentists on the spot.

Almost all doctors in the region will have a good level of English – or at least know the medical terms. However, there may be occasions when you need to explain your problem in Arabic or use the tables on pages 164–165.

Doctor/General دكتور/عام

Where can I find a doctor/dentist?	ayn ajid duktoor/duktoor asnaan
	أين أجد دكتور/دكتور أسنان؟
Where's there a doctor/dentist who speaks English?	ayn ajid duktoor/duktoor asnaan yatkallam al-injileezeeya
	أين أجد دكتور/دكتور أسنان يتكلم الإنجليزية؟
What are the office [surgery] hours?	maa hiya mawaaAHeed al-AHiyaada
	ما هي مواعيد العيادة؟
Could the doctor come to see me here?	hal yumkin lid-duktoor an yuzoornee huna
	هل يمكن للدكتور أن يزورني هنا؟
Can I make an appointment ...?	mumkin aakhud mauAHid
	ممكن آخذ موعدا ...؟
for today/tomorrow	lil-yaum/ghadan لليوم/غدا
as soon as possible	li-aqrab furSa mumkina
	لأقرب فرصة ممكنة
It's urgent!	innahaa Haala mustAHjila
	إنها حالة مستعجلة!
I've got an appointment with Doctor ...	AHndee mauAHid mAHa duktoor
	عندي موعد مع دكتور...

– mumkin aakhud mauAHid li-aqrab
furSa mumkina?
– naHnu maHjoozeen tammaaman al-yaum.
hal al-Haala mustAHjila?
– nAHm.
– mumkin nAHmil lak Hajz as-sAHa AHshara wa
rubAH mAHa ad-duktoor shareef.
– as-sAHa AHshara wa rubAH. shukran jazeelan.

Accident and injury   حادث وإصابة

... is injured.	... أصيب/أصيبت. ... uSeeb/uSeebat
my husband / wife	زوجي/زوجتي zaujee/zaujatee
my son / daughter	ابني/بنتي ibnee/bintee
my friend	صديقي Sadeeqee
my baby	رضيعي raDeeAHee
He / She is ...	هو/هي ... huwa/hiya ...
unconscious	فاقد الوعي faaqid al-wAHee
injured (seriously)	أصيب (خطيرة) uSeeb (khaTeera)
He / She is bleeding.	huwa/hiya yanzif/tanzif
	هو/هي ينزف/تنزف.
I have a / an ...	عندي ... AHndee ...
blister	كيس ماء kees maa'
boil	خراج khuraaj
bruise	كدمة kadma
burn	حرق Harq
cut	قطع qaTAH
graze	سلخ salkh
insect bite	لدغة حشرة ladghat Hashara
lump	ورم waram
rash	طفح جلدي TafH jildee
sting	حرقان Harqaan
strained muscle	تمزق عضلي tamazzuq AHDalee
swelling	ورم waram
wound	جرح jurH
My ... hurts.	... يؤلمني. ... yu'limnee

Symptoms الأعراض

I've been feeling ill for ... days.	ashAHur bil-maraD munzu ... ayyaam
	أشعر بالمرض منذ ... أيام.
I feel faint.	ashAHur bi-ighmaa' أشعر بإغماء.
I feel feverish.	ashAHur bi-Humaa أشعر بحمى
I've been vomiting.	kunt atqayya' كنت أتقيء.
I've got diarrhea.	AHndee ishaal عندي إسهال.
It hurts here.	innahu yu'lim huna إنه يؤلم هنا.
I have a/an ...	AHndee ... عندي
backache	alam feeZ-Zahr ألم في الظهر
cold	bard برد
cramps	taqalluSaat تقلصات
earache	alam feel uzun ألم في الأذن
headache	SudaAH صداع
sore throat	alam feel Halq ألم في الحلق
stiff neck	alam feel AHunuq ألم في العنق
stomachache	alam feel baTn ألم في البطن
sunstroke	Darbat shams ضربة شمس

Health conditions الأوضاع الصحية

I have arthritis.	AHndee iltihaab bil-mafaaSil عندي التهاب بالمفاصل.
I have asthma.	AHndee rabw عندي ربو.
I am ...	ana ... أنا
deaf	aSamm أصم
diabetic	muSaab bis-sukaree مصاب بالسكري
epileptic	muSaab biS-SarAH مصاب بالصرع
handicapped	muAHaq معاق
(... months) pregnant	Haamil (bish-shahr al ...) حامل (بالشهر الـ ...)
I have a heart condition.	ana mareeD bil-qalb أنا مريض بالقلب.
I have high blood pressure.	AHndee irtifaAH bi-DaghT ad-dam عندي ارتفاع بضغط الدم.
I had a heart attack ... years ago.	kaan AHndee azma qalbeeya min ... sineen كان عندي أزمة قلبية من ... سنين.

163

Doctor's inquiries أسئلة الدكتور

منذ متى تشعر هكذا؟	How long have you been feeling like this?
هل هذه أول مرة تصاب بهذا؟	Is this the first time you've had this?
هل تأخذ أي أدوية أخرى؟	Are you taking any other medication?
عندك حساسية من أي شيء؟	Are you allergic to anything?
هل أنت ملقح ضد التيتانوس؟	Have you been vaccinated against tetanus?
هل فقدت الشهية للطعام؟	Have you lost your appetite?

Examination الفحوص

سأقيس لك الحرارة/ضغط الدم.	I'll take your temperature/ blood pressure.
ارفع كمك، لو سمحت.	Roll up your sleeve, please.
اخلع ملابسك العليا لو سمحت.	Please undress to the waist.
استلق، لو سمحت.	Please lie down.
افتح فمك.	Open your mouth.
تنفس بعمق.	Breathe deeply.
أسعل، لو سمحت.	Cough, please.
أين تؤلمك؟	Where does it hurt?
هل يوجد ألم هنا؟	Does it hurt here?

Diagnosis التشخيص

أريدك أن تأخذ صورة بالأشعة.	I want you to have an X-ray.
أريد عينة من دمك/برازك/بولك.	I want a specimen of your blood/stools/urine.
أريدك أن ترى أخصائي.	I want you to see a specialist.
أريدك أن تذهب إلى المستشفى.	I want you to go to hospital.
إنها مكسورة/ملتوية.	It's broken/sprained.
إنها مخلوعة/ممزقة.	It's dislocated/torn.

عندك ...	You've got ...
التهاب الزائدة الدودية	appendicitis
التهاب المثانة	cystitis
انفلونزا	flu
تسمم غذاء	food poisoning
كسر	a fracture
حموضة في المعدة	gastritis
البواسير	hemorrhoids
فتاق	a hernia
التهاب في ...	an inflammation of ...
حصبة	measles
التهاب رئوي	pneumonia
عرق النسا	sciatica
التهاب اللوزتين	tonsilitis
ورم	a tumor
مرض تناسلي	venereal disease
إنه ملوث.	It's infected.
إنه معد.	It's contagious.

Treatment علاج

سأعطيك ...	I'll give you ...
مطهر	an antiseptic
مسكن	a painkiller
سأصف لك ...	I'm going to prescribe ...
مضادات حيوية	a course of antibiotics
بعض التحاميل/اللبوس	some suppositories
هل عندك حساسية من أي دواء؟	Are you allergic to any medicine?
خذ حبة واحدة ...	Take one pill ...
كل ... ساعات	every ... hours
... مرات في اليوم	... times a day
قبل/بعد كل وجبة	before/after each meal
عندما تتألم	in case of pain
لمدة ... أيام	for ... days
استشر طبيبا عندما تعود.	Consult a doctor when you get home.

Parts of the body أعضاء من الجسم

English	Transliteration	Arabic
appendix	az-zaa'ida ad-doodeeya	الزائدة الدودية
arm	ziraaAH	ذراع
back	Zahr	ظهر
bladder	mathaana	مثانة
bone	AHuZma	عظمة
breast	thady	ثدي
chest	Sidr	صدر
ear	uzun	أذن
eye	AHyn	عين
finger	iSbAH	إصبع
foot	qadam	قدم
hand	yad	يد
head	ra's	رأس
heart	qalb	قلب
jaw	fakk	فك
joint	mifSal	مفصل
kidney	kilya	كلية
knee	rukba	ركبة
leg	saaq	ساق
liver	kibd	كبد
mouth	fam	فم
muscle	AHDala	عضلة
neck	raqaba	رقبة
nose	anf	أنف
rib	DilAH	ضلع
shoulder	kitif	كتف
skin	jild	جلد
stomach	baTn	بطن
thigh	fakhd	فخذ
throat	Hanjara	حنجرة
toe	iSbAH al-qadam	إصبع القدم
tongue	lisaan	لسان
tonsils	luwaz	لوز
vein	wareed	وريد

Gynecologist الطبيب النسائي

I have …	AHndee …عندي
abdominal pains	amraaD jaufeeya آلام جوفية
period pains	alam al-AHaada ash-shahreeya ألم العادة الشهرية
a vaginal infection	talawwuth feel mahbal تلوث في المهبل
I haven't had my period for … months.	al-AHaada ash-shahreeya inqatAHat… min … shuhoor العادة الشهرية انقطعت من … شهور.
I'm on the Pill.	aakhud Huboob manAH al-Haml آخذ حبوب منع الحمل.

Hospital المستشفى

Please notify my family.	AHlim AHa'iltee, lau samaHt أعلم عائلتي، لو سمحت.
I'm in pain.	ana AHndee alam. أنا عندي ألم
I can't eat/sleep.	laa astaTeeAH al-akl/an-naum لا أستطيع الأكل/النوم.
When will the doctor come?	matta sa-ya'tee ad-duktoor متى سيأتي الدكتور؟
Which ward is … in?	fee ayy jinaaH …؟ في أي جناح
I'm visiting …	ana azoor … أنا أزور

Optician نظاراتي

I'm short-sighted/ far- [long-] sighted.	ana qaSeer an-naZar/Taweel an-naZar أنا قصير النظر/طويل النظر.
I've lost …	faqadt … فقدت
one of my contact lenses	iHda AHdsaatee al-laaSqa إحدى عدساتي اللاصقة
my glasses/a lens	naZaartee/AHdsa نظاراتي/عدسة
Could you give me a replacement?	mumkin tAHTeenee badeel ممكن تعطيني بديلاً؟

167

I have toothache.	AHndee alam fee sinnee
	عندي ألم في سني.
This tooth hurts.	haazas sinn yu'allimnee
	هذا السن يؤلمني.
I've lost a filling / tooth.	faqadt Hashw/sinna. فقدت حشوا/سنة
My gums are swollen.	AHndee iltihaab feel litha
	عندي التهاب في اللثة.
My gums are bleeding.	AHndee nazeef feel litha
	عندي نزيف في اللثة.
Can you repair this denture?	mumkin iSlaaH hazaaT Taqm
	ممكن إصلاح هذا الطقم؟
I don't want it extracted.	laa ureed khalAHhaa
	لا أريد خلعها.

سأعطيك حقنة/مخدر موضعي.	I'm going to give you an injection / a local anesthetic.
أنت تحتاج حشو/تاج الضرس	You need a filling / cap (crown).
يجب أن أخلعه.	I'll have to take it out.
أستطيع معالجته مؤقتا.	I can only fix it temporarily.
لا تأكل أي شيء لمدة ... ساعات.	Don't eat anything for ... hours.

Payment and insurance الدفع والتأمين

How much do I owe you?	kam al-Hisaab؟ كم الحساب
I have insurance.	AHndee ta'meen. عندي تأمين
Can I have a receipt for my health insurance?	mumkin tAHTeenee eeSaal li-ta'meenee aS-SiHHee
	ممكن تعطيني إيصال لتأميني الصحي؟
Would you fill in this health insurance form, please?	min faDlak, mumkin tamla istimaarat at-ta'meen aS-SiHHee
	من فضلك ممكن تملأ استمارة التأمين الصحي؟

Dictionary
English - Arabic

To enable correct usage, most terms in this dictionary are either followed by an expression or cross-referenced to pages where the word appears in a phrase. The notes below provide some basic grammar guidelines.

Nouns

Nouns are either masculine or feminine. It is easy to tell them apart as almost all feminine nouns either refer to female people or end with **a**.

al- (the) is used for both genders. There is no equivalent of the English "a(n)".

masculine	**al-walad**	the boy	*feminine*	**al-bint**	the girl
	markib	a boat		**madeena**	a city

Plurals are complicated and follow a number of different patterns. The plural can sound significantly different from the singular (▶ 216). The dictionary gives the plural for words you are most likely to encounter in this form.

Adjectives

Adjectives come after the noun and agree in gender with the noun they are describing. Feminine adjectives, like nouns, usually end in **a**. If the noun has **al-**, then the adjective should also:

markib kabeer	a big boat	**madeena kabeera**	a big city
al-markib al-kabeer	the big boat	**al-madeena al-kabeera**	a big city

Feminine adjectives are used with all plurals except people:

maraakib kabeera	big boats	**al-mudun al-kabeera**	the big cities

Verbs

Verbs are generally shown in the dictionary in present tense "he" form (*third person singular*). Different prefixes and endings are added to a present or past "stem". Although there are some variations, generally these prefixes and endings are as shown underlined below:

	present	*past*
	yaktub (write)	**katab** (wrote)
ana (I)	**a**ktub	katabt**(u)**
anta (you, m.)	**t**aktub	katabt**(a)**
anti (you, f.)	**t**aktub**ee(na)**	katabt**i**
huwa (he/it, m.)	**y**aktub	katab
hiya (she/it, f.)*	**t**aktub	katab**at**
naHnu (we)	**n**aktub	katab**naa**
antum (you, pl.)	**t**aktub**oo(na)**	katab**tum**
hum (they)	**y**aktub**oo(na)**	katab**oo**

*All non-human plurals are grammatically *feminine singular* and so will also take this part of the verb:

al-rijaal wasal<u>oo</u>	the men arrived	**al-maraakib wasal<u>at</u>**	the boats arrived

a little قليل
qaleel 15

a lot كثير
kateer 15

a.m. صباحاً sabaaHan

about *(approximately)*
تقريباً taqreeban 15

abroad خارج الحدود
khaarij al-Hudood

accept, to يقبل yaqbal 136

accident حادث Haadis 92, 152

accidentally بدون قصد bidoon qaSd 28

accompany, to يرافق yuraafiq 65

accountant محاسب muHaasib

acne حب الشباب Habb ash-shabaab

actor/actress ممثل / ممثلة
mumassil / mumassila

adapter محول muHawwil 148

address عنوان AHunwaan 84, 126;
your ~ عنوانك AHunwaanak 93

adjoining rooms غرفتان مفتوحتان
ghurfatayn maftooHatayn 22

admission charge رسم الدخول
rasm ad-dukhool 114

adults كبار kubaar 81

aerobics تمرينات رياضية tamreenaat
riyaaDeeya 114

after بعد bAHd 13, 95, 165

after shave عطر بعد الحلاقة AHiTr
bAHd al-Hilaaqa 142

afternoon, in the بعد الظهر
bAHd aZ-Zuhr 221

agree: I don't ~ أنا لا أوافق
ana laa uwaafiq

air conditioning تكييف هواء takyeef
hawaa 22, 25

air pump مضخة الهواء maDakhkhat
al-hawaa 87

airmail بريد جوي bareed
jauee 155

airport مطار maTaar 96

aisle seat مقعد قرب الممر maqAHd
qurb al-mamarr 73

alarm clock منبه munabbih 149

Algeria الجزائر al-jazaa$ir

Algerian جزائري jazaa'iree

all جميع / كل jameeAH / kull

allergy حساسية Hasaaseeya 164

almost تقريباً taqreeban

alone وحيدا waHeedan

also أيضا ayDan

alter, to يعدل yuAHaddil 137

alumin(i)um foil رقائق ألمنيوم
raqaa'iq aluminyoom 148

always دائما daa'iman 13

am: I am أنا ana

amazing مدهش mudhish 101

ambassador سفير safeer

ambulance سيارة إسعاف sayyaarat
isAHaaf 92

American أمريكي amreekee 150, 152

amount *(of money)* مبلغ mablagh 42

amusement arcade قاعة تسلية
qaAHat tasleeya 113

and و wa

anesthetic: (local) anesthetic مخدر
(موضعي) mukhaddir (mawDiAHee) 168

angling صيد السمك Sayd as-samak 114

animal(s) حيوان (حيوانات)
Hayawaan(aat) 106

anorak معطف المطر mAHTaf
al-matar

another آخر aakhar 21

antibiotics مضادات حيوية
muDaadaat Hayaweeya 165

antique store محل أنتيكات
maHall anteekaat 129

antique(s) أنتيكا(ت) anteekaa(t) 157

antiseptic مطهر muTahhir 165;
~ cream كريم مطهر kreem
muTahhir 141

any أي ayy

anything else? أي شئ آخر؟
ayy shay aakhar

apartment(s) شقة (شقق) shaqqa (shuqaq)
28, 123

appendix *(part of body)* الزائدة الدودية
az-zaa'ida ad-doodeeya 166

apples تفاح tufaaH 49

appointment موعد mauAHid 147, 161

approximately تقريبا taqreeban 152

apricots مشمش mishmish 49

Arabic عربي AHrabee 11;
~ **language** اللغة العربية al-lugha
al-AHrabeeya 126; ~ **music**
موسيقى عربية mooseeqaa
AHrabeeya 111

architect مهندس معماري muhandis
mAHmaaree 103

are there ...? هل هناك ... ؟ hal hunaak 17

area code الرقم النداء الدولي raqm
an-nidaa' ad-daulee 127

arm ذراع ziraaAH 166

around *(time)* حوالي Hawaala 13

arrive (in), to يصل إلى yaSil
ilaa 68, 70, 75

art gallery معرض الفنون mAHraD
al-funoon 99

arthritis التهاب المفاصل iltihaab
al-mafaaSil 163

artificial sweetener سكر صناعي
sukkar SinaAH-ee 38

artist فنان fanaan 103

ashtray منفضة سجاير manfaDat
sajaayir 39

ask: I asked for طلبت Talabt 41

aspirin أسبرين asbireen 141

asthma ربو rabw 163

at *(place)* عند AHnda 12;
(time) الساعة as-sAHa 13

at last! أخيرا akheeran 19

athletics ألعاب القوى alAHaab
al-quwa 114

ATM آلة سحب النقود aalat saHb
an-nuqood 139

attack اعتداء iAHtidaa 152

attractive جذاب jazaab

aubergine باذنجان
baazinjaan 47

aunt خالة khaala *(maternal)* 120;
عمة AHmma *(paternal)* 120

Australia استراليا ostraalyaa 119

authenticity أصلية aSleeya 157

automatic *(car)*
otomateek 86 أوتوماتيك

automobile(s)
سيارة (سيارات)
sayyarra(at)

autumn الخريف
al-khareef

awful مرعب murAHib 101;
شنيع shaneeAH 122

B **baby** طفل (رضيع) Tifl
(radeeAH) 39, 113, 162;
~ **food** طعام الأطفال TAHaam
al-aTfaal 142; ~ **wipes**
مساحات الأطفال masaaHaat
al-aTfaal 142

babysitter حاضنة HaaDina 113

back *(part of body)* ظهر Zahr 166;
(rear) الخلف al-khalf 147

backache ألم في الظهر alam
feeZ-Zahr 163

backpacking
السفر بحقيبة ظهر
as-safar bi-Haqeebat Zahr

bad سيء sayyi' 14

badminton تنس الريشة tanis
ar-reesha 114

bag *(luggage)* حقيبة Haqeeba 67;
(packet) باكيت baakeet 159

blocked مسدود masdood 25

blood دم dam 164; **~ group** فصيلة الدم faSeelat ad-damm; **~ pressure** ضغط الدم DaghT ad-dam 164

blouse بلوزة bilooza 144

blow-dry تنشيف tansheef 147

blue أزرق azraq 143

boarding card بطاقة الصعود baTaaqat aS-SuAHood 70

boat مركب markib 81; **~ trip** رحلة بالمركب riHla bil-markib 81, 97

body جسم jism 166

boil (medical) خراج khuraaj 162

boiler سخان sakh-khaan 29

bone عظمة AHaZma 166

bonnet (of car) غطاء المحرك ghaTaa al-muHarrik 90

book(s) كتاب (كتب) kitaab (kutub) 11, 150

booklet of tickets كتيب من التذاكر kutayyeb min at-tazaakir 79

bookshop مكتبة maktaba 129

boot (of car) صندوق السيارة Sundooq as-sayyaara 90

booted: my car has been booted سيارتي ربطت بملزم sayyaaratee rubiTat bi-mulzim 87

boots بوت boot 145

boring ممل mumill 101

born: I was born in ... ولدت في ... wulidt fee

botanical garden حديقة النبات Hadeeqat an-nabaat 99

bottle(s) زجاجة (زجاجات) zujaaja(at) 37; **~-opener** فتاحة زجاجات fattaaHat zujaajaat 148

bowel أمعاء amAHaa

bowl(s) سلطانية (سلطانيات) sulTaaneeya(at) 148

boxing (sport) الملاكمة al-mulaakma 114

boy(s) ولد (أولاد) walad (awlaad) 120, 157

boyfriend صاحب SaaHib 120

bra حمالة صدر Hamaalat Sidr 144

bracelet سوار sawaar 149

brake pad تيل الفرامل teel al-faraamil 82

brakes فرامل faraamil 91

bread خبز khubz 38, 43

break, to يكسر yaksar 28; **~ down, to** يعطل yAHTal 28; **~down** عطل AHTl 88; **~down truck** ونش winsh 88; **~in** اقتحام iqtiHaam 153

breast (part of body) ثدي thady 166

breathe, to يتنفس yatnaffas 92, 164

bridge جسر jisr 96, 107

Britain بريطانيا bireeTaanya 119

British بريطانية bireeTaanee 152

broken مكسور maksoor 25, 137, 164

bronchitis التهاب شعبي iltihaab shuAHbee

brooch بروش broosh 149

brother أخ akh 120

brown بني bunnee 143

browse, to يتفرج yatfarraj 133

bruise كدمة kadma 162

brush فرشاة fursha 142

bucket دلو dilw 157

building مبنى mabnaa

built: was built بُني buniya 103

bulletin board لوحة البيانات lauHat al-bayyaanaat 26

bureau de change مكتب تغيير عملات maktab taghyeer AHumlaat 138

burn حرق Harq 162

A-Z

caravan بيت متنقل bayt mutanaqqil 30, 81

cards *(game)* كوتشينة kootsheena 121

careful: be careful! احترس! iHtaras

carpet سجادة sijaada

carrier bag كيس البضائع kees al-baDaa'iAH

carrots جزر jazar 47

cart(s) عربة (عربات) AHraba(at) 158

carton كرتونة kartoona 159

cash desk خزينة khazeena 132

cash machine آلة سحب النقود aalat saHb an-nuqood 139

cash, to يصرف yaSraf 138

cash: by cash نقدا naqdan 136;
in cash نقدا naqdan 17

cashier خزينة khazeena 132

casino صالة القمار Saalat al-qumaar 112

cassette شريط كاسيت shareeT kaaseet 157

castle قلعة qalAHa 99

cave كهف kahf 107

CD سي دي "CD"; **CD-player** جهاز سي دي jahaaz "CD"

cemetery مقبرة maqbara 99

center (of town) وسط (المدينة) wasT (il-madeena) 21

central heating تدفئة مركزية tadfi'a markazeeya

ceramics الخزف al-khazaf

certificate شهادة shahaada 149, 157

chain سلسلة silsila 149

change *(coins)* صرافة Sarraafa 87;
keep the ~ احتفظ بالباقي iHtafiZ bil-baaqee 84

change, to يغير yughayyir 68, 74, 76, 78, 79, 80, 84, 138; *(baby)* يغير الفوط yughayyir al-fuwaT 39

changing facilities *(for babies)* تسهيلات لتغيير الفوط tas-heelaat li-tahgyeer al-fuwaT 113

charcoal فحم faHm 31

charge *(fee)* سعر siAHr 30;
حساب Hisaab 115

cheap رخيص rakheeS 14, 134

cheaper أرخص arkhaS 21, 24, 109, 134

check in, to يسجل yasajjil 69

check [cheque] book دفتر الشيكات daftar ash-sheekaat

check [cheque] guarantee card بطاقة ضمان الشيكات baTaaqat Damaan ash-sheekaat

check-in desk مكتب التسجيل maktab at-tasjeel 69

checking in تسجيل tasjeel 69

cheers! في صحتك! fee SaHHitak

cheese جبنة jibna 48, 160

chemist أجزخانة/صيدلية ajzakhaana/ Saydaleeya 131

chess شطرنج shaTranj 121, 157

chest صدر Sidr 166

chewing gum لبان libaan 150

chicken دجاج dajaaj 46; **~ soup** شوربة فراخ shoorbit firaakh 43

chickpeas حمص HumuS 48

child (children) طفل (أطفال) Tifl (aTfaal) 22, 74, 81, 100, 120, 133, 152; **~ seat** كرسي للطفل kursee liT-Tifl 39

chili شطة shaTTa 38

Chinese صيني Seenee 35

chocolate شوكولاتة shokoolaata 40; **~ bar** لوح شوكولاتة lauH shookoolaata 150

church كنيسة kaneesa 96, 99, 105

cigarette(s) سجائر (سجارة) sijaara (sajaa'ir); **~ kiosk** كشك سجائر kushk sajaa'ir 129; **packet of cigarettes** علبة سجائر AHulbat sajaa'ir 150

cigars سيجار seejaar 150

coolbox علبة تبريد AHulbat tabreed

copper نحاس naHaas 149

corkscrew فتاحة نبيذ fattaaHat nabeet 148

corn ذرة dura 47

corner زاوية zaaweeya 95

correct صحيح SaHeeH

cosmetics مستحضرات تجميل mustHDaraat tajmeel

cot سرير للطفل sareer lil-Tifl 22

cottage شالية shaalay 28

cotton قطن quTn 145; [cotton wool] قطن طبي quTn Tibbee 141

cough (noun) سعال suAHaal 141

cough, to يسعل yasAHl 164

could I have? ممكن آخذ؟ mumkin aakhud 18

country (countries) (دول) دولة dawla (duwal)

courgette كوسة koosa 47

courier (guide) مرشد murshid

course (of meal) طبق Tabaq; (of medicine) دورة علاج daurat AHilaaj

crab كبوريا kaaboorya 44

cracked wheat برغل burghul 48

cramps تقلصات taqalluSaat 163

crèche دار الحضانة daar al-HaDaana

credit card بطاقة الائتمان baTaaqat al-itimaan 42, 136

crib سرير للطفل sareer lil-Tifl 22

crockery أواني awaanee 29, 148

crossroad تقاطع taqaaTiAH 95

crowded مزدحم muzdaHim 31

crown (dental) (أسنان) تاج taaj (asnaan) 168

cruise (noun) رحلة بحرية riHla baHreeya

crutches عكازات AHkkaazaan

crystal بلور balloor 149

cucumber خيار khiyaar 47

cup(s) فنجان (فناجين) finjaan (fanaajeen) 39, 148

cupboard خزانة khazaana

curlers مشابك لف الشعر mushaabik laff ash-shAHr

currency عملات AHumlaat 67; ~ **exchange office** مكتب تغيير عملات maktab taghyeer AHumlaat 138

curtains ستائر sataa'ir

customer service خدمة الزبائن khidmat az-zabaa'in 133

customs (airport) جمارك jamaarik 67, 157; ~ **declaration** شهادة الجمرك shihaadat al-jumruk 155

D **damaged** تالف taalif 28
damn! لعين! lAHeen 19

damp (n/adj) رطوبة / رطب rutooba / raTib

dance (n) رقص raqS 111

dance, to يرقص yurqus 124

dangerous خطر khaTir

dark (without light) مظلم muZlim 24; (color) غامق ghaamiq 14, 134, 143

darker (color) أغمق aghmaq 143

dates (fruit) بلح balaH 49

daughter بنت bint 120, 162

dawn فجر fajr 221

day(s) (أيام) يوم yaum (ayyaam) 97, 122; ~ **ticket** تذكرة لطول اليوم tazkara li-Tool al-yaum; ~ **trip** رحلة لطول اليوم riHla li-Tool al-yaum

dead (battery) (بطارية) فارغة faargha 88

deaf أصم aSamm 163

deck chair كرسي الشاطئ kursee ash-shaaTi' 117

deep عميق AHmeeq

degrees (temperature) درجات الحرارة darajaat al-Haraara

delay تأخير ta'kheer 70

delicious لذيذ lazeez 14

denim جينز jeenz 145

dental floss شريط لتنظيف الأسنان shareeT li-tanZeef al-asnaan

dentist طبيب أسنان Tabeeb asnaan 131, 161, 168

dentures طقم (أسنان) Taqm (asnaan) 168

deodorant مزيل لرائحة العرق muzeel li-raa'iHat al-AHraq 142

department قسم qism 132; **~ store** محل تجاري maHall tijaaree 129

departure lounge قاعة الرحيل qaaAHa ar-raHeel 69

deposit عربون AHraboon 24, 83

describe, to يصف yaSif 152

desert صحراء SaHraa' 106, 107; **~ track(s)** طريق (طرق) صحراوي Tareeq (Turuq) SaHraawee 106

destination وجهة wijha

details تفاصيل tafaaSeel

detergent منظف munaZZif

detour تحويل taHweel 96

developing (photos) تحميض taHmeeD 151

diabetes مرض السكري marD as-sukkaree

diabetic مصاب بالسكري muSaab bis-sukkaree 39, 163

diagnosis تشخيص tashkheeS 164

dialling code رقم النداء الدولي raqm an-nidaa ad-daulee 127

diamond الماس al-maas 149

diapers حفاضات HafaaDaat 142

diarrhea إسهال ishaal 141, 163; **I have ~** عندي إسهال AHndee ishaal

dice زهر اللعب zahr al-lAHb

dictionary قاموس qaamoos 150

diesel ديزل deezil 87

diet: I'm on a diet أنا أتبع نظام غذائي ana atbAH naZaam ghizaa'ee

difficult صعب SAHb 14

dining car عربة الطعام AHrabit aT-TAHaam 77

dining room حجرة الطعام Hujrat aT-TAHaam 26

dinner jacket سترة العشاء sutrat al-AHashaa'

dinner: to have dinner يتعشى yatAHashshaa 124

direct مباشر mubaashir 74

direction(s) اتجاه (اتجاهات) ittijaah(aat) 94; **in the ~ of** باتجاه bittijaah 95

director (of company) مدير mudeer

dirty وسخ wisikh 14, 28

disabled معاق muAHaaq 22

discotheque ديسكو deeskoo 112

discount(s) تخفيض (تخفيضات) takhfeeD(aat) 24, 74, 100

disgusting مقرف muqrif

dish cloth منشفة صحون minshafat SuHoon 148

dishwashing detergent سائل لغسيل الصحون saa'il li-ghaseel aS-SuHoon 148

dislocated مخلوع makhlooAH 164

display cabinet خزانة العرض khazaanat al-AHrD 149

display case صندوق العرض Sundooq al-AHrD 134

distilled water مقطرة مياه miyaah muqaTTara

dive, to يغطس yaghTas 117

diversion تحويل taHweel 96

divorced مطلق muTallaq 120

dizzy: I feel dizzy أشعر بدوار
ashAHur bi-dawaar

doctor دكتور doktoor 92, 131, 161, 167

doctor's office [surgery] عيادة
AHiyaada 161

doll دمية dumya 157

dollar(s) دولار(ات) dolaar(aat) 67, 138

door(s) باب (أبواب) baab (abwaab) 25, 29

double (cabin) لشخصين li-shakhSayn 81;
~ bed سرير مزدوج sareer muzdawij 21;
~ room غرفة لشخصين ghurfa
li-shakhSayn 21

downstairs تحت taHt 12

downtown area وسط المدينة wasT
al-madeena 99

draught (wind) تيار الهواء tayyaar
al-hawaa

dress فستان fustaan 144

drink(s) مشروب(مشروبات) mashroob(aat)
37, 70, 125, 126

drink, to يشرب yishrab 37

drinking water ماء الشرب maa'
ash-shurb 30

drive, to يسوق yasooq 93

driver سائق saa'iq

driver's license شهادة السواقة
shahaadat as-sawaaqa 93

drowning: someone is drowning!
هناك شخص يغرق! hunaak shakhS yaghriq

drugstore صيدلية Saydaleeya 129

dry cleaner محل تنظيف ملابس maHall
tanZeef malaabis 131

dubbed (movie) مدبلج mudablaj 110

duck بط baTT 46

during خلال khilaal

dustbin صندوق الزبالة Sundooq
iz-zibaala 30

duvet غطاء سميك للنوم ghaTaa'
sameek li-naum

~ address
عنوان في الإي-ميل
AHunwaan feel eemayl 155

ear أذن uzun 166; **~ drops**
نقط للأذن nuqaT lil-uzun; **~ache**
ألم في الأذن alam feel uzun 163

earlier أبكر abkar 147

early مبكر mubakkir 221

earrings حلق Halaq 149

east شرق sharq 95

easy سهل sahl 14

eat, to يأكل ya'kul 41, 139, 167

economy class
الدرجة السياحية
ad-daraja as-siyaaHiyya 68

eggs بيض bayD 160; **boiled ~**
بيض مسلوق bayD maslooq 43;
fried ~ بيض مقلي bayD maqlee 43;
scambled ~ بيض ممزوج bayD
mamzooj 43

eggplant باذنجان baazinjaan 47

Egypt مصر muSr 119

Egyptian مصري muSree

elastic (adj) مطاطي maTaaTee

electric outlet(s) مواقع لأخذ الكهرباء
mauqiAH (mawaaqiAH) li-akhd
al-kahrabaa 30

electric shaver آلة حلاقة كهربائية aalat
Halaaqa kahrabaa'eeya

electricity كهرباء kahrabaa' 28
~ meter عداد الكهرباء AHddaad
al-kahrabaa 28

electronic إلكتروني iliktroonee;
~ game لعبة إلكترونية lAHba
iliktrooneeya 157

elevator(s) مصعد (مصاعد) maSAHd
(maSaaAHid) 26, 132

A-Z

else: something else
شئ آخر shay aakhir
embassy سفارة sifaara
emergency exit
مخرج طوارئ makhraj
Tawaari' 132

Emirates الإمارات al-imaaraat;
from the ~ إماراتي
imaaraatee

empty فارغ faarigh 14
end, to ينتهي yantahee 108
engaged (to be married) خاطب
khaaTib 120
engine محرك muHarrik 82, 91
engineering هندسة handasa 121
England إنجلترا injilteraa 119
English إنجليزي injileezee 67; (language)
الإنجليزية al-injileezeeya 150, 152, 161;
~-speaking يتكلم إنجليزي yatkallam
injileezee 98, 152

enjoy, to يستمتع yastamtiAH 123
enough كفاية kifaaya 15, 42, 136
ensuite bathroom حمام تابع للغرفة
Hamaam taabiAH
lil-ghurfa
entertainment guide دليل لأماكن الترفيه
daleel li-amaakin at-tarfeeh
entry visa تأشيرة الدخول ta'sheerat
ad-dukhool
envelope(s) ظرف (أظرف) Zarf
(aZruf) 150
epileptic مصاب بالصرع muSaab
biS-SarAH 163
equipment معدات muAHidaat 116
error خطأ khaTa'
escalator سلم كهربائي sillim
kahrabaa'ee
essential ضروري Darooree 89
estate agent وكيل عقاري wakeel
AHqaaree

evening المساء al-masaa 221;
in the ~ في المساء feel masaa 221;
~ dress ملابس السهرة malaabis
as-sahra 112
every day كل يوم kull yaum
every week كل أسبوع kull
usbooAH 13
examination (medical) فحص (طبي)
faHS (Tibbee)
example: for example مثلا masalan
except ما عدا maa AHdaa
excess baggage أمتعة زيادة amtiAHa
ziyaada 69
exchange rate سعر الصرف siAHr
aS-Sarf 138
exchange, to يغيّر yughayyir 137, 138
excluding بدون bidoon 24
excursion جولة سياحية منظمة
jaula siyyaaHeeya munaZZama 97
excuse me (apology) آسف aasif 10;
(attention) لو سمحت lau
samaHt 10, 94
exhausted (very tired) منهك
munhak 106
exit مخرج makhraj 70, 132
expensive غالي ghaalee 14, 134
expiration [expiry] date
تاريخ الانتهاء taareekh
al'intihaa 109
exposure (photos) صورة Soora 151
extension (telephone) امتداد
imtidaad 128
extra (adj) إضافي iDaafee 27
eye عين AHyn 166

F **fabric** قماش qumaash 145
facial تنظيف للوجه tanZeef
lil-wajh 147

facilities تسهيلات tas-heelaat 22

faint: to feel faint
يشعر بإغماء
yashAHur bi-ighmaa' 163

fairground مدينة الملاهي madeenat
al-malaahee 113

falconry صيد بالصقور SayD
biS-Suqoor 115

fall (season) الخريف al-khareef 219

family (families) عائلة (عائلات)
AH'ila(at) 74; **my ~** عائلتي
AH'iltee 66, 120, 167

famous شهير shaheer

fan (cooling) مروحة marwaHa 25, 91

far بعيد bAHeed 95; **how ~ is it?**
كم تبعد؟ kam tabAHud 72

fare أجرة ujra 78

farm مزرعة mazrAHa 107

fast بسرعة bi-surAHa 93

fast food وجبات سريعة
wajbaat sareeAHa 35, 40

fat دهن duHn 39

father أب ab 120

faucet حنفية Hanafeeya 25

favorite مفضل mufaDDal

fax فاكس faaks 155

feeding bottle زجاجة الرضيع
zujaajat ar-raDeeAH

feel ill, to يشعر بالمرض yashAHur
bil-maraD 163

ferry معدية mAHdeeya 81;
by ~ بالمعدية bil-mAHdeeya 123

feverish, to feel يشعر بحمى
yashAHur bi-Huma 163

few بعض bAHD 15

fiancé(e) خطيب/خطيبة
khaaTeeb/khaaTeeba

field حقل Haql 107; **~ hockey**
الهوكي al-hookee 115

fifth خامس khaamis 217

fight (brawl) مشاجرة mushaajara

figs تين teen 49

fill in, to (a form)
يملأ yamla 168

filling (dental)
حشو (أسنان) Hashw
(asnaan) 168

film (camera) فيلم (كاميرا) feelm
(kaameeraa) 151; فيلم (movie)
feelm 108, 110; **black and white ~**
فيلم أسود و أبيض feelm aswad
wa abyaD 151; **color ~**
فيلم ألوان feelm alwaan 151

filter فلتر filtir 151

find, to يجد yajid 18

fine (going well) بخير bi-khayr 19;
~, thanks بخير، الحمد لله
bi-khayr, al-Hamdu lilaah 118

fine (penalty) غرامة gharaama 93

finger إصبع iSbAH 166

fire حريق Hareeq; **~ alarm**
إنذار الحريق inzaar al-Hareeq;
~ department [brigade] المطافئ
al-muTaafi' 92; **~ escape**
سلم الحريق sillim al-Hareeq;
~ extinguisher طفاية الحريق
Tafaayat al-Hareeq

firewood حطب HaTab

first [أولى] أول awwil [fem: oolaa] 68, 75,
132, 217; **~ class** الدرجة الأولى
ad-daraja al-oolaa 68, 73

fish سمك samak; **~ restaurant** مطعم سمك
matAHm amak 35; **~ soup**
شوربة سمك shoorbit samak 43;
~ store محل سمك maHall samak 129

fishing rod سنارة sinaara

fishing, to go يذهب لصيد السمك
yazhab li-Sayd as-samak

fit, to (clothes) يلائم yulaa'im 146

fitting room غرفة القياس ghurfat
al-qiyaas 146

A-Z

fix, to يصلح yuSalliH 168

flannel فوطة صغيرة fooTa Sagheera

flash (electronic) فلاش (اليكتروني) flaash (ileektroonee) 151

flashlight بطارية جيب baTaareeyat jayb 31

flat (tire) ثقب thuqb 83, 88

flea برغوث barghoot

flight رحلة riHla 68, 70; **~ number ...** الرحلة رقم ... ar-riHla raqm 68

flip-flops شبشب حمام shibshib Hammaam 145

floor (level) طابق Taabiq 132

florist محل زهور maHall zuhoor 129

flour طحين TaHeen 39

flower(s) زهرة (زهر) zahra (zahr) 106

fly (insect) ذبابة dubaaba

follow, to يتبع yitbAH 95, 152

food طعام TAHaam 39, 41; **~ poisoning** تسمم tasammum 165

foot قدم qadam 166; **~ path** ممر المشاة mamarr al-mushaa

football (soccer) كرة القدم kurat al-qadam 115

for (+ length of time) لمدة li-muddat 13, 23

foreign currency عملات أجنبية AHumlaat ajnabeeya 138

forest غابة ghaaba 107

forget: I've forgotten نسيت naseet 42

fork(s) شوكة (شوك) shauka (shuwak) 39, 41, 148

form استمارة istimaara 168

fortnight اسبوعان usbooAHayn

fortunately لحسن الحظ liHusn al-HaZZ 19

fountain نافورة naafoora 99

four-wheel drive الدفع الرباعي ad-dafAH ar-rubaaAHee 86

fourth رابع raabiAH 217

foyer (hotel/theater) بهو bahw

fracture كسر kasr 165

frame إطار iTaar

free (not busy) فاضي faaDee 124

freezer فريزر fireezir 29

French dressing صلصة الخل SalSat al-khall 38

French fries بطاطس مقلية baTaaTis maqleeya 38

frequent: how frequent ...? كم عدد ...؟ kam AHdad 75

frequently مرارا miraaran

fresh (food) طازج Taazij 41

Friday (يوم) الجمعة (yaum) al-jumAHa 218

fridge ثلاجة tallaaja

fried مقلي maqlee

friend(s) صديق (أصدقاء) Sadeeq (aSdiqaa') 162

frightened, to be يخاف yukhaaf

from من min 12, 119; **from ... to** من ... إلى min ... ilaa 13

front الأمام al-amaam 147; **~ door** الباب الرئيسي al-baab ar-ra'eesee 26

fruit فواكه fawaakih 49; **~ juice** عصير فواكه AHseer fawaakih 43

frying pan مقلاة maqlaa 29

fuel (gasoline) وقود wuqood 86

full مليان malyaan 14; **~ board** إقامة كاملة iqaama kaamla 24

fun: to have fun يستمتع yastamtiAH

furniture أثاث athaath

fuse(s) (electric) صمام الكهرباء (صمامات) Samaam(aat) al-kahrabaa; **~ box** علبة صمامات الكهرباء AHilbat Samaamaat al-kahrabaa 28

G game (*match*) ماتش maatsh 114

garage كراج garaaj 88

garbage bag(s) قمامة (أكياس) kees (akyaas) qammaama 148

garden حديقة Hadeeqa

gas bottle(s) أنبوبة (أنابيب) الغاز anbooba (anaabeeb) al-ghaaz 28

gas station محطة بنزين maHaTTat banzeen 87

gasoline بنزين benzeen 88

gate (*airport*) بوابة bawwaaba 70

genuine أصلي aSlee 134

get off, to (*bus*) ينزل yanzil 79

get to, to يصل إلى yaSil ilaa 70, 77; how do I get to ...? كيف أصل إلى ...؟ kayf aSil ilaa 72, 94

gift هدية hadeeya 67, 156; ~ shop محل هدايا maHall hadaayaa 129

girl(s) بنت (بنات) bint (banaat) 120, 157

girlfriend صاحبة Saahba 120

give, to يعطي yuAHTee

glass(es) كوب (أكواب) koob (akwaab) 37, 39, 148

glasses (*optical*) نظارات naZaara 167

gloves قفاز qafaaz

go, to يذهب yaz-hab 18; let's go! هيا بنا نذهب! hayyaa bina naz-hab; ~ back يرجع yirjAH 95 ~ for a walk يتمشى yatmashshaa 124

goggles نظارات بحر naZaaraat baHr

gold ذهب dahab 149; ~ plate قشرة ذهب qishrat dahab 149

golf الجولف al-goolf 115; ~ course أرض الجولف farD al-gool 115

good جيد jayyid 14, 35; ~ afternoon مساء الخير masaa al khayr 10; ~ evening مساء الخير masaa al khayr 10;

~ morning صباح الخير sabaaH al khayr 10; ~ night تصبح على خير tiSbaH AHla khayr 10; **Good God!** يا إلهي! yaa ilaahee 19

good-bye مع السلامة maAH as-salaama 10

gram غرام ghraam 159

grandparents الجد والجدة al-jadd wal-jadda

grapes عنب AHinab 49, 160

grass عشب AHushb

gratuity بقشيش baqsheesh

gray رمادي ramaadee 143

graze سلخ salkh 162

greasy (*hair*) دهني dihnee

green أخضر akhDar 143; ~ beans فاصوليا خضراء faSoolya khaDra 47; ~ pepper فلفل أخضر filfil akhDar 47; ~grocer محل خضار maHall khuDaar 129

ground (*noun*) أرض arD 31; (*adj*) أرضي arDee 132; ~cloth حصيرة HaSeera 31; ~sheet حصيرة HaSeera 31

group مجموعة majmooAH 66

guarantee ضمان Dammaan 135

guavas جوافة jawaafa 49

guide (tour) مرشد (سياحي) murshid (siyyaaHee) 98

guidebook دليل سياحي daleel siyaaHee 150

guitar جيتار geetaar

Gulf (Persian) الخليج al-khaleej 119

guy rope حبل الخيمة Habl il-khayma 31

gynecologist طبيب نسائي Tabeeb nisaa'ee 167

A-Z **H**

hair شعر shAhr 147; ~ spray
اسبراي للشعر isbraay lish-shAhr 142;
~cut حلاقة الشعر Halaaqat
ash-shAhr; ~dresser صالون حلاقة
Saaloon Hallaaqa 131, 147;
~stylist مزين (للشعر) muzayyin
(lish-shAhr)

half نصف nuSf 217; ~ an hour
نصف ساعة nuSf saAha 217;
~ board نصف إقامة nuSf iqaama 24
~ past ... ونصف ... ... wa nuSf 220

hammer مطرقة miTraqa 31

hand يد yad 166; ~ washable
يغسل باليد yughsal bil-yad 145

handbag حقيبة يد Haqeebat yad 153

handicapped معاق muAHaq 163

handkerchief منديل mindeel

hanger (clothes) علاقة AHlaaqa 27

happen: what happened? ماذا حدث؟
maazaa Hadas 93

harbor ميناء بحري meenaa baHree

hat قبعة qubAha 144

have: can I have? ممكن آخذ؟ mumkin
aakhud 18

have to (must) يجب أن yajib an 79

hay fever حمى القش Huma
al-qash 141

head رأس ra's 166; ~ waiter
المتر al-mitr 41; ~ache صداع
SudaAh 163

health صحة SiHHa; ~ food store
محل أطعمة صحية maHall aTAHima
SiHHeeya 129; ~ insurance
تأمين صحي ta'meen SiHHee 168

hear, to يسمع yasmAh

hearing aid سماعة (لثقيلي السمع)
samaaAha

heart قلب qalb 166; ~ attack
أزمة قلبية azma qalbeeya 163;
~ condition مريض بالقلب mareeD
bil-qalb 163

heat تدفئة tadfi'a 25

heating تدفئة tadfi'a 25

heavy ثقيل taqeel 14, 69, 134

height طول Tool 152

hello السلام عليكم as-salaam
AHlaykum 10; مرحبا marHaban 118

helmet خوذة khooza 82

help: can you help me? ممكن تساعدني؟
mumkin tusaAhidnee 18, 92

hemorrhoids البواسير al-bawaaseer 165

her ها haa (on end of word) 16;
hers لها lahaa 16

here هنا hunaa; here it is
ها هو هنا haa huwa huna 17

hi! أهلا! ahlan 10

high مرتفع martafiAh 122; ~ blood
pressure (ارتفاع) ضغط الدم (irtifaAh)
DaghT ad-dam 163

highlighted (hair) مميش
mumayyish 147

hill تل tall 107

his ـه uh (on end of word) 16; له lahu 16

hitchhiking طلب توصيل Talb tauSeel 83

hobby(-ies) (هوايات) هواية
hiwaaya(at) 121

holiday إجازة ijaaza 123; ~ resort
في إجازة muntajAh; on ~
fee ijaaza 66

home بيت bayt; we're going home
سنعود إلى بيتنا sa-nAhood ilaa baytnaa

homosexual (adj) شاذ جنسيا shaazz
jinseeyan

honey عسل AHsal 43; ~moon
شهر العسل shahr al-AHsa1;

hood (of car) غطاء المحرك ghaTaa
al-muHarrik 90

hopefully أتمنى atmanna 19

horn (of car) آلة التنبيه aalat at-tanbeeh 91

horse حصان HuSaan; **~back riding**
ركوب الخيل rukoob al-khayl 115, 116;
~racing سباق الخيل sibaaq
al-khayl 115

hospital مستشفى mustashfa 131, 164, 167

hot ساخن saakhin 14; (weather) حار
Harr 122; **~ dog**
ساندويش سجق sandweesh sujuq 110; **~ spring**
(عين (ماء ساخن AHyn (maa' saakhin);
~ water ماء ساخن maa' saakhin 25

hotel(s) (فندق (فنادق funduq (fanaadiq)
21, 123

hour ساعة saAHa 97; **in an ~**
بعد ساعة bAHd saAHa 84;
~s of opening المواعيد
al-mawaaAHeed 161

house(es) بيت (بيوت) bayt (buyoot)

housewife ربة منزل rabbat manzil 121

how? كيف kayf 17; **~ are things?**
كيف الأمور؟ kayf al-umoor 19;
~ are you? كيف حالك؟
kayf Haalak 118; **~ far?**
كم المسافة؟ kam al-masaafa 94, 106;
~ long? (time) كم المدة kam
il-mudda 23, 75; **~ long?** (distance)
كم المسافة؟ kam al-masaafa 77;
~ many? كم؟ kam 15, 80;
~ much? بكم bikam 15, 21, 65,
84, 100, 109; **~ often?** كم مرة؟
kam marra 140, 165; **~ old are you?**
عمرك كم؟ kam AHumrak

hundred مئة mi'a 217

hungry جوعان jauAHaan

hurry: I'm in a hurry أنا في عجلة
ana fee AHjala

hurt, to يؤلم yu'allim 164;
my ... hurts يؤلمني ...
... yu'limnee 162

husband زوج
zauj 120, 162

hypermarket سوق شامل
sooq shaamil

I **ice** ثلج talj 38, 49
ice cream آيس كريم aayis
kreem 40, 160; **~ parlor** محل
aayis kreem 35 محل آيس كريم

I'd like ... أريد ... ureed 36, 37, 40

ill مريض mareeD

illegal غير قانوني ghayr qaanoonee

imitation تقليد taqleed 134

immediately فورا fauran 13

in في fee 12, 13

included مشمول mashmool 98;
is ... included? هل ...مشمول؟
hal ... mashmool 86

indicate, to يشير إلى yusheer ilaa

indigestion عسر هضم AHusr haDm

inexpensive رخيص rakhees 35

infected ملوث mulawwas 165

infection تلوث talawwuth 167

inflammation التهاب iltihaab 165

informal (dress) (ملابس) غير رسمية
(malaabis) ghayr rasmeeya

information معلومات mAHloomaat 97;
~ desk مكتب الاستعلامات maktab
al-istiAHlaamaat 72; **~ office**
مكتب الاستعلامات maktab
al-istiAHlaamaat 96

injection حقنة Huqna 168

injured مصاب muSaab 92

innocent بريء baree'

insect(s) (حشرة (حشرات Hashara
(Hasharaat) 25; **~ bite**
لدغة حشرة ladghat Hashara 162; **~ repellent**
طارد للحشرات Taarid lil-Hashsraat 141

inside داخل daakhil 12

186

kilo(gram) كيلو keeloo 159

kilometer كيلومتر keeloomatr

kind (*pleasant*) لطيف laTeef

kind: what kind of ... ... ما نوع هذا الـ maa nooAH haazal ...

kiosk كشك kushk

kitchen مطبخ maTbakh 29

knapsack حقيبة الظهر Haqeebat iZ-Zahr 31, 145

knee ركبة rukba 166

knife (**knives**) سكين (سكاكين) sikkeen (sakaakeen) 39, 41, 148

knight (*chess*) حصان الشطرنج HuSaan ash-shaTranj

Kuwait الكويت al-kuwayt

Kuwaiti كويتي kuwaytee

L **ladder** سلم sillim

ladies' fingers بمية bamya 47

lake بحيرة buhayra 107

lamb ضاني Daanee 46

lamp مصباح miSbaaH 25, 29

language course دورة لدراسة لغة daura li-diraasat lugha

large كبير kabeer 40, 110

larger أكبر akbar 134

last أخير akheer 68, 75; آخر aakhir 80

last, to يدوم yadoom

later متأخر mutakhkhar 147, 221

laugh, to يضحك yaDHak 126

laundromat مغسلة (خدمة ذاتية) maghsala (khidma zaateeya) 131

laundry (*service*) مغسلة maghsala 22

lawyer محام muHaamee 152

laxative مسهل musahhil

lead, to يؤدي إلى yu'addee ilaa 94

lead-free (*gas/petrol*) دون رصاص doon raSaaS 87

learn, to يتعلم yatAHallam

leather جلد jild 145

leave, to (*depart*) يغادر yughaadir 32, 70, 81; (*deposit*) يترك yatruk 72; **leave me alone!** اتركني وحدي! utruknee waHdee 126; **I've left my bag** تركت حقيبتي tarakt Haqeebtee

Lebanese لبناني lubnaanee 35

Lebanon لبنان Lubnaan

left يسار yasaar 95; **on the ~** على اليسار AHlal yasaar 95

left-luggage office مكتب الأمانات maktab al-amaanaat 71

leg ساق saaq 166

legal قانوني qaanoonee

lemon ليمون laymoon 38

lemonade ليمونادة laymoonaada

length طول Tool

lens عدسة AHdasa 151, 167; **~ cap** غطاء للعدسة ghiTaa' lil-AHdasa 151

lentils عدس AHds 48; **lentil soup** شوربة عدس shoorbit AHds 43

less أقل aqall 15

lesson(s) درس (دروس) dars (duroos)

letterbox صندوق الخطابات Sundooq al-khaTaabaat

lettuce خس khass 47

level (*even*) مستو mustawee 31

library مكتبة maktaba

Libya ليبيا leebeeyaa

Libyan ليبي leebee

lifeguard منقذ munqiz 117

lift (*elevator*) مصعد miSAHad 26

light(s) نور (أنوار) noor (anwaar) 82, 83; **~ bulb** لمبة lamba 148

light (*adj. – color*) فاتح faatiH 14, 134, 143; (*adj. – weight*) خفيف khafeef 14, 134

lighter (color) أفتح aftaH 143; (with more light) أكثر إنارة aktar inaara 24
lighter (cigarette) ولاعة walaAHa 150
like (similar to) مثل misl
like, to يحب yuHibb 111, 119, 121;
  I like it أحبه uHibbuh 101;
  I don't like it لا أحبه laa uHibbuh 101;
  I'd like أريد ureed 18
limousine ليموزين leemoozeen
linen كتان kittaan 145
lipstick أحمر شفاة aHmar shifaa
liter(s) لتر(ات) litr(aat) 87, 159
little (small) صغير Sagheer
live, to يسكن yaskun 119
liver كبد kibd 166
living room غرفة جلوس ghurfat juloos 29
loaf of bread رغيف خبز ragheef khubz 160
lobby (theater/hotel) قاعة qaAHa
lobster استاكوزا istaakooza 44
local محلي maHallee 35, 37
lock قفل qifl 25, 82, 90
long طويل Taweel 144, 146
look for, to يبحث عن yabHas AHn 133, 143
loose واسع waasiAH 146
lorry شاحنة shaaHina
lose, to يفقد / يضيع yafqad / yuDeeAH
  I've lost ... فقدت ... faqadt 138, 153
lost property office مكتب المفقودات maktab al-mafqoodaat 72
lost-and-found مكتب المفقودات maktab al-mafqoodaat 72
love: I love you أنا أحبك ana uHibbak
lovely ممتاز mumtaaz 122
low منخفض munkhafiD 122
low-fat قليل الدهن qaleel ad-dihn

luck: good luck حظ سعيد HaZZ sAHeed 219
luggage check مكتب الأمانات maktab al-amaanaat 71
luggage locker(s) خزانة (خزائن) الحقائب khazaanat (khazaa'in) al-Haqaa'ib 71
lump ورم waram 162
lunch غداء ghadaa 98
lung رئة ri'a

M **madam** مدام madaam
  magazine مجلة majalla 150
magnificent جميل جدا jameel jiddan 101
maid خادمة khaadima
mail بريد bareed 27; **by ~** بالبريد bil-bareed 22; **~box** صندوق البريد Sundooq al-bareed 154
mail, to يرسل بالبريد yarsil bil-bareed
main رئيسي ra'eesee 129, 154
make-up مكياج mikyaaj
mallet مطرقة خشبية miTraqa khashabeeya 31
man (men) رجل (رجال) rajul (rijaal)
manager مدير mudeer 25, 41, 137
mango منجا manga 40, 49
manicure تجميل الأظافر tajmeel al-aZaafir 147
manual (car) يدوي yadawee
map خريطة khareeTa 94, 106, 150
mark مارك maark 67
market(s) سوق (أسواق) sooq (aswaaq) 99, 131
married متزوج mutzawwij 120
mascara مسكارا maskaaraa
mask (diving) قناع الغوص qinaaAH al-ghauS
massage تدليك tadleek 147

matches كبريت kibreet 31, 148, 150

matter: it doesn't matter لا يهم laa yuhimm; what's the matter? ماذا بك؟ mazaa bik

mattress مرتبة martaba 31

may I? ممكن؟ mumkin 18

maybe ربما rubbamaa

me أنا ana

meal(s) وجبة (وجبات) wajba(at) 38, 42, 125, 165

mean, to يقصد yaqSud; what does this mean? ما معنى هذا؟ maa maAHna haaza 23

measles حصبة HaSba 165

measurement قياس qiyaas

meat لحم laHm 41; ~ soup شوربة لحم shoorbit laHm 43; ~balls كفتة kufta 46

medication دواء dawaa 164, 165

medium متوسط mutawassiT 122

meet, to يلتقي yaltaqee 125; pleased to meet you تشرفنا tasharrafnaa 118; meeting place نقطة اللقاء nuqTit al-liqaa' 12

member(s) (of club) عضو (أعضاء) ADoo (AHDaa) 112, 116

mention: don't mention it عفوا AHfwan 10

menu قائمة الطعام qaa'imat aT-TAHaam

message(s) رسالة (رسائل) risaala (rasaa'il) 27

metal معدن mAHdan

meter (taxi) عداد AHdaad 84

metro (أنفاق) مترو metroo (anfaaq) 80; ~ station محطة المترو maHaTTit al-metroo 80

microwave (oven) فرن الميكروويف furn al-meekroowayf

midday منتصف النهار muntaSaf an-nahaar

midnight منتصف الليل muntaSaf al-layl 220

migraine صداع شديد SudaaAH shadeed

mileage مسافة masaafa 86

milk حليب Haleeb 43, 160

million مليون milyoon 217

mind: do you mind? هل عندك مانع؟ hal AHndak maaniAH 76; I don't mind لا أمانع laa umaaniAH 19

mine لي lee 16; it's mine! هذا لي! hazaa mulkee

mineral water مياه معدنية miyaah mAHdaneeya

mini-bar البار الصغير al-baar aS-Sagheer 32

mint tea شاي بنعنع shaay bi-nAHnAH 51

minute دقيقة daqeeqa

mirror مرآة miraaya 82

missing مفقود mafqood 137, 152

mistake خطأ khaTa 32, 41, 42

mobile home بيت متنقل bayt mutanaqqil

modern حديث Hadees 14

Modified American Plan (M. A. P.) نصف إقامة nuSf iqaama 24

moisturizer (cream) كريم مرطب kreem muraTTib

monastery دير dayr 99

Monday (يوم) الاثنين (yaum) al-itnayn 218

money فلوس fuloos 42; نقود nuqood 136, 153; ~ order حوالة نقدية Huwaala naqdeeya; ~-belt حزام حفظ النقود Hizaam HafZ an-nuqood

month(s) شهر (أشهر) shahr (ashhur) 218

monthly شهري shahree 79

moped دراجة نارية صغيرة
darraaja naareeya
Sahgeera 83

more أكثر aktar 15; **I'd like
some more ...** أريد المزيد من ...
ureed al-mazeed min 39

morning صباح SabaaH; **in the ~**
صباحا SabaaHan 221

Moroccan مغربي maghribee

Morocco المغرب al-maghrib 119

Moslem مسلم muslim

mosque جامع jaamiAH 96, 99, 105

mosquito bite لدغة الباعوض
ladghat al-baaAHooD

mother أم umm 120

motorbike دراجة نارية darraaja
naareeya 83

motorboat زورق بخاري zauraq
bukhaaree 117

mountain جبل jabal 107; **~ pass**
ممر جبلي mamarr jabalee 107;
~ range سلسلة جبلية silsila
jabaleeya 107

mountaineering تسلق الجبال
tasalluq al-jibaal 115

moustache شوارب shawaarib

mouth فم fam 164, 166

movie (سينمائي) فيلم feelm (seenamaa'ee)
108, 110; **~ theater** سينما
seenimaa 96, 110

Mr. السيد as-sayyid

Mrs. السيدة as-sayyida

mugging سلب salb 152

muscle عضلة AHDla 166

museum متحف matHaf 99

music موسيقى mooseeqaa 111, 121
~ store محل كاسيتات maHall
kaaseetaat 131

musician عازف الموسيقى AHaazif
al-mooseeqaa

mussels بلح البحر balaH al-baHr 44

must: I must لابد أن laa budd an

mustard مسطردة musTarda 38

my ي ee (on end of word) 16

myself: I'll do it myself سأفعل هذا بنفسي
sa'afAHal haaza bi-nafsee

N name اسم ism 22, 36, 118, 120;
my name is ... اسمي ismee ...
22, 118; **what's your name?** ما اسمك؟
maa ismak 118

napkin منديل المائدة mindeel
al-maa'da 39

nappies حفاضات HafaaDaat 142

narrow ضيق Dayyiq 14

national وطني waTanee

nationality جنسية jinseeya

near قريب من qareeb min 12;
nearby قريب qareeb 21;
nearest أقرب aqrab 80, 88, 92, 129,
140, 154

neck رقبة raqaba 147, 166; **round ~**
ياقة مستديرة yaaqa mustadeera 144;
V-~ ياقة سبعة yaaqa sabAHa 144

necklace عقد AHuqd 149

need: I need to ... أحتاج أن ... 18
aHtaaj an ...

nephew ابن الأخ أو الأخت ibn al-akh
aul ukht

nerve عصب AHSab; **nervous system**
الجهاز العصبي al-jahaaz al-AHaSabee

never أبدا abadan 13; **~ mind**
ولا يهمك walaa yuhimmak 10

new جديد jadeed 14; **New Year**
رأس السنة ra's as-sana 219

newspaper جريدة jareeda 150

newsstand [newsagent] بائع جرائد
baa'iAH jaraa'id 150

next قادم qaadim 68, 75, 77, 80;
~ **to** بجانب bijaanib 12, 95

nice لذيذ lazeez

niece ابنة الأخ أو الأخت ibnat al-akh
au al-ukht

night ليلة layla; **at** ~ بالليل bil-layl
221; ~**club** نادٍ ليلي naadee
laylee 112

no لا laa 10; **no way!** لا مجال!
laa majaal 19

no-one لا أحد laa aHad 16

noisy مزعج muzAHij 14

non-alcoholic بدون كحول bidoon
kuHool 50

non-smoking عدم التدخين AHdam
at-tadkheen 36

none لا شيء laa shay 15, 16

noon ظهر Zuhr 220

normal عادٍ AHdee 67

north شمال shamaal 95

nose أنف anf 166

not yet ليس بعد laysa bAHd 13

nothing لا شيء laa shay 15;
~ **else** لا شيء آخر laa shay aakhar 15

notify, to يعلم yuAHlim 167

now الآن al-aan 13,84

number(s) رقم (أرقام) raqm (arqaam)
138; **sorry, wrong number**
آسف، النمرة غلط aasif, an-nimra ghalaT

nurse ممرضة mumarriDa

nylon نايلون naayloon

O o'clock: it's ... o'clock.
... الساعة as-saAHa ... 220

oasis واحة waaHa 102, 107

occasionally من حين إلى آخر min Heen
ilaa aakhar

occupied (busy) مشغول mashghool 14

octopus أخطبوط
akhTabooT 44

of course طبعا
TabAHan 19

office مكتب maktab

often كثيرا kateer 13

oil زيت zayt

okay حسنا Hasanan 10

okra بمية bamya 47

old (non-human) قديم qadeem 14;
(human) عجوز AHjooz 14;
~**fashioned** قديم (زي) qadeem 14

olive oil زيت زيتون zayt zaytoon

Oman عمان AHumaan

Omani عماني Omanee

omelette عجة AHjja 43

on (+ day, date) في fee 13;
~ **foot** ماشيا maashiyan 17, 95;
~ **my own** وحدي
waHdee 120; ~ **the left**
على اليسار AHlal
yasaar 12; ~ **the right**
على اليمين AHlal
yameen 12; ~ **the spot**
فورا fauran 93; **on/off switch**
مفتاح التشغيل miftaaH at-tashgheel

once مرة marra 217

one واحد waaHid; **one like that**
واحد مثل ذلك waaHid misl
zaalik 16

one-day (ticket) يومية yaumeeya 79

one-way (ticket) ذهاب zahaab 65, 68, 73;
~ **street** طريق باتجاه واحد
Tareeq bittijaah waaHid 96

onion بصل baSal 47

open مفتوح mafTooH 14; ~**air**
مكشوف makshoof 117

open, to يفتح yaftaH 76, 132, 140

opening hours المواعيد
al-muwaaAHeed 100

opera أوبرا oobraa 108, 111; **~ house**
دار الأوبرا daar
al-oobraa 99, 111

operation عملية
AHamaleeya

opposite مقابل muqaabil 12

optician نظاراتي naZaaraatee 131, 167

or أو au

orange (color) برتقالي burtuqaalee 143

oranges برتقال burtuqaal 49

orchestra أوركسترا oorkistraa 111

order, to (request) يطلب yaTlub 32, 37, 41, 135

our نا naa (on end of word) 16

ours لنا linaa 16

outrageous جنوني junoonee 89

outside خارج khaarij 12;
في الخارج feel khaarij 36

oval بيضاوي bayDaawee 134

oven فرن furn

over there هناك hunaak 36, 76

overcharge: I've been overcharged
دفعت أكثر من اللازم dafAHt
aktar min al-laazim

overdone (food) كثير السوا
kateer as-siwaa 41

overheat تسخين أكثر من اللازم
taskheen aktar min
al-laazim

own: on my own وحدي waHdee 65

owner المالك al-maalik

oyster محار maHHaar 44

P **p.m.** بعد الظهر baAHd aZ-Zuhr
pack of cards
علبة من ورق اللعب
AHulba min waraq al-lAHb

package طرد Tard 155

packet of cigarettes علبة سجائر
AHulbat sajaa'ir 150

paddling pool مسبح للأطفال
masbaH lil-aTfaal 113

padlock قفل qifl

pail دلو dilw 157

pain ألم alam 167; **~killer** (الألم) مسكن
musakkin (al-alam) 141, 165

paint, to يرسم بالألوان yarsim
bil-alwaan; **painter** رسام rassaam;
painting لوحة lauHa

pajamas [pyjamas] بيجاما beejaamaa

palace قصر qaSr 99

Palestine فلسطين filasTeen

Palestinian فلسطيني filasTeenee

palpitations ضربات القلب المتزايدة
Darabaat al-qalb al-mutzaayida

pants (U.S.) بنطلون banTaloon 144

panty hose شراب حريمي طويل shuraab
Hareemee Taweel 144

paper ورق waraq 150;
~ napkins مناديل ورق manaadeel
waraq 148

paraffin بارافين baaraafeen 31

paralysis شلل shalal

parents: my parents والديّ
waalidayya 120

park حديقة عامة Hadeeqa AHama
96, 99, 107

parking ركن rakn 87; **~ lot**
ركن السيارات rakn as-sayyaaraat 87, 96;
~ meter عداد الركن AHdaad
ar-rakn 87

parliament building مبنى البرلمان
mabna al-barlamaan 99

party (social) حفلة Hafla 124

passport جواز سفر jawaaz safar 66, 69;
joint ~ جواز (سفر) مشترك
jawaaz (safar) mushtarak 66

pasta مكرونة makaroona 48

pastry store محل حلويات maHall Halweeyaat 131

patch, to يرقع yuraqqiAH 137

patient (*sick person*) المريض al-mareeD

pavement رصيف raSeef; **on the ~** على الرصيف AHlar raSeef

pay, to يدفع yadfAH 42, 67, 136;

payment (مبلغ) سداد saddaad (mablagh)

pay phone هاتف عام haatif AHaam

peaches خوخ khookh 49

peak قمة qimma 107

pearl اللؤلؤ al-lu'lu' 149

peas بسلة bisilla 47

pebbly (*beach*) صخري Sakhree 117

pedal (*bicycle/car*) دواسة dawaasa 82, 91

pedestrian crossing ممر للمشاة mamarr lil-mashaah 96

pedestrian zone منطقة المشاة manTiqat al-mashaah 96

pedicure تجميل أظافر القدمين tajmeel aZaafir al-qadamayn

pen(s) (أقلام) قلم qalam (aqlaam) 150

penicillin بنسلين binisileen 165

penknife مطواة miTwaa 31

people ناس naas 92, 119

pepper فلفل filfil 38

per: ~ day باليوم bil yaum 83, 86;

~ hour في الساعة fees saAHa 155;

~ night لليلة li-layla 21; **~ week** بالأسبوع bil usbooAH 83, 86

perhaps ربما rubbamaa 19

period (*menstrual*) العادة الشهرية al-AHaada ash-shahreeya 167

~ pains ألم العادة الشهرية alam al-AHaada ash-shahreeya 167

permed (*hair*) موج mumawwaj 147

petrol بنزين banzeen 87, 88; **~ station** محطة بنزين maHaTTat banzeen 87

pharmacy أجزخانة/صيدلية ajzakhaana/Saydaleeya 131, 140, 158

phone, to يطلب بالهاتف yaTlub bil-haatif

photo صورة Soora 116; **to take a ~** يأخذ صورة ya'hkud Soora

photocopier آلة نسخ aalat naskh 155

photograph(s) (صور) صورة Soora (Suwar) 98

photographer مصور muSawwir

photography تصوير taSweer 151

phrase عبارة AHibaara 11

pickup truck شاحنة صغيرة shaaHina Sagheera

piece قطعة qiTAHa 69, 159

pigeon حمام Hamaam 46

pill حبة Habba 165; **the Pill** (*contraceptive*) حبوب منع الحمل Huboob manAH al-Haml 167

pillow وسادة wisaada 27;

~ case كيس الوسادة kees al-wisaada

pineapples أناناس anaanaas 49

pink وردي wardee 143

pizzeria محل بيتزا maHall beetza 35

plain (*not patterned*) سادة saada

plane طائرة Taa'ira 68; **by ~** بالطائرة biT-Taa'ira 123

plant (*noun*) نبات nabaat

plastic bag(s) كيس (أكياس) بلاستك kees (akyaas) balaastik

plate(s) (صحون) صحن SaHn (SuHoon) 39, 148

platform(s) (أرصفة) رصيف raSeef (arSifa) 72, 76

platinum بلاتين balaateen 149

play (*theater*) مسرحية masraHeeya 110;

~wright كاتب المسرحية kaatib al-masraHeeya 110

A-Z

play, to يلعب yalAHb 121; (music) يعزف yAHzif 111; **~ group** مجموعة لعب majmooAHat lAHb 113

playground ملعب malAHb 113

playing field أرض الملعب arD al-malAHab 96

pleasant مرض murDee 14

please من فضلك min faDlak 10

plug سدادة saddaada 148

plumber سباك sabbaak

plums برقوق barqooq 49

pneumonia التهاب رئوي iltihaab ri'awee 165

point to, to يشير إلى yusheer ilaa 11

poison سم samm; **poisonous** سام saamm

police شرطة shurTa 92, 152; **~ station** مركز الشرطة markaz ash-shurTa 96, 152

pollen count نسبة غبار الطلع nisbat ghubaar aT-TalAH 122

pomegranates رمان rummaan 49

pond بركة birka 107

pop (music) البوب al-boob 111

popular مشهور mash-hoor 111

port (harbor) ميناء بحري meenaa' baHree

porter شيال shayyaal 71

portion مقدار miqdaar 39

possible: as soon as possible بأسرع ما يمكن bi-asrAH maa yumkin

post (mail) بريد bareed; **~ office** مكتب البريد maktab al-bareed 96, 131, 154; **~box** صندوق البريد Sundooq al-bareed 154; **~card** كرت (بوستال) kart (boostaal) 154, 156; **~man** ساعي البريد saaAHee al-bareed; **postage** أجرة البريد ujrat al-bareed 154

potatoes بطاطس baTaaTis 38, 47

pound(s) sterling جنيه (جنيهات) إسترليني junayh(aat) istarleenee 67, 138

power cut انقطاع التيار الكهربائي inqiTaAH at-tayyaar al-kahrabaa'ee

power point(s) مواقع لأخذ الكهرباء mauqiAH (mawaaqiAH) li-akhd al-kahrabaa 30

prawn جمبري/قريدس jambaree/ quraydis 44

pregnant حامل Haamil 163

premium (gas/petrol) ممتاز mumtaaz 87

prescribe, to يصف (الدواء) yaSif 165

prescription (طب) وصفة waSfa 140, 141

present (gift) هدية hideeya

press, to يكوي yakwee 137

pretty جميل jameel

price سعر sAHr 24

primus stove موقد البريموس mauqad il-bareemoos 31

prison سجن sijn

probably من المحتمل min al-muHtamal 19

produce store بقالة baqqaala 131

program برنامج barnaamij 109

pronounce, to ينطق yanTuq

pullover كنزة kanza

pump مضخة maDakhkha 82, 87

puncture ثقب thuqb 83, 88

pure (cotton) قطن (خالص) (quTn) khaalis 145

purple بنفسجي banafsijee 143

purse (Brit.) محفظة maHfaZa 153

put: where can I put ...? أين أضع الـ...؟ ayn aDAH al ...

pyramid(s) هرم (أهرام) haram (ahraam) 102

194

Q Qatar قطر qaTar
Qatari قطري qaTaree
quality (type) نوع nauAH 134
quantity كمية kimmeeya 134
quarter ربع rubAH 217
  quarter past ... والربع
  ... war-rubAH 220; **quarter to ...**
  ... إلا ربعا ilaa rubAH 220
question سؤال su'aal
queue, to يصطف yaSTaff 112
quick سريع sareeAH 14
quickest: what's the quickest way?
  ما هي أسرع طريقة؟ maa hiya
  asrAH Tareeqa
quickly بسرعة bi-surAHa 17
quiet هادئ haadi' 14
quieter أهدأ ahda' 24, 126

R rabbit (meat) أرانب araanib 46
race سباق sibaaq;
racetrack [racecourse]
  مضمار السباق
  miDmaar as-sibaaq 114
racket (sports) مضرب miDrab 116
radiator خزان الماء khazaan
  al-maa' 91
railroad [railway] سكك حديدية
  sikak Hadeedeeya
rain, to تمطر tumTir 122
raincoat معطف للمطر miAHTaf
  lil-maTar 144
rape اغتصاب ightiSaab 152
rare (steak) قليل السواء qaleel
  as-siwaa'; (unusual) نادر naadir
rash (skin) طفح جلدي TafH
  jildee 162
rate: special rate أسعار خاصة
  asAHaar khaaSSa 86

razor موس الحلاقة
  moos al-Hilaaqa;
  ~ blade شفرة الحلاقة
  shafrat al-Hilaaqa 142
reading قراءة qiraa'a 121
ready جاهز jaahiz 89, 137, 151
real (genuine) حقيقي Haqeeqee 149
really? بجد؟ bijadd 19
receipt وصل waSl 32, 89, 136, 151
reception (desk) مكتب الاستقبال
  maktab al-istiqbaal
receptionist موظف الاستقبال muwaZZaf
  al-istiqbaal
recommend, to ينصح yinSaH 21,
35, 141; **can you recommend ...?**
  ممكن تنصحنا ... ؟ mumkin tinSaHnaa 108;
  what do you recommend?
  بماذا تنصحنا؟ bi-maaza tinSaHnaa 37
record (music) أسطوانة ustuwaana 157
red أحمر aHmar 143; **~ wine**
  نبيذ أحمر nabeet aHmar 49
reduction(s) (in price) تخفيض (تخفيضات)
  takhfeeD(aat) 68
refrigerator ثلاجة tallaaja 29
refund (نقود) استرجاع istirjaAH
  (nuqood) 137
refuse bag(s) كيس (أكياس) قمامة kees
  (akyaas) qimaama 148
region منطقة minTaqa 106
registered mail البريد المسجل al-bareed
  al-musajjal
registration number رقم السيارة
  raqm as-sayyaara 88
regular (gas/petrol) عادي AHdee 87;
  (size) متوسط mutawassiT 110
religion ديانة diyyaana
remember يتذكر yatzakkar; **I don't**
  remember أنا لا أتذكر ana laa atzakkar
rent, to يستأجر yasta'jir 29, 86, 116;
  I'd like to rent أريد استئجار ureed
  isti'jaar 83

sales rep. مندوب مبيعات
mandoob mabeeAHaat

sales tax ضريبة Dareeba 24

salt ملح malH 38, 39

salty مالح maaliH

same: the same ... نفس الـ...
nafs al-... 74; **same-day** بنفس اليوم
bi-nafs al-yaum 74

sand رمل raml; **~ dune** كثيب رملي
kuthayb ramlee 107; **sandy** (beach)
رملي ramlee 117

sandals صندل Sandal 145

sandwich سندويتش sandawitsh 40

sanitary napkins [towels]
فوطة صحية للسيدات fuwaT SiHHeeya
lis-sayyidaat 142

satellite TV تلفزيون فضائي tilifizyoon
faDaa'ee

satin (قماش) الساتان (qumaash)
as-saataan

satisfied: I'm not satisfied with this
أنا غير راض عن هذا ana ghayr
raadee AHn haaza

Saturday (يوم) السبت (yaum)
as-sabt 218

sauce صلصة SalSa 38

saucepan إناء صغير inaa' Sagheer 29

Saudi سعودي sAHoodee

Saudi Arabia السعودية as-sAHoodeeya

sauna السونا as-sauna 26

sausages سجق sujuq 46, 160

say يقول yaqool; **how do you say ...?**
كيف تقول ...؟ kayf taqool ...

scarf لفاح lifaaH 144

scheduled flight رحلة طيران مجدولة
riHlat Tayaraan mujadwala

school مدرسة madrasa 96

scissors مقص miqaSS 148

Scotland اسكوتلندا iskootlandaa 119

screwdriver مفك mifakk 148

sea بحر baHr 107;
~front على البحر
AHlal baHr;
~sick: I feel seasick
أشعر بدوار البحر
ashAHur bi-dawaar al-baHr

season ticket تذكرة موسمية
tazkara mausimeeya

seat(s) مقعد (مقاعد) maqAHd
(maqaa'id) 73, 76, 108, 109; **~ belt**
حزام الأمان Hazaam al-amaan 90;
aisle ~ مقعد بقرب الممر maqAHd
bi-qurb al-mamarr 69; **window ~**
مقعد بجانب الشباك maqAHd bi-jaanib
ish-shibaak 69

second ثاني taanee 217; **~ class**
درجة ثانية daraja tanya 73;
~-hand مستعمل mustAHmal

secretary سكرتيرة sakriteera

sedative مهدئ mahaddi'

see, to يشاهد yara 18; (witness)
yashaahid 93; **see you soon!**
إلى اللقاء! ilaal liqaa 126

self-employed صاحب مهنة حرة
SaaHib mihna Hurrah 121

self-service خدمة ذاتية khidma
zaateeya 87, 133

sell, to يبيع yabeeAH 133

send, to يرسل yursil 155

senior citizen(s) مسن (مسنين)
musinn(een) 74

separated (in marriage) منفصل
munfaSil 120

separately منفصلين munfasileen 42

serious جاد jaadd

service(s) خدمات khidma(at) 131;
is service included?
هل الخدمة ضمن الحساب؟
hal il-khidma Dimn
il-Hisaab 42

skiing التزحلق على الجليد at-tazaHluq AHlaal jaleed 115

skin جلد jild 166

skirt تنورة tannoorra 144

sleep, to ينام yanaam 167

sleeper car عربة نوم AHrabit naum 73

sleeping bag حقيبة للنوم Haqeeba lil-naum 31

sleeping pill منوم munawwim

sleeve(s) كم (أكمام) kumm (akmaam) 144

slippers شبشب shibshib 145

slow بطيء baTee' 14; **slow down!** هدئ السرعة! hadi' as-surAHa; **slowly** ببطء bi-buT' 11, 17, 94

small صغير Sagheer 14, 24, 40, 110, 134; **smaller** أصغر aShgar 136

smoke, to يدخن yudakhkhin 126

smoking تدخين tadkheen 36

snacks وجبات خفيفة wajbaat khafeefa

snack bar مطعم سناك maTAHm snaak 72

sneakers حذاء رياضة Hizaa riyaaDa

snorkel أنبوبة التنفس anboobat at-tanaffus

soap صابون Saaboon 27, 142; **~ powder** مسحوق الغسيل masHooq al-ghaseel

soccer كرة القدم kurat al-qadam 115

socket فيش كهرباء feesh kahrabaa'

socks شراب shuraab 144

soft drink كازوزة kaazooza 110, 160

solarium شرفة حمام شمسي shurfat Hammaam shamsee 22

sole (shoes) نعل nAHl

some بعض bAHD

someone أحد ما aHad maa 16

something شيء ما shay maa 16

sometimes أحيانا aHyaanan 13

somewhere أي مكان ayy makaan 108

son ابن ibn 120, 162

soon قريبا qareeban 13; **as soon as possible** أقرب فرصة ممكنة aqrab furSa mumkina 161

sore ملتهب multahib; **~ throat** ألم في الحلق alam feel Halq 141, 163

sorry آسف aasif 10

sort(s) صنف (أصناف) Sanf (aSnaaf) 134

soup شوربة shoorba 43

sour حاذق Haaziq 41

south جنوب janoob 95

South Africa جنوب أفريقيا janoob afreeqyaa

South African جنوب أفريقي janoob afreeqee

souvenir تذكار tizkaar 98, 156 **~ store** محل هدايا تذكارية maHall hadaayaa tizkaareeya 131

space (e.g. in campsite) مكان makaan 30

spade جاروف jaaroof 157

spare (extra) إضافي iDaafee

speak, to يتكلم yatkallam 11, 18, 41, 67, 128; **~ to s.o.** يتكلم مع yatkallam mAHa 128; **do you speak English?** تتكلم إنجليزي؟ tatkallam injileezee 11

specialist أخصائي akhSaa'ee 164

spectacles نظارات naZaaraat

spicy كثير البهار kateer al-buhaar

sponge إسفنج isfinj 148

spoon(s) ملعقة (ملاعق) milAHaqa (malaAHiq) 39, 41, 148

sport رياضة riyaaDa 114, 121;
sports club نادٍ رياضي naadee riyaaDee 115; **sports ground** أرض الملعب arD al-malAHab 96; **sporting goods store** محل أدوات رياضية maHall adawaat riyaaDeeya 131

sprained ملتوٍ multawee 164

spring (season) الربيع ar-rabeeAH 219

square مربع murabbAH 134

squash الإسكواش al-iskwaash 115

squid سبيط subbayT 44

stadium مدرج mudarraj 96

stain بقعة buqAHa

stairs سلم sillim 132

stamp(s) طابع (طوابع) TaabiAH (TawaabiAH) 150, 154

stand in line, to يصطف yaSTaff 112

start, to يبدأ yabda' 98, 108

station محطة maHaTTa 96

statue تمثال timthaal 99

stay (noun) إقامة iqaama 32

stay, to (remain) يبقى yibqaa 65; (reside) يقيم yuqeem 23, 123

steak house مطعم لحم ستيك maTAHm laHm steek 35

steering wheel عجلة القيادة AHjalat al-qiyaada 90

sterilizing solution سائل معقم saa'il muAHaqqim 142

still: I'm still waiting أنا لا أزال منتظرا ana la azaal muntaZiran

sting حرقان Haraqaan 162

stockings جوارب حريمي jawaarib Hareemee 144

stolen: ... has been stolen سُرق ... suriqa ... 71

stomach بطن baTn 166; ~ache ألم في البطن alam feel baTn 163

stop (bus/metro) محطة maHaTTa 79, 80;
next stop! المحطة القادمة! al-maHaTTa al-qaadima 79; **which stop?** أي محطة؟ ayy maHaTTa 80

stop, to يتوقف yatwaqqaf 77; يقف yaqif 98; **stop at** يقف عند yaqif AHnd 75, 77

stopcock محبس maHbas 28

store(s) محل (محلات) maHall(aat) 129; ~ guide دليل المحل daleel al-maHall 132

stove فرن furn 28, 29

straight ahead على طول AHla Tool 95

strained muscle تمزق عضلي tamazzuq AHDalee 162

strange غريب ghareeb 101

straw (drinking) ماصة maaSSa

strawberries فراولة faraawla 49

stream جدول jadwal 107

street شارع shaariAH; **main [high]** ~ الشارع الرئيسي ash-shaariAH ar-ra'eesee 96; **side** ~ طريق جانبي Tareeq jaanibee 95

strong (potent) قوي المفعول qawee al-mafAHool

student(s) طالب (طلاب) Taalib (Tulaab) 74, 100, 121

study, to يدرس yadrus 121

stunning مذهل muzhil 101

subtitled (movie) مترجم mutarjam 110

subway (metro) مترو (أنفاق) metro (anfaaq) 80; ~ station محطة المترو maHaTTit metro 80

Sudan السودان as-soodaan

Sudanese سوداني soodaanee

sugar سكر sukkar 38, 39

suggest, to يقترح yaqtariH 123

suit بدلة badla 144

suitable (for) مناسب (لـ) munaasib (li)

summer الصيف aS-Sayf 219

sun شمس shams; **~bathe, to**
يأخذ حمام شمس ya'khud Hamaam
shams; **~burn** حرقة الشمس
Harqat ash-shams 141; **~glasses**
نظارات شمس naZaarat shams;
~stroke ضربة شمس Darbat
shams 163; **~tan cream**
كريم الشمس kreem ash-shams 142;
sunny مشمس mushmis 31

Sunday (يوم) الأحد (yaum) al-aHad 218

superb ممتاز mumtaaz 101

supermarket سوبرماركت
soobarmaarkat 131, 158

supervision إشراف ishraaf 113

supplement(s) إضافة (إضافات)
iDaafa(at) 68

suppositories تحاميل/لبوس
taHaameel/luboos 165

sure: are you sure?
هل أنت متأكد؟ hal anta mutakkid

surfboard لوح ركوب الموج lauH
rukoob al-mauj 117

surname اسم العائلة ism al-AHaaila

sweater كنزة kanza 144

sweatshirt سويت شيرت sweet
sheert 144

sweet (taste) حلو Hilw

sweets سكاكر sakaakir 150

swelling ورم waram 162

swim, to يسبح yasbaH 117

swimming السباحة as-sibaaHa 115;
~ pool حمام سباحة HamMaam
sibaaHa 117; **~ trunks** مايوه رجالي
maayoo rijaalee 144

swimsuit مايوه نسائي maayoo
nisaa'ee 144

switch (light) مفتاح النور miftaaH an-noor 25

swollen, to be متورم mutwarrIm

symptoms أعراض AHraaD 163

synthetic
اصطناعي
iSTinaAHee 145

Syria سوريا sooreeyaa

Syrian سوري sooree

T-shirt تي-شيرت tee-sheert 144, 156
table مائدة maa'da 36, 112;

table tennis تنس الطاولة tanis
aT-Taawla 115

tablet(s) قرص qurS (aqraaS) 140

take, to يأخذ yakhud; **~ medicine**
يأخذ دواء yakhud dawaa 140;
I'll take it سآخذه sa-aakhuduh 135;
taken (reserved) محجوز maHjooz 76

talcum powder بودرة تلك boodrat talk

talk, to يتكلم yatkallam

tall طويل Taweel 14

tampons صمامات قطنية للسيدات
Samaamaat qutneeya lis-sayyidaat 142

tan سمرة الشمس sumrat ash-shams

tap حنفية Hanafeeya 25

taxi(s) تاكسي (تاكسيات) taaksee(yaat)
70, 71, 84; **shared ~**
سرفيس sarfees 78; **~ stand [rank]**
موقف تاكسي mawqif taaksee 96

tea شاي shaay 51; **~ bags**
أكياس شاي akyaas shaay 160; **~ towel**
فوطة مطبخ fooTat maTbakh 156; **~spoon**
ملعقة صغيرة milAHaqa Sagheera 140

teacher مدرس mudarris

team(s) فريق (فرق) fareeq
(firaq) 114

teddy bear دمية بشكل دب dumya
bi-shakl dubb 157

telephone تلفون tilifoon 22, 92, 127;
~ number رقم التلفون raqm
at-tilifoon 127

tissues مناديل ورق manaadeel
waraq 142

to (place) إلى ilaa 12

toast خبز محمص khubz
muHammaS 43

tobacco تبغ tabgh 150

today اليوم al-yaum 124, 161, 218

toe إصبع القدم iSbAH al-qadam 166

toilet مرحاض marHaaD 29; **~ paper**
ورق الحمام waraq al-Hammam 25, 29

tomatoes طماطم TamaaTim 47

tomato soup شورية طماطم shoorbit
TamaaTim 43

tomorrow غدا ghadan 84, 161, 218

tongue لسان lisaan 166

tonight الليلة al-layla 110, 124;
for tonight لهذه الليلة li-haazihil
layla 108

tonsilitis التهاب اللوزتين iltihaab
al-lauzatayn 165

tonsils لوز luwaz 166

too جداً jiddan 93, 135; كثيرا kateer 146;
~ much كثير جدا kateer jiddan 15

tooth (teeth) سنة (أسنان) sinna
(asnaan) 168; **~brush** فرشاة الأسنان
furshat al-asnaan; **~ache** ألم الأسنان
alam al-asnaan; **~paste** معجون أسنان
mAHjoon asnaan 142

top قمة qimma 147

torch بطارية جيب baTaareeyat
jayb 31

torn مقطوع maqTooAH; **~ muscle**
تمزق tamazzuq

tough (food) عسير المضغ
AHseer al-maDgh 41

tour جولة jaula 97;
~ representative مندوب سياحي
mandoob siyaaHee 27

tourist(s) سائح (سائحون) saa'iH (saa'iHeen);

~ office
مكتب السياحة
maktab
as-siyyaaHa 97

tow truck ونش winsh 88

tower برج burj 99

town مدينة madeena 70, 94;
~ hall دار البلدية daar al-baladeeya 99;
old ~ مدينة قديمة madeena
qadeema 96, 99

toy لعبة lAHba 157; **~ store**
محل لعب maHall luAHb 131

traditional تقليدي taqleedee 35

traffic حركة المرور Harakat al-muroor;
~ jam احتقان المرور iHtiqaan
al-muroor; **~ violation [offence]**
مخالفة مرور mukhaalfat muroor

trailer بيت متنقل bayt mutanaqqil 30, 81

train قطار qiTaar 72, 75, 76;
~ station محطة القطار maHaTTat
al-qiTaar 72; **by ~** بالقطار
bil-qiTaar 123

trainers حذاء رياضة Hizaa riyaaDa 145

tram ترام traam

transfer تحويل taHweel

transit, in ترانزيت traanzeet

translate, to يترجم yutarjim 11

translation ترجمة tarjama

translator مترجم mutarjim

trash زبالة zibaala 28;
~can صندوق الزبالة Sundooq
iz-zibaala 30

travel سفر safar; **~ agency**
مكتب سفر maktab safar 131;
~ sickness دوار السفر dawwaar
as-safar 141

traveler's check(s) [cheque(s)]
شيك (شيكات) سياحي (سياحية)
sheek(aat) siyaaHee(ya) 136, 138

tray صينية Seeneeya

A-Z

A-Z

tree(s) (شجر) شجرة
shajara (shajar) 106

trim (hair) تقليم
taqleem 147

trip (journey) رحلة riHla
75, 77, 97, 123

trolley(-ies) (عربات) عربة
AHraba(at) 158

trousers بنطلون banTaloon 144

truck شاحنة shaaHina

true: that's true هذه الحقيقة
hazihil Haqeeqa 19; that's not true
هذا غير صحيح haazaa ghayr SaHeeH

trunk (of car) صندوق السيارة Sundooq
as-sayyaara 90

try on, to يجرب yajarrib 146

Tuesday (يوم) الثلاثاء (yaum)
at-talaat 218

tumor ورم waram 165

Tunisia تونس toonis

Tunisian تونسي toonisee

tunnel نفق nafaq

turkey ديك رومي deek roomee 46

turning منعطف munAHTaf 95

TV تلفزيون tilifizyoon 22

tweezers ملقاط milqaaT

twice مرتان marratayn 217

twin bed بسريرين bi-sareerayn 21

type نوع nauAH 109

typical تقليدي taqleedee 37

U U.S. أمريكا amreeka 119
ugly قبيح qabeeH 14, 101

U.K. المملكة المتحدة al-mamlaka
al-mutaHida

ulcer قرحة qurHa

uncle عم/خال AHmm (paternal) /
khaal (maternal) 120

unconscious فاقد الوعي faaqid
al-wAHee 92, 162

under تحت taHt

underdone (food) قليل السوا qaleel
as-siwaa 41

underpants لباس داخلي libaas
daakhilee 144

underpass نفق nafaq 96

understand, to يفهم yafham 11;
do you understand? هل تفهم؟
hal tafham 11; I don't understand
لا أفهم laa afham 11

uneven (ground) غير مستو ghayr
mustawee

unfortunately للأسف lil-asaf 19, 126

United States الولايات المتحدة
al-wilaayaat al-mutaHida

unleaded petrol بنزين خالي الرصاص
banzeen khaalee ar-raSaaS

unlimited mileage دون تحديد المسافة
doon taHdeed al-masaafa

unlock, to (القفل) يفتح yaftaH (al-qifl)

unpleasant غير مرض ghayr
murDee 14

unscrew, to (بمفك) يفك yafakk
(bi-mifakk)

until لغاية li-ghaayat 221

up to حتى Hatta 12

upset stomach ألم في البطن alam
feel baTn 141

upstairs فوق fouq 12

urgent مستعجل mustAHjil 161

use, to يستعمل yastAHmil 139

V vacant فارغ faarigh 14
vacate, to يخلي yukhlee 32

vacation إجازة ijaaza 123;
on ~ في إجازة fee ijaaza 66

204

vaccinated against ملقح ضد mullaqaH Didd 164

validate, to يوثق yuwassiq

valley وادي waadee 107

value قيمة qeema 155

valve محبس maHbas 28

vanilla فانيلا faneela 40

VAT ضريبة Dareeba 24

veal بتلو bitiloo 46

vegetables خضار khuDaar 38; **vegetable soup** شوربة خضار shoorbit khuDaar 43

vegetarian نباتي nabaatee 35, 39

vehicle registration document أوراق السيارة awraaq as-sayyaara 93

vein وريد wareed 166

ventilator فتحة تهوية fatHat tahweeya

very جداً jiddan 17; **very good** ممتاز mumtaaz 42

video game ألعاب الفيديو alAHaab al-feedyoo

video recorder مسجل الفيديو mussajil al-feedyoo

viewpoint مكان مرتفع للمشاهدة makaan murtifiAH lil-mushaahda 99

village قرية qarya 107

vinaigrette صلصة الخل SalSat al-khall 38

visa تأشيرة ta'sheera

visit (noun) زيارة ziyaara 119, 123

visit, to يزور yazoor 167; **places to ~** أماكن للزيارة amaakin liz-ziyaara 123; **visiting hours** مواعيد الزيارة mawaaAHeed az-ziyaara

vitamin tablets أقراص فيتامين aqraS feetaameen 141

volleyball الكرة الطائرة al-kura aT-Taa'ira 115

voltage فولت foolt

vomit, to يتقيأ yatqayya' 163

W wait ينتظر yantaZir 41, 89, 140; **wait!** انتظر! intaZir 98;

waiting room صالة الانتظار Saalit il-intiZaar 72

Waiter! يا جرسون! yaa garsoon 37

Waitress! يا آنسة! yaa aanisa 37

wake someone, to يصحّي yuSaHHee 27

wake-up call مكالمة الإيقاظ mukaalmat al-eeqaaZ

Wales ويلز waylz 119

walk home, to يمشي للبيت yimshee lil-bayt 65

walking boots بوت للمشي boot lil-mashy

wallet محفظة maHfaZa 42, 153

want, to يريد yureed 18

ward (hospital) جناح jinaaH 167

warm ساخن saakhin 14

washbasin حوض الغسيل HauD al-ghaseel

washing machine غسالة الملابس ghasaalat al-malaabis 29

washing powder مسحوق غسيل الملابس mas-Huq ghaseel al-malaabis 148

washing-up liquid سائل لغسيل الصحون saa'il li-ghaseel aS-SuHoon 148

wasp دبور dabboor

watch ساعة saAHa 149, 153

water ماء maa' 87; **~ bottle** زجاجة مياه zujaajat miyaah **~ heater** سخان الماء sakh-khaan al-maa' 28; **~ pipe** شيشة sheesha 51; **~ skis** لوح التزحلق على الماء lauH at-tazaHluq AHlaal maa' 117; **mineral ~** مياه معدنية miyaah mAHdaneeya 50

water melons بطيخ baTTeekh 49

waterfall شلال shallaal 107

waterproof مقاوم للماء muqaawim lil-maa'; **~ jacket** جاكيت واقية من الماء jaakeet waaqeeya min al-maa' 145

wave(s) موجة (موج) mauja (mauj)

waxing إزالة الشعر بالشمع izaalat ash-shAHr bish-shamAH 147

way: I've lost my way أنا تهت ana tuht 94

we نحن naHnu

wear, to يرتدي yartadee 152

weather طقس Taqs 122; **~ forecast** تنبؤات الجو tanabu'aat al-jau 122

wedding (زواج) فرح faraH (zawaaj); **~ ring** خاتم الزواج khaatim az-zawaaj

Wednesday (يوم) الأربعاء (yaum) al-arbAHa 218

week(s) (أسابيع) أسبوع usbooAH (asaabeeAH) 97, 218

weekend نهاية الأسبوع nihaayat al-usbooAH 218

weekly (ticket) أسبوعي usbooAHee 79

weight وزن wazn

welcome مرحبا marHaban

well I never! مش معقول! mish maAHqool 19

well-done (steak) كثير السواء kateer as-siwaa'

Welsh (adj.) ويلزي waylzee

west غرب gharb 95

wetsuit بذلة غوص badlat ghauS

what? ما/ماذا؟ maa/maaza; **what's your name?** ما اسمك؟ maa ismak; **what do you do?** (job) بماذا تعمل؟ bi-maaza tAHmil 121; **what kind of?** من أي نوع؟ min ayy nauAH 106

wheel (عجلة) دولاب doolaab (AHjala)

wheelchair كرسي متحرك kursee mutHarrik

when? متى matta 13

where? أين؟ ayn 12; **where are you from?** من أين أنت؟ min ayn anta 119

which? أي؟ ayy 15

white أبيض abyaD 143; **~ wine** نبيذ أبيض nabeet abyaD 49

who? مَن؟ man 16

whole: the whole day طول النهار Tool an-nahaar

whose? لمن؟ liman 16

why? لماذا؟ limaaza 14

wide واسع waasiAH 14

wife زوجة zauja 120, 162

wildlife الحياة البرية al-Hayaat al-barreeya

window(s) (شبابيك) شباك shibbaak (shabaabeek) 25, 76, 90, 149; **~ seat** مقعد بجانب الشباك

windshield [windscreen] الزجاج الأمامي az-zujaaj al-amaamee 90

windy مذرو بالرياح mazroo bir-riyaaH 122

winter الشتاء ash-shitaa 219

with مع maAH 17

withdraw, to (money) يسحب yasHab 139

within (time) خلال khilaal 13

without بدون bidoon 17

witness(es) (شهود) شاهد shaahid (shuhood) 93

wood خشب khashab 149

wood (forest) غابة ghaaba 107

wool صوف Soof 145

work, to يعمل yAHmil 83; **this doesn't work** هذا لا يعمل haaza laa yAHmal 137; **~ for** يعمل لحساب yAHmal li-Hisaab 121

worse أسوأ aswa' 14

worst الأسوأ al-aswa'

wound (cut) جرح jurH 162

write down, to يكتب yaktub 136

wrong (incorrect) خطأ khaTaa 88, 136;

~ **number** رقم غلط raqm ghalaT 128

 x-ray صورة بالأشعة Soora bil-ashiAHa 164

yacht يخت yakht

year سنة sana 218

yellow أصفر aSfar 143

Yemen اليمن al-yaman

Yemeni يمني yamanee

yes نعم naAHm 10

yesterday أمس ams 218

yoghurt لبن زبادي laban zabaadee

you (masc./fem./plural) أنت/أنتِ/أنتم anta/anti/antum

young صغير السن Sagheer as-sinn 14

your ك ak (fem: ik) (on end of word) 16

yours لك lak (fem: lik) 16

youth hostel بيت الشباب bayt ash-shabaab 29

zero صفر Sifr 216

zipper سوستة soosta

zuchini كوسة koosa 47

Glossary
Arabic - English

This Arabic-English glossary covers all the areas where you may need to decode written Arabic: hotels, public buildings, restaurants, stores, ticket offices, airports, and stations. The Arabic is written in large type to help you identify the word(s) from the signs you see around you.

General عام

Arabic	Transliteration	English
يسار	*yasaar*	LEFT
يمين	*yameen*	RIGHT
دخول	*dukhool*	ENTRANCE
خروج	*khurooj*	EXIT
دورة المياه	*daurat al-miyaah*	TOILETS
رجال	*rijaal*	MEN (TOILETS)
سيّدات	*sayyidaat*	WOMEN (TOILETS)
ممنوع التدخين	*mamnooAH at-tadkheen*	NO SMOKING
خطر	*khaTar*	DANGER
ممنوع الدخول	*mamnooAH ad-dukhool*	NO ENTRY

اجذب/ادفع	*ijzib/idfAH*	PULL/PUSH
المفقودات	*al-mafqoodaat*	LOST PROPERTY
ممنوع السباحة	*mamnooAH as-sibaaHa*	NO SWIMMING
ماء للشرب	*maa' lish-shurb*	DRINKING WATER
خاصّ	*khaaSS*	PRIVATE
انذار الحريق	*inzaar al-Hareeq*	FIRE ALARM
ممنوع السير على الحشائش	*mamnooAH as-sayr AHlal Hashaa'ish*	KEEP OFF THE GRASS
احترس من البوية	*iHtaris min al-booya*	WET PAINT
درجة أولى	*daraja oolaa*	FIRST CLASS
درجة ثانية	*daraja taanya*	SECOND CLASS
سقف منخفض	*saqf munkhafiD*	LOW CEILING

علامات الطريق Road Signs

قف	qif	STOP
الزم اليمين	ilzam al-yameen	KEEP RIGHT
الزم اليسار	ilazam al-yasaar	KEEP LEFT
اتجاه واحد	ittijaah waaHid	ONE WAY
لا تتخطى	laa tatkhaTa	NO PASSING
ممنوع الوقوف	mamnooAH al-wuqoof	NO PARKING
طريق سريع	Tareeq sareeAH	HIGHWAY [MOTORWAY]
بوابة رسوم	bawaabat rusoom	TOLL
اشارات مرور	ishaaraat muroor	TRAFFIC LIGHTS
تقاطع	taqaaTuAH	JUNCTION
هدى السرعة	Hidee as-surAHa	SLOW

معلومات	mAHloomaat	INFORMATION
رصيف ١	raSeef waaHid	PLATFORM 1
بوابة ١	bawaaba waaHid	GATE 1
الجمارك	al-jamaarik	CUSTOMS
الجوازات	al-jawaazaat	IMMIGRATION
وصول	wuSool	ARRIVALS
مغادرة	mughaadara	DEPARTURES
خزائن الأمتعة	khazaa'in al-amtiAHa	LUGGAGE LOCKERS
استلام الحقائب	istilaam al-Haqaa'ib	LUGGAGE RECLAIM
باصات	baaSaat	BUSES
تأجير السيّارات	ta'jeer as-sayyaaraat	CAR RENTAL
القطارات	al-qiTaaraat	TRAINS

ARABIC ➤ ENGLISH

211

Hotel/Restaurant الفندق/المطعم

معلومات	*mAHloomaat*	INFORMATION
الاستقبال	*al-istiqbaal*	RECEPTION
محجوز	*maHjooz*	RESERVED
مخرج الطوارئ	*makhraj aT-tawaari'*	EMERGENCY/ FIRE EXIT
ماء ساخن	*maa' saakhin*	HOT (WATER)
ماء بارد	*maa' baarid*	COLD (WATER)
للعاملين فقط	*lil-AHaamileen faqaT*	STAFF ONLY
قسم للعائلات	*qism lil-AHaa'ilaat*	FAMILY SECTION
الشرفة/ الحديقة	*ash-shurfa/al-Hadeeqa*	TERRACE/GARDEN
بار	*baar*	BAR

<u>Stores</u> محلات

مفتوح	maftooH	OPEN
مغلق	mughlaq	CLOSED
غداء	ghadaa	LUNCH
قسم الـ...	qism al …	… DEPARTMENT
دور	door	FLOOR
مصعد	maSAHd	ELEVATOR [LIFT]
سلّم كهربائي	sillim kahrabaa'ee	ESCALATOR
صرّاف	Sarraaf	CASHIER
تخفيضات	takhfeeDaat	SALE

الدخول مجاناً	ad-dukhool majaanan	FREE ADMISSION
للكبار	lil-kubaar	ADULTS
للأطفال	lil-aTfaal	CHILDREN
للطلبة	liT-Talaba	STUDENTS
هدايا تذكارية	hidaayaa tizkaareeya	SOUVENIRS
مرطبات	muraTTibaat	REFRESHMENTS
ممنوع اللمس	mamnooAH al-lams	DO NOT TOUCH
ممنوع التصوير	mamnooAH at-taSweer	NO PHOTOGRAPHY
سكوت	sukoot	SILENCE
ممنوع الدخول	mamnooAH ad-dukhool	NO ACCESS

Public Buildings المباني العامة

مستشفى	*mustashfaa*	HOSPITAL
طبيب	*Tabeeb*	DOCTOR
طبيب أسنان	*Tabeeb asnaan*	DENTIST
شرطة	*shurTa*	POLICE
بنك	*bank*	BANK
مكتب البريد	*maktab al-bareed*	POST OFFICE
حمام السباحة	*Hamaam as-sibaaHa*	SWIMMING POOL
مبنى البلدية	*mabnaa al-baladeeya*	TOWN HALL
موقف تاكسي	*mauqaf taaksee*	TAXI STAND [RANK]
متحف	*matHaf*	MUSEUM

Numbers

GRAMMAR

1. Unlike the rest of the script, Arabic numbers are written from left to right (as in English). Arabic numbers vary from Western numerals (although they are related) as shown here:
   0 = • 1 = ١ 2 = ٢ 3 = ٣ 4 = ٤ 5 = ٥ 6 = ٦ 7 = ٧ 8 = ٨ 9 = ٩

2. When counting nouns, Arabic uses a special "dual" ending **-ayn** (or **-tayn** for words which end in the feminine **a**) rather than the number 2. So "a book" is **kitaab**, "2 books" is **kitaab<u>ayn</u>**; "a city" is **madeena**, "2 cities" is **madeena<u>tayn</u>**.

3. Plurals are made by using a large number of different patterns. They can sound very different from the singular, e.g., **kitaab** (book)/**kutub** (books). They are shown for the most important words in the dictionary if you need them (➤ 169–207).

4. Numbers 3–10 are followed by the *plural*, but numbers above 10 are followed by the *singular*:

a (1) book **kitaab**	10 books	**AHshara kutub**
2 books **kitaabayn**	11 books	**Hadashar kitaab**
3 books **talaata kutub**	100 books	**mi'a kitaab**

0	*Sifr* صفر	6	*sitta* ستة
1	*waaHid* واحد	7	*sabAHa* سبعة
2	*itnayn* اثنان	8	*tamaanya* ثمانية
3	*talaata* ثلاثة	9	*tisAHa* تسعة
4	*arbAHa* أربعة	10	*AHshara* عشرة
5	*khamsa* خمسة	11	*Hadashar* أحد عشر

12	itnashar اثنا عشر	70	sabAHeen سبعون
13	talaatashar ثلاثة عشر	80	tamaaneen ثمانون
14	arbAHatashar أربعة عشر	90	tisAHeen تسعون
15	khamastashar خمسة عشر	100	mi'a مئة
16	sittatashar ستة عشر	101	mi'a wa waaHid مئة وواحد
17	sabAHatashar سبعة عشر	201	mi'a wa itnayn مئة واثنان
18	tamaantashar ثمانية عشر	200	mi'atayn مائتان
19	tisAHtashar تسعة عشر	500	khamsa mi'a خمسمائة
20	AHishreen عشرون	1,000	alf ألف
21	waaHid wa AHishreen واحد وعشرون	10,000	AHsharat aalaaf عشرة آلاف
22	itnayn wa AHishreen اثنان وعشرون	1,000,000	milyoon مليون
23	talaata wa AHishreen ثلاثة وعشرون	first	awwal/oola أول/أولى
24	arbAHa wa AHishreen أربعة وعشرون	second	taanee ثاني
25	khamsa wa AHishreen خمسة وعشرون	third	taalit ثالث
26	sitta wa AHishreen ستة وعشرون	fourth	raabiAH رابع
27	sabAHa wa AHishreen سبعة وعشرون	fifth	khaamis خامس
28	tamaanya wa AHishreen ثمانية وعشرون	once	marra مرة
29	tisAHa wa AHishreen تسعة وعشرون	twice	marratayn مرتان
30	talaateen ثلاثون	three times	talaat marraat ثلاث مرات
31	waaHid wa talaateen واحد وثلاثون	a half	nuSf نصف
32	itnayn wa talaateen اثنان وثلاثون	half an hour	nuSf saAHa نصف ساعة
40	arbAHeen أربعون	a quarter	rubAH ربع
50	khamseen خمسون	a third	tult ثلث
60	sitteen ستون	a pair of ...	zauj min ... زوج من ...
		a dozen	dazayna دزينة
		1999	alf wa tisAHa mi'a wa tisAHa wa tisAHeen ألف وتسعمائة وتسعة وتسعون
		2001	alfayn wa waaHid ألفان وواحد
		the 1990s	al-tisAHeenaat التسعينات

الأيام Days

	Monday	(yaum) al-itnayn (يوم) الاثنين
	Tuesday	(yaum) at-talaat (يوم) الثلاثاء
	Wednesday	(yaum) al-arbAHa (يوم) الأربعاء
	Thursday	(yaum) al-khamees (يوم) الخميس
Friday		(yaum) al-jumAHa (يوم) الجمعة
Saturday		(yaum) as-sabt (يوم) السبت
Sunday		(yaum) al-aHad (يوم) الأحد

Months الشهور

Following are the Arabic names for the months of the Christian calendar (with alternatives used in some Arab countries, e.g., Syria). The Islamic lunar **hijra** calendar (➤ 219) also has 12 months, but is 10 to 11 days shorter. A.D. 2000 is A.H. 1419/1420 in the **hijra** calendar.

January	yanaayir (kaanoon at-taanee) يناير (كانون الثاني)
February	fabraayir (shabbaT) فبراير (شباط)
March	maaris (azaar) مارس (آذار)
April	abreel (neesaan) إبريل (نيسان)
May	maayoo (ayyaar) (مايو) أيار
June	yoonyoo (Hazeeraan) يونيو (حزيران)
July	yoolyoo (tamooz) يوليو (تموز)
August	aghusTus (aab) أغسطس (آب)
September	sibtambir (aylool) سبتمبر (أيلول)
October	uktoobar (tishreen al-awwal) أكتوبر (تشرين الأول)
November	noofambir (tishreen at-taanee) نوفمبر (تشرين الثاني)
December	deesimbir (kaanoon al-awwal) ديسمبر (كانون الأول)

تواريخ Dates

It's ...	innahu ... إنه ...
July 10	AHshara yoolyoo (tamooz) ١٠ يوليو (تموز)
yesterday	ams أمس
today	al-yaum اليوم
tomorrow	ghadan غدا
next week	al-usbooAH al-qaadim الأسبوع القادم
on [at] the weekend	fee AHTlat nihaayat al-usbooAH في عطلة نهاية الأسبوع

Seasons فصول السنة

spring	ar-rabeeAH الربيع
summer	aS-Sayf الصيف
fall [autumn]	al-khareef الخريف
winter	ash-shitaa الشتاء
in spring	feel rabeeAH في الربيع
during the summer	khilaal aS-Sayf خلال الصيف

Greetings تحيات

A general greeting that you can use on someone's birthday and on most major festivals is **kull sana wa anta bi-khayr**, meaning "Every year and you are well."

Happy birthday!	AHeed meelaad sAHeed! عيد ميلاد سعيد
Happy New Year!	AHaam saAheed! عام سعيد
Congratulations!	mabrook! مبروك
Good luck!	HaZZ sAHeed! حظ سعيد

Public holidays العطلات الرسمية

National holidays vary from country to country, but most observe both the Western and Islamic New Years and other major Islamic holidays. As the Islamic months are shorter, Muslim festivals will move in relation to the Gregorian calendar, but for the foreseeable future the Islamic year begins in spring. The Muslim months and major festivals are:

Islamic month	Major Islamic holidays
al-muharram	1st: Islamic New Year
	10th: Ashura
safar	
rabee al-awwal	12th: Prophet's birthday
rabee at-taanee	
jumadee al-awwal	
jumadee al-aakhra	
rajab	27th: Laylat al-ma'raj
shabaan	
ramadaan	
shawwaal	1st-4th: Eid al-Fitr
zuu al-qa'da	
zuu al-Hijja	10th-16th Eid al-Adha

<u>Time</u> الساعة

Excuse me, can you tell me the time?	*kam as-saAHa, lau samaHt* كم الساعة، لو سمحت؟
It's …	*as-saAHa* … الساعة …
five past one	*waaHda wa khamsa* الواحدة وخمس
ten past two	*itnayn wa AHshara* الثانية وعشرة
a quarter past three	*talaata war-rubAH* الثالثة والربع
twenty past five	*khamsa wa tult* الخامسة وثلث
twenty-five past four	*arbAHa wa khamsa wa AHishreen daqeeqa* الرابعة وخمسة وعشرون دقيقة
half past six	*sitta wa nuSf* السادسة والنصف
twenty-five to seven	*sabAHa wa khamsa wa talaateen daqeeqa* السادسة وخمسة وثلاثون دقيقة
twenty to eight	*tamaanya ilaa tult* الثامنة إلا ثلث
a quarter to nine	*tisAHa ilaa rubAH* التاسعة إلا ربعا
ten to eleven	*Hadashar ilaa AHshara* الحادية عشرة إلا عشر
five to ten	*AHshara ilaa khamas daqaa'iq* العاشرة إلا خمس دقائق
twelve o'clock noon/midnight	*itnashar Zuhran/muntaSaf al-layl* الثانية عشرة ظهرا/منتصف الليل

at dawn	fajran	فجرا
in the morning	SabaaHan	صباحا
during the day	khilaal an-nahaar	خلال النهار
before lunch	qabl al-ghadaa	قبل الغداء
after lunch	bAHd al-ghadaa	بعد الغداء
in the afternoon	bAHd aZ-Zuhr	بعد الظهر
in the evening	feel masaa	في المساء
at night	bil-layl	بالليل

I'll be ready in five minutes.
sa-akoon jaahiz bAHd khamas daqaa'iq
سأكون جاهز بعد خمس دقائق.

He'll be back in a quarter of an hour.
sa-yarjAH khilaal rubAH saAHa
سيرجع خلال ربع ساعة.

She arrived half an hour ago.
waSalat munzu nuSf saAHa
وصلت منذ نصف ساعة.

The train leaves at 13:04.
yughaadir al-qiTaar as-saAHa waaHda wa arbAH daqaa'iq
يغادر القطار الساعة الواحدة وأربع دقائق.

10 minutes late / early
mutakhkhar/mubakkir bi-AHshar daqaa'iq
متأخر/مبكر بعشرة دقائق

from 9:00 to 5:00
min as-saAHa tisAHa ilaa khamsa
من الساعة ٩ إلى٥.

between 8:00 and 2:00
bayn as-saAHa tamaanya wa itnayn
بين الساعة ٨ و٢.

Will you be back before …?
hal sa-tirjAH qabl
هل سترجع قبل ...؟

We'll be here until …
sa-nakoon huna li-ghaayat
سنكون هنا لغاية ...

Quick reference مراجعة سريعة

Good morning.	SabaaH al-khayr.	صباح الخير.
Good afternoon/ evening.	masaa al-khayr	مساء الخير.
Hello.	ahlan/salaam.	أهلا/سلام.
Good-bye.	mAHas salaama.	مع السلامة.
Excuse me! (getting attention)	lau samaHt!	لو سمحت!
Pardon?	AHfwan?	عفوا؟
Sorry!	aasif!	آسف!
Please.	min faDlak.	من فضلك.
Thank you.	shukran.	شكرا.
Do you speak English?	hal tatkallam al-injileezeeya	هل تتكلم الإنجليزية؟
I don't understand	laa afham.	لا أفهم.
Where is/are ...?	ayn ...?	أين ...؟
Where are the bathrooms [toilets]?	ayn al-Hammaamaat	أين الحمامات؟

Emergency حالات طارئة

Help!	an-najda!	النجدة!
Go away!	inSarif/imshee!	انصرف!/امشي!
Leave me alone!	utruknee waHdee!	اتركني وحدي!
Call the police!	ittaSil bish-shurTa!	اتصل بالشرطة!
Stop thief!	imsik Haraamee!	امسك حرامي!
Get a doctor!	ittaSil bi-duktoor!	اتصل بدكتور!
Fire!	Hareeq!	حريق!
I'm ill.	ana mareeD.	أنا مريض.
I'm lost.	ana tuht.	أنا تهت.
Can you help me?	hal mumkin tusaAHidnee	هل ممكن تساعدني؟